D1242939

Strategy and Conscience

A PUBLICATION FROM THE
CENTER FOR RESEARCH ON CONFLICT RESOLUTION,
THE UNIVERSITY OF MICHIGAN

Strategy
and
Conscience

ANATOL RAPOPORT

*Mental Health Research Institute, University of Michigan,
Ann Arbor, Michigan*

Introduction by
KARL W. DEUTSCH

HARPER & ROW, PUBLISHERS
NEW YORK, EVANSTON
AND LONDON

To My Father

CONTENTS

~~~~~~

Part III. The Two Worlds

INTRODUCTION

by KARL W. DEUTSCH

Professor of Political Science, Yale University

This book is important, urgent and unfinished. It has been written by one of the best minds of our time. Anatol Rapoport is a scientist in the field of mathematical biology, a philosopher in the field of semantics and general systems theory, a leading specialist in the application of mathematics in the social sciences, and an original and creative contributor to political theory and social science. His book on *Fights, Games and Debates* is the best general book on the theory of games and conflicts that I know. He has the analytical power of the mathematician and the scientist, together with the sensitivity and perceptiveness of the artist and the wide knowledge of the man of letters—perhaps one of the most fortunate combinations for the study of human affairs.

Strategy and Conscience has been written out of urgency and anguish, no less than out of study and reflection. Like Jonathan Swift's *Modest Proposal* it is written as a protest against a glib and shallow fashion of contemporary thought that embodies and enhances man's inhumanity to man. In Swift's day, lives in Ireland were wasted in accordance with policies and theories of mercantilism which—as we know now—mainly codified the contemporary ignorance of economics, but which lead to economic decisions and practices as heartless as they were ignorant. Today, Rapoport suggests many of our theories of strategic deterrence have hardly more claim to intellectual respectability than did the crude and misleading economic theories of the eighteenth century. Yet today's widely publicized invitations to "think the unthinkable" and to compute the "acceptable cost" of some course of foreign policy at the level of sixty million dead in American cities in the event of a "thermonuclear exchange" may be intellectually no less superficial and morally even more callous than were the pseudo-economic beliefs and policies that once called forth Swift's savage indignation.

Professor Rapoport's critique of present-day strategic thinking fills most of this book, but a few points may be indicated here. In their frequent appearance in mathematical language, he points out, strategic thinking and writing often misuse the concepts of probability and "calculated risk." They hide and misrepresent the subjective character of many of the probability estimates with which they operate. "Probability" means usually one of two things. It means either "frequency of an event within a defined class of events"—but the assignment of an event (such as "Will the Russians fire on our planes?") to such a class may contain a major element of subjective and even arbitrary judgement. "Probability" then may be a cover name for glorified belief. Or "probability" may be openly labeled as subjective "degree of belief," but there is no clearly defined psychological degree of belief that can be assigned to different levels of low probability of a rare event. There is very little difference in our feeling of skepticism when we say that in a certain situation the likelihood of a nuclear attack would seem to us equal to one chance in a thousand, or one in ten thousand, or one in a hundred thousand, but the figures might make a decisive difference to the outcome of the calculation.

A deterrent policy or weapons system is often described by an analogy to some arrangement of insurance safety engineering. This is doubly misleading, Rapoport insists. First of all, insurance schemes are based on known frequencies of the events insured against, and engineering equipment is expected to be safe within tested limits of reliability. No frequencies of thermonuclear war are known, and no limits of deterrent systems can be tested short of catastrophy. In the second place, insurance policies are taken out against nature which is indifferent to our moves. Taking out hail insurance does not increase the likelihood of hail storms, nor do automobile seat belts provoke other drivers to crash into our car. Building a large number of air raid shelters, by one country, however, may signal *to its human adversary* that its government is now more impressed with the likelihood of war, than it was earlier. This may increase international tension and make war somewhat more likely, so that mass shelters would leave it, on balance, more endangered and not less.

Strategic thinking aims at influencing human behavior by means of threats, and it thus assumes a knowledge of how men behave when threatened or provoked. Yet strategists have paid little or no attention to relevant psychological research. The ignorance of psychology among most of them, Dr. Rapoport concludes is appalling.

Many strategic theories are modeled upon games. Such games and classic game theory models usually assume the unlimited ability of each party to think and to compute with no limit or cost of time or effort—something not found among real generals or politicians. Such models usually further assume complete accuracy in the execution of all moves and policies—something not found in real governments or armies. Yet if terms for probable error in the execution of all moves were introduced into such game models, their outcomes—and the policies suggested—might well be different.

More basically, strategic thinking compares war and politics to games—that is, to contests in which the goals of each party are single, simple and unchanging: to win against the adversary—where "winning" is usually well defined and easily discernible. This disregards the experience of history that most major contests—and particularly most ideological contests—have not ended with a clearcut victory of either side. Even where more sophisticated models of variable sum games and of more-than-two person games are introduced, the assumption of fixed and single goals remains. This assumption ignores the findings of psychology and social science that most individuals and groups have plural goals and values, none of which may be pursued to the complete detriment or sacrifice of the others; further, that such goals and values often change in the course of time, or even in the course of their pursuit; and that goals and values certainly are not independent of the means used to preserve or pursue them.

By ignoring these considerations, strategic thinking often accepts uncritically the current goals and interests of the actors as fixed and given, regardless of their genesis and their probable change in the future. It disregards the interdependence between goals, the chosen means for their pursuit, and the personality structures and group arrangements of the actors. It thus often commits the fallacy of the irrelevance of ethics, or the related fallacy the ethical scruples as to means represent nothing but obstacles, costs or "luxuries" in the pursuit of policy, or even the ancient fallacy that ends justify all means, and that hence any means—including the most ruthless mass slaughter—could be used successfully to safeguard or attain "good" purposes.

In directing so much of our time and attention—and of the nation's time and attention—to images of terror and ruthless destruction, and so little to any images of moderation, compromise, and mutual accommodation, Dr. Rapoport charges, the strategists are making some headway in making us over in the image of their craft. Our minds tend to become, he thinks, at least somewhat influenced by their subjects of preoccupation. Phantasies of thermonuclear war may gradually lead us in our own minds to accept acts of cruelty and ruthlessness from which earlier we might have shrunk in horror— similar to the process of growing moral indifference toward the bombardment of civilian populations during World War II, culminating in the nuclear bombing of Hiroshima, and described step by step in Robert Batchelder's study *The Irreversible Decision*. By weakening or removing now, in the 1960's, on one or both sides of the international contest any still effective psychological inhibitions against nuclear mass killing, the indoctrination of the peoples with strategic modes of thought might increase the likelihood of bringing on in actuality the horrors envisaged in its theoretic calculations.

The strategic thinkers whom Rapoport criticizes are clearly identifiable from his text. Yet he does not attack them as persons. A strategist, he insists, is not a person but a social role. This is an argument in the spirit of Ralph Waldo Emerson's address on "The American Scholar" in which he opposed the use of such terms as "the farmer," "the worker," or "the thinker," and suggested as preferable "man farming," "man working," and "man thinking." Strategic thinking is then only one mode of thought—the mode, according to Rapoport, in which men seek "answers," that is, imposing their current values upon their environment, rather than seeking for "insights," that is, gaining a deeper and more critical insight into their own values, and thus an improved chance to change them toward something better. Strategic thinking tells us how to get what we want; conscience might tell us what we ought to want, that is, what it would be good or right for us to want.

Much of this critique is telling, and some of it is devastating. It seems to me that after the appearance of *Strategy and Conscience,* intellectually respectable strategic discourse will not be quite the same again. Dr. Rapoport has said much that needed saying, and that needed saying now.

It is against this urgency of its substance that the imperfections of the book must be assessed. If Dr. Rapoport had revised it for another year or two, it would then have been a more finished but perhaps less useful book. His discussions of game theory and probability are remarkably lucid, even though a few of the technical arguments are somewhat telescoped, and even those have a way of standing up when explicated and examined in more detail. The author is writing in order to be heard, and he admits freely that he sometimes has overstated his points in order to ensure them attention. Many of his critical remarks about the competitiveness in American culture and about the deficiencies of the public sense of social responsibility and moral purpose in the United States seem to me to fall in this category—surely David Riesman's "other-directed" men, "keeping down with the Joneses," are not quite as competitive as Dr. Rapoport sees them.

Dr. Rapoport defines ideology as "essentially a commitment to some particular aspect of the human condition," and stresses the complementary elements in American and Soviet ideology. He suggests similarities in the outlook of "liberals" in America and Russia, who have trust in the future development of their respective national societies, and another set of similarities between American ultra-conservatives and Russian Stalinists:

In short, both future-oriented views, the American and the Soviet, assume the perfectibility or at least the workability of the respective systems. Both conservative (actually reactionary) views are obsessed with the corruption of primitive virtues brought about by "modernistic" innovations.

He then points out differences, including the one which to him seems decisive: manipulation of the human psyche under Communist regimes; "the frank espousal of such manipulation by the Communists"; and the intellectual climate of dogmatism, that makes it almost impossible for Communists to learn readily from their own experiences and experiments. Dr. Rapoport sees some hope in the humanizing elements in Soviet culture, which he is finding in its children's books and in the classic literary and humanistic values communicated to all Russian youngsters in the early years of their schooling. He expects, therefore, the spirit of de-Stalinization to continue and prevail in the long run, and he suggests that efforts be made toward some "ideological disarmament" between America and the Soviet Union, without in any way abandoning or jeopardizing "the core of the ethos" of either of these societies.

Here again Dr. Rapoport has stated his points strongly in order to counteract, as he says, the "Devil image" which he finds dominating American and Russian views of one another. I would find somewhat less complementarity, and many more differences between American and Soviet politics and culture; and since I agree with Dr. Rapoport on the vital need for America—and presumably similarly for Russia—to preserve and defend the core of its values and its culture, it seems to me that what we might reasonably hope for would be not so much "ideological disarmament" between the two countries but at best something like a state of "ideological arms control." This, however, is Dr. Rapoport's book, not mine, and he has a full claim to our careful attention to the case he states.

In attacking the one-sidedness of much of strategic thinking, Dr. Rapoport himself has been stressing, it seems to me, chiefly one side in his own argument. He points out the intellectual and moral weaknesses of this overly narrow and only formally rational mode of thought, but in the same discussion he seems far less critical of the intuitive, insight-seeking, and "conscience-driven" mode of thinking which he recommends as an antidote for the inhuman calculations of many strategists. But there is little evidence that intuition and conscience would necessarily lead to wiser or more humane results. Intuition is notoriously fallible: conscience is very largely culture-bound; and both are determined in good part by the personality and the past and present existential conditions of each individual. Blind prejudice, bigoted fanaticism, and crusading self-righteousness often have operated under the style of intuition and of conscience. Even with the inefficient weapons of the past, they led to thousands of killings. They could kill many millions with the weapons of today. The ideological fanatic who would tolerate no compromise with evil, the general who will accept "no substitute for victory"—all these may well be following what they sincerely perceive to be the voice of their conscience.

Strategic thinking has been an important asset for the United States in overcoming the clamor of crackpots and crusaders. It has taught people to look at both sides of the contest and to take some account of the options and capabilities of the nation opposite them in international politics. It has made explicit much that was merely implied in the popular assumptions about national defense and foreign policy.

If strategic reasoning must be criticized also in terms of insight, wisdom and conscience, then conscience in its turn must be criticized by confrontation with reality, in the sense of biblical injunction, "By their fruits ye shall know them." If we may think of strategic reasoning as a first-order strategy, seeking means to attain given goals, then we may perhaps think of the problem of the right conscience—that is, the realistic and viable conscience—as a problem for a higher order strategy; that is to say, for the search for a principle or decision rule in accordance with which future lower order strategic decisions should be made.

Beyond demolishing some of the myths of strategic thinking, and establishing an eloquent and imaginative case for peace research, however, Dr. Rapoport has made this book a mine of insights and ideas in political and social science. His remarks on the proper relation of theories and experiments in the development of the social sciences deserve to become classic. His explanation of the importance of the "prisoner's dilemma" game as a model of conflict behavior and of international politics, and his preliminary report on the results of many thousands of controlled experiments which he and his collaborators have conducted with the aid of this new instrument should be of the utmost interest to political and social scientists.

Dr. Rapoport's remark that human behavior could be explained better in terms of past psychic commitments rather than of objective frequency of rewards suggests a very promising line of analysis as well as of empirical research. His emphasis on the subjective element in the assigning of classes for the estimation of probabilities and his discussion of the St. Petersburg paradox may eventually lead us to more adequate models for the making of rational decisions of this kind. Such models might include explicit terms for time horizons and time discounts, noise levels, resources and reserves of actors relevant to the gambler's ruin problem; and thus they might permit a more adequate separation of an actor's subjective psychological preferences, on the one hand, and his objective personal resources and capabilities, on the other.

Any such intellectual prospects should not distract us, however, from Dr. Rapoport's main points. The more effective our weapons have become, he concludes, the less intense or stable need be our intent for their use, and yet it will suffice to produce the same destruction. To butcher a million people with knives would require extreme motivation and perseverance. To kill the same number with a multi-megaton bomb might be done by pushing a few buttons; some day a casual error, a mechanical malfunctioning, or a fit of absentmindedness might be enough. Yet just as a lesser willingness to kill comes to suffice for an equally deadly result, many theorists of deterrence are urging to increase and display publicly our willingness to use nuclear weapons including some "credible first strike capability," in order to make more credible the threats which are to serve us as means of foreign policy; and as we are thus being urged closer to the brink of incalculable risk, other nations are being urged by their strategists to acquire their own nuclear weapons and the willingness to use them.

Under these conditions the poverty and rigidity of policy goals and intellectual resources admitted into strategic calculations is becoming a detriment to national security and to world peace. Strategic thinking has produced thus far at best something like "The Intelligent

Robot's Guide to International Politics." It is high time, Dr. Rapoport suggests, that thinking about war and peace became again a matter of the human conscience, of human insights, and of the multiple, interdependent, and developing values of mankind.

Dr. Rapoport's book is the first comprehensive and fundamental criticism of general present-day strategic thinking. It will not be the last one. Many of the problems he has opened up will occupy many of us for a long time to come. If we emerge in the end with a broader and more balanced way of thinking about international politics—a way that combines science and ethics, and insight and reason, compassion and competence—then we shall all owe a debt to Dr. Rapoport for having given a new urgency and direction to the search.

PREFACE

~~~~~~

To Clausewitz, war was the continuation of politics by other means. Had he lived to our day, he might have observed that international politics has become the continuation of war by other means.

In a way, the situation is not new. The foreign policies of the great powers have always been conceived as war is conceived and pursued as war is waged, by maneuvers, conspiracies, and coups. However, another factor has entered international politics since Clausewitz's time. In our day, not just the statesmen, the politicians, the diplomats, and the generals, but entire populations are involved in international politics. This is understandable, because war and peace have become not just alternative ways of pursuing "national interests" (once of concern only to specialists) but matters of life and death for all of us.

When a matter becomes everyone's concern, discussions of it tend to reflect deep-seated attitudes, predilections, and commitments rather than reasoned positions supported by rigorous argument. The increasing public concern with foreign policy in the United States has been reflected in just such trends. There is a "peace movement" consisting of scattered groups, whose leadership is recruited mainly among intellectuals and religious leaders. These groups stress the senselessness of the destruction which a major war is sure to bring. They propose various "just" solutions to the problems arising from the confrontation of powerful opposing blocs. Diametrically opposed to these groups are those of the extreme right. These people invoke an image of an implacably evil Enemy and urge the utmost exertion of will and armed right, which they envisage as leading to a final "victory."

Aloof from this clash of commitments stands the modern professional strategist. He is a master of a new science, whose principles are spelled out in abstract, often mathematical, terms. His expertness does not derive necessarily from experience with practical political or military matters but from training in physics, economics, political science, or the abstract principles of strategic thinking. His influence in decision-making quarters is evidenced by the flourishing state of the profession, by the lavish financing of gigantic research organizations devoted to the working out of diplo-military strategies, and by the predominance of "modern" strategic thinking in international affairs. He has also attained fame and with it a share of influence on public opinion. Accordingly, the books he writes and the testimony he gives in hearings deal not only with traditional problems of strategy (how to utilize sound strategic principles in the conduct of foreign policy, how to prepare for war, how to wage it) but also with the problem of assuaging the fear of war, which has become endemic in the population, especially the fear of nuclear war.

In combating the fear and the abhorrence of war, the modern strategist appeals to the qualities of thinking which characterize the scientific outlook and displays these qualities himself. In fact, claims to objectivity, maturity, realism, and courageous imagination sometimes appear explicitly in his writings.

One strategist, for example, defends his approach to problems related to nuclear war on the basis of a declaration that he has dared to "think of the unthinkable," and he has invited others to do likewise. Such declarations often give the impression of objectivity and composure, not only by the absence of invective directed against the "enemy" but also by an ascription of the same degree of "rationality" to the enemy that we ourselves possess.

Against the background of this discourse, both the ravings of the hate groups and the pleadings of the pacifists appear childish. The voice of strategy appears as the voice of reason and tolerance. Sophisticated strategic thinking tends to eschew dogmatic prescriptions. The strategist treats goals and costs as flexible parameters in his calculations. There appears to be room in the strategist's format for many policies, ranging over the entire spectrum from surrender through accommodation to toughness. Wars of graduated severity appear simply as a range of policies on one end of a scale. Nor is the other end of the scale excluded from consideration or, at least, from mention.

It appears, then, that the strategic mode of thought in the field of international conflict resembles only superficially the old-fashioned great-power diplomacy. Both may seem "coldly calculating," devoid of moral considerations, opportunistic, etc. But where old-fashioned diplomacy was content-oriented and tradition-bound, the modern "science of strategy" appears to be general and emancipated. In its sweep over the scale of goals and values, it appears to have included all possible positions.

"Name your figure," writes the strategist in effect. "How many lives is it worth to us to achieve such and such objectives? Ten, fifty, one hundred million? There is a policy for every objective." He might have gone on: "Pacifist? No need to shout. Just plug in your values and follow the method. No need to stop with pacifism. There are positions beyond—antivivisectionism, vegetarianism, anti-insecticidism, anti-antibioticism . . . Between these positions and the advocacy of a doomsday machine is only a scale of values."

Faced with such talk, many have been moved to anger. The strategist thrives on the anger of his opponents. It makes him appear objective and rational. It puts the opponents of the strategic mode of thought into the camp of scandalized defenders of obsolete prejudices, together with the antievolutionists and the decency-leaguers.

On occasions I have found myself in this position. One day, a strategist came to our university to give a lecture on "Defense and Strategy in the Nuclear Age." The seminar room was packed with standees. The tense atmosphere revealed itself in the ripples of nervous laughter which punctuated the lecturer's ghoulish jokes. In the all-too-brief question period, waving hands were clamoring for the chairman's attention. Several of the questions were exactly of the sort the lecturer might have anticipated. He was asked why instead of engaging in research applicable exclusively to war and to preparations for war (which the strategist maintained he abhorred "as much as any other father of small children") the strategists did not direct their talents to research aimed at averting war. Why did the "unthinkable," which the strategist so bravely faced, include only "scenarios" of massive destruction? Why did his scheme not include other "un-thinkable" situations, for example, the consequences of complete sur-render, etc.?

The strategist's replies were exactly to the point. Much strategic research, he averred, *was* directed at preventing war. The possibilities of surrender *were* being considered. At any rate, there was nothing in the strategic approach that prevented such alternatives from being considered. If any scientist picked up one line of research rather than another, this was because of the nature of scientific endeavor, which demands a division of labor based on differentiated spheres of competence. Far from discouraging peace research, he maintained, the strategic mode of thinking actually encouraged effective peace research, in fact guaranteed that recommendations for peaceful or accommodating moves in the game of diplomatic maneuver were in effect conducive to the aims they were supposed to serve. Thereby the discussion was kept on the rails.

Like many others (who later told me of their impressions), I felt engulfed by a wave of repugnance. I felt as if someone had taken Swift's *Modest Proposal* seriously and had proceeded to defend it by ridiculing prejudice, by invoking the principle of "the greatest good for the greatest number," and by dismissing moral indignation as a symptom of sentimentalism.

Succumbing to my feelings, I asked the speaker whether he would agree to a definition of "genocide" as a deliberate slaughter of helpess populations for political ends, adding that I was bringing up this subject only because he himself had mentioned it in his talk. The speaker accepted the definition. I then asked him whether he realized that in view of the several precedents set at Nuremberg, Warsaw, Jerusalem, and elsewhere, genocide was a hanging offense, and, if so, how would he defend himself if at some future time he were a co-defendant in a genocide trial.

Again the reply was dignified and to the point. He said that if mass destruction resulted, despite expectations, from policies based on his and others' analyses, and if on these grounds he were held responsible, he would plead "partially guilty." The purpose of his research, he kept saying, was to avert war, not to kill people more efficiently. If war nevertheless broke out, he would be "genuinely sorry." (Those were his words.)

After the meeting I learned that many of my colleagues thought my question inappropriate. This feeling was shared, I was told, by the chairman, a convinced and active pacifist. The basis of the feeling was obvious. I had violated the standards of academic discourse. These standards include the constraint of keeping the discussion within the mode of reasoned argument and within the sphere circumscribed by the subject of the discussion. It was expected, therefore, that questions would be confined to matters pertaining to the accuracy of asserted facts, the consistency of stated assumptions, the validity of drawn inferences, and the like. Questions of morality, while possibly crucially important in themselves, should have been excluded, because they were not pertinent to the subject of discussion. Personal attacks on the speaker were altogether taboo.

As a member of the academic community, I could not but acknowledge the correctness of this criticism. I had no doubt that one belonged to the academic community (as to any other community) by virtue of accepting its standards of value. I knew also that freedom of inquiry was one of the most cherished of the standards I was bound to respect. This implies that anyone's serious intellectual exercises had a right to a serious hearing and that granting this right carried an obligation of following the man who asked to be heard from his assumptions to his conclusions. I knew also that accepting for the sake of argument someone's assumptions carried no implication of agreement; that the rules of the game required one to defer the criticism of the assumptions until the inferences had been drawn.

Yet I could not escape the feeling that something was wrong somewhere if these standards were to be indiscriminately applied to all controversy as long as it formally fell within the scientific mode. I returned once more to the hypothetical case which I felt was analogous to the present one. I tried to imagine what would happen if a scientist carried out and reported investigations that led to the arguments once presented by Jonathan Swift in his morbid essay.[1]*

Suppose, I thought, a scientist felt concerned about the food problem in the post-nuclear-attack period and carried out calculations on how many adult lives could be saved by judicious utilization of babies' flesh. Being of a humanitarian disposition, the scientist would also be understandably concerned with the moral problem, but being a

* Superscripts refer to the Notes at the end of this volume.

scientist, he would try to "solve" this problem also. At first he would convince himself that as far as the *babies* were concerned, there would be no suffering to speak of. The slaughtering could be carried out without the infliction of pain, and, of course, the babies would not be subjected to any mental anguish either, being unaware of what was happening. The real problem would be seen to lie in the attitudes of the adults, particularly of the parents of babies. Clearly then, our scientist would conclude, research should be directed along lines aimed at discovering means, possibly conditioning procedures, possibly narcotics, to remove the psychological obstacles to a rational solution of the food problem. If, say, a drug could be found that would do the trick (make parents less resistant to the scheme), the solution would be almost within grasp. Of course, the problem would still remain of how to induce adults to take the drug. But this problem could also be treated as a technological problem (as every problem can be made to appear), and its solution could be referred to appropriate specialists.

Suppose now the scientist presented his findings and recommendations to the scientific community. How should this information be received? How *would* it be received? Would consternation inspired by sentiment override the compulsion of keeping the discussion within the confines of academic etiquette? Would any one insist that some sort of bounds have been transgressed and that therefore the standards of free discussion were simply not tenable under these circumstances?

I have discussed these matters with a colleague who abhors the idea of nuclear war but who feels that somehow the choice of a "right strategy" can preserve peace. He has on several occasions invited me to participate in seminars on arms control, technological problems of inspection, and the like. For the most part, I have declined these invitations, for I could not bring myself, even tentatively, to assume that such discussions are relevant to the problem of preserving peace, and I knew that speaking in another mode in the environment of such seminars would serve no constructive purpose.

My colleague keeps taking me to task for refusing to "do my part." Taking the attitude that I do, he says, cuts me off completely from quarters where decisions are made. I ought to be putting out effort to exert at least a minimal influence on these quarters instead of staying ineffectively on the side of the angels. I have no chance of being listened to, he says, so long as I keep insisting that the moral issues are central. These issues are deliberately excluded from defense policy. I ask him whether "they" listen to *him* when he criticizes strategic thinking in the language of strategy. He admits that "they" do not, but at least that he talks to someone who talks to someone who is listened to.

There is a great deal of merit in my colleague's argument. To be sure, I am not convinced, as he seems to be, that the only hope lies in reaching the "decision-makers." But I am equally unconvinced that a dent can be made upon anybody by persistently calling attention to the moral issue. For the moral issue is something to think about only when it is not a hindrance. It is a hindrance in strategic thinking and therefore must be dismissed either scornfully ("Sentiments! Naiveté!") or regretfully ("Something to think about, but we live in a different kind of world.") Therefore the strategic thinker cannot be reached with moral arguments. The sincere and competent strategic thinker, however, can be reached with "rational" arguments because he is involved with what he believes to be rational procedures. Indeed he takes pride in the "rationality" of strategic thinking, in which he invests his professional competence. (In our age no involvement is more complete than professional involvement.) Therefore if strategic thinkers and all those who listen only to them are to be reached at all, their adamant demand must be met. Any crossing of swords must take place on their own territory. This I have attempted to do in Parts I and II of this book.

The last chapters, however, are devoted to what I believe to be the real issues of the Cold War. There I make a plea to come to grips with these issues instead of playing games of strategy for enormous and unrecoverable stakes.

ACKNOWLEDGMENTS

This book grew out of two papers contributed to a five-week conference on international conflict sponsored by the American Academy of Arts and Sciences in 1962. My first debt is to the Academy and the thirteen colleagues, the participants in the conference, who stimulated, challenged, and inspired me. They are:

Kenneth E. Boulding M.A. (Oxon), codirector, Center for Research in Conflict Resolution, and Professor of economics, University of Michigan, Ann Arbor, Mich.; author of *Conflict and Defense, The Image, Economic Analysis, The Economics of Peace,* etc.

Urie Bronfenbrenner, professor of psychology and of child development and family relationships, Cornell University; Fellow, Center for Advanced Study in the Behavioral Sciences, 1955–1956.

Morton Deutsch, Ph.D., social psychologist, Bell Telephone Laboratories, Murray Hill, N.J.; coeditor of *Preventing World War III, Some Proposals.*

Erik Erikson, professor of human development, lecturer on psychiatry, Harvard University; author.

Amitai Etzioni, assistant professor of sociology and staff member of Institute of War and Peace Studies, Columbia University, New York City; author of *Comparative Analysis of Complex Organizations,* and *The Hard Way to Peace.*

Roger Fisher, B.V., LL.B., professor of law, Harvard Law School; assistant to the Solicitor General of the United States, 1956–1958; author of "Constructing Rules that Affect Governments," in *Arms*

Control, Disarmament and National Security, etc.; consultant, Department of Defense.

William A. Gamson, Ph.D., social psychology; research associate in social psychiatry, jointly at the Department of Social Relations and the School of Public Health, Harvard University; author of "A Theory of Coalition Formation," *American Sociological Review;* "The Fluoridation Dialogue: Is It an Ideological Conflict?," *Public Opinion Quarterly,* etc.

Kathleen Gough, Ph.D., associate professor of anthropology, University of Oregon; field work on Indian kinship systems and Indian religion; publications include fifteen or sixteen professional papers, the most recent, "When the Saints Go Marching In: An Account of the Ban the Bomb Movement in England."

Lester Grinspoon, M.D.; senior research psychiatrist, Massachusetts Mental Health Center, Boston; assistant in psychiatry, Harvard Medical School; publications in social psychiatry, group therapy, psychopharmacology, and medicine.

E. James Lieberman, M.D.; fellow in psychiatry, James Jackson Putnam Children's Center, Boston; research and training in social psychiatry; author of "Psychochemicals as Weapons," *Bulletin of the Atomic Scientists;* "The Moral Context of Psychiatry" and "Non-Violence vs. Pacifism," *American Association for Social Psychiatry,* etc.

Elliot G. Mishler, Ph.D., social psychology; director of psychological research, Massachusetts Mental Health Center, Boston; research associate, Department of Psychiatry, Harvard Medical School; publications in social psychiatry, epidemiology, and social organization.

James A. Robinson, Ph.D., assistant professor of political science and staff member of the program of graduate training and research in international relations, Northwestern University, Evanston, Illinois; author of *The Monroney Resolution: Congressional Initiative in Foreign Policy Making.*

Arthur Waskow, historian and staff member, Peace Research Institute; author of *The Limits of Defense.*

Subsequently I had lengthy conversations on the subject of this book with J. David Singer, whose office is three doors down the hall from mine, and with Karl W. Deutsch of Yale University, separately and together during the latter's frequent visits to the Mental Health Research Institute during 1962–1963. Many ideas contained here have been instigated, modified, and frequently criticized by these two political scientists and philosophers.

Valuable editorial suggestions were offered by my wife, by Mrs. Claire Adler, and by the editors of Harper & Row.

The Mental Health Research Institute placed generous secretarial help at my disposal.

Permission to incorporate material from my earlier papers (included in *International Conflict and Behavioral Science,* "The Craigville Papers," Roger Fisher, editor) was gratefully received from Basic Books, Inc.

Ann Arbor, Michigan   A.R.
February 1964

Part I. Theories of Rational Decision

CHAPTER 1

INTRODUCTION

The widespread interest which game theory has attracted in the United States may have been instigated by some deep-seated attitudes pervasive in this country.

One such attitude is our ready acceptance of competition as a way of life. In common usage, the term "competition" refers to conflicts in which either (1) the conflicting parties recognize certain rules or constraints, hence "cooperate," at least in the sense of keeping the conflict within certain limits; or (2) the acts of the conflicting parties are not directed explicitly against each other. Examples of conflicts under self-imposed constraints are the many forms of competitive games. Examples of the second kind of conflicts are "contests," in which contestants match prowess or skill but are not permitted (or have no opportunity) to impede the efforts of their competitors. For example, track runners are not allowed to trip each other; pole vaulters cannot affect each other's performance, etc. We shall refer to such conflicts as *non-interactive*.

Business competition is frequently pictured as having both of these features. Such competition must function within limits prescribed by law and sometimes by professional ethics.

Competition thus appears to be a form of conflict from which hostility and viciousness have been eliminated. This "civilized" garb, together with the well-known survival-of-the-fittest principle (long used as a justification of economic competition) has made competition eminently acceptable in our society.

As it will turn out (cf. page 36), the voluntary acceptance of rules is not a necessary feature of situations to which the theory of games can be applied. As for non-interactive conflicts, to which contests and many forms of the struggle for existence belong, they fall altogether outside the scope of game theory.

There is, however, another attitude, prevalent in the United States, which is also conducive to promoting interest in game theory, namely, a faith in science as a tool for mastering the environment. Here game theory seems especially pertinent, for it purports to be a science of rational decision in conflict situations.

A key concept in game theory is that of *strategy*. Although this concept is not relevant to certain forms of competition, namely non-interactive contests (which, as we have said, fall outside the scope of game theory), this distinction is not made among non-specialists. Frequent mentions of game theory in popular writings on related subjects have given the impression that a basis has finally been found for uniting in a single conceptual scheme all situations where parties vie for positions of advantage or compete for prizes: points in a parlor game, profits or shares of the market in business competition, or, in the context of international relations, the real or imagined gains in security, power, prestige, and strategic advantage in future contests. Once game theory is defined as the "science of rational conflict," it is easy and tempting to conclude that a mastery of the theory makes one a successful competitor.

In this light, the widespread interest in a theory which was first presented in an involved and abstruse mathematical treatise becomes understandable. Game theory is a codification of strategic thinking, and strategic thinking, particularly in conflict situations, appears to be a paradigm of rational analysis.

Rational analysis, in turn, is almost by definition the basis of effective thinking. This view is dictated by both scientific and practical experience. Specifically:

1. Rational analysis is *realistic*. It takes into account verifiable facts. It guards against mistaking our wishes for facts. It separates questions about what is from questions about what ought to be.

2. Rational analysis is *deductive*. It uses all the available techniques of logical reasoning, including calculations and mathematical inference.

3. Rational analysis is *predictive* and therefore *productive*. On the basis of established facts, reasonably valid inductions, and rigorous deductions, rational analysis provides us with the most reliable

estimates and expectations of future events, thereby conferring upon us a measure of control over our environment.

4. Rational analysis is unencumbered, not only by sentiments (in which we usually find strong admixtures of wishful thinking) but also by awe of authority, by superstitions, dogmas, and neurotic fears. It is therefore conducive to *free* and *courageous* thinking.

5. Rational analysis is indicative of *sanity*, because mentally disturbed people are the ones who violate the principles of rational analysis most conspicuously.

In short, rational analysis is conducted in the *problem-solving* mode, hence in the framework of *mature* thinking.

Nevertheless, rational analysis, like every other tool, has its limitations. Failure to realize these can lead us into grave errors, for the very power of rational analysis inspires confidence in the results of any theory based on it and so makes errors resistant to correction. Errors frequently result from applying a level of decision theory inappropriate to the situation examined and also from confusing the modes of the theory. For, as we shall see, rational decision theory has at least three different modes and several levels of complexity, to each of which a different level of analysis applies. Erroneous estimates of the level of analysis appropriate in a given case can result in a gross distortion of the problem under consideration; confusing the modes of the theory can lead to a misinterpretation of the results of the analysis.

The three modes of decision theory which we shall need to distinguish are the formal, the prescriptive (or normative), and the descriptive (or empirical).

The formal mode is purely deductive. Like mathematics, of which it frequently appears as a branch, formal decision theory does not depend on data. The axioms of the theory, as well as all the pertinent variables in any problem, are always assumed to be given. The task of the theory is confined to the construction of a deductive apparatus to be used in deriving logically necessary conclusions from given assumptions.

Prescriptive theory, on the other hand, is concerned with the determination of *optimal* decisions. It depends on a set of given *goals*. Only when goals are specifically stated and when a situation is explicitly described can the method of prescriptive theory be applied in the pursuit of such goals. The existence of "best" decisions (in the sense of furthering given goals) does not by any means imply that real people are always or predominantly guided by them. Thus, discrepancies between prescriptive theory and observed behavior do not refute a prescriptive theory. Such a theory says how people ought to act, not how they do act.

A descriptive theory seeks to find principles which guide real people's decisions. It must therefore rely on *behavioral data*. Such a theory acomplishes its aims if it can say (and support the statement with empirical evidence) something like this: "People make decisions, *as if* they were guided by the following such and such decision rules . . ." Since the decision patterns of different people may be different, the descriptive theory will rely in part on classifications, typologies, and other groupings of decision-makers.

It follows that formal decision theory (which includes the mathematical theory of games) is most nearly related to the deductive disciplines (logic and mathematics); prescriptive decision theory, to applied "hard" sciences (e.g., engineering and operations research); and descriptive decision theory, to the behavioral sciences.

In the chapters which constitute Part I, we shall deal with the theories of rational decision, as they apply to various situations confronting the decision-maker, in the order of increasing complexity, namely, decisions under certainty, under risk, under uncertainty, and in conflicts of various types. In each case, we shall first present a formal theory of rational decisions. These formal theories, as we have said, bypass the problem of collecting and evaluating data on which the decisions are to be based, because formal theories do not depend on data. In order to construct a prescriptive theory on the basis of a formal one, certain types of data are needed, depending on the nature of the problem. We shall therefore examine the problem of obtaining data required in the solutions of different types of decision problems. In some cases it will turn out that such data cannot be obtained without a descriptive theory of decision. This will lead us to some of the problems inherent in descriptive theory. Part I, then, purports to be a short survey of the present state of the theory of rational decision and, in addition, an inventory of requirements which such a theory must satisfy if it is to serve as an effective guide to action.

CHAPTER 2

THE OUTCOMES ARE CERTAIN

The simplest example of a decision problem involves the choice of one of several courses of action, where the outcome of each course is uniquely determined. That is, if we choose action A_1, we are sure to get outcome O_1; if A_2, we shall get O_2, etc. In this context, the choice of action which leads to the most preferred outcome is called a rational decision.

Already in this simplest problem we can see the distinctive features of the formal, prescriptive, and descriptive approaches. The formal theory does no more than *define* the rational decision in this context, as has just been done. Prescriptive theory must prescribe. It can therefore be applied only after the most preferred outcome has been determined, which may require no more than an introspective "scanning" on the part of the decision-maker. Descriptive theory, on the other hand, must relate many people's preference schemes and many decision schemes. It is by no means certain that such comparisons will immediately enable the investigator to organize his data into a theory; i.e., a set of general propositions consistent with observed facts. In short, it is not certain whether a descriptive theory of rational decisions even when the outcomes of actions are certain is at all possible. To assume that it is possible is to affirm the basic faith inherent in the scientific enterprise.

To deserve being called "rational" (as we usually understand the term), decisions must satisfy at least three criteria, namely consistency, instrumentality, and transitivity.

Consistency means that if we prefer outcome O_1 to outcome O_2, we do not at the same time prefer O_2 to O_1.

Instrumentality means that if we prefer outcome O_1 to outcome O_2, we also prefer action A_1 (if it guarantees O_1) to action A_2 (if it leads to O_2).

Transitivity means that if we prefer O_1 to O_2 and O_2 to O_3, we also prefer O_1 to O_3.

In the context of formal theory, these criteria are only a restatement of the definition of a rational decision. In the context of a prescriptive theory, they are rules for ordering preferences and choosing actions. What role do the criteria play in descriptive theory? Clearly they cannot be general descriptions of our gross observations of how people order preferences and choose actions. Violations of these principles are all too common, as the examples we are about to list will show. Confronted with such violations, we could, of course, draw the conclusion that the violators are not behaving "rationally." However, we can usually do better than that. We can often redefine the situation so as to remove the violations. Usually such a redefinition will involve a revision of the list of outcomes, so that outcomes which were first assumed to be simple turn out to be complex. If the redefinition of the decision situation removes the apparent violations of the criteria of rationality, the criteria are thereby vindicated. That is to say, people are seen to act more rationally than it first appeared. We might therefore say that an aim of descriptive decision theory is to describe people's decisions in such a way as to make them appear "rational."

Can such a theory be justified? Is it not true that people often act "irrationally?" We must take care here to distinguish between different meanings of "rational." People do, in fact, often act irrationally in the sense that their actions lead to outcomes which they themselves deplore. However, our definition of rationality was in terms of extremely weak criteria. Such "rationality" is by no means to be identified with prudence or wisdom or intelligence. The criteria we have offered are only different aspects of consistency. They are nothing but a minimal framework within which decisions must be made in order to make *some* sense. They leave the widest latitude to the decision-maker's perception of the situation and to his value system. In this way, the axioms define the task of descriptive theory: to discover the perceptual framework and the value system of the decision-maker, in the light of which his decisions will make sense.

VIOLATIONS OF THE CRITERIA OF RATIONALITY

Consistency seems to be violated when a decision-maker changes his mind for no apparent reason. At times, however, we discover additional features of the situation which make the change of preference understandable. If we can *codify* these features, that is, state a rule which governs the changes of preference, the consistency criterion is restored. What happens is that more outcomes appear in the situation than were originally discerned.

Suppose a man, confronted with a menu, sometimes chooses meat and sometimes fish. We could describe this "inconsistency" to momentary shifts of preference; that is, essentially to whim. Choices dictated by whim are by definition not rational. It may happen, however, that we discover perfectly consistent patterns: The man orders fish only on Fridays and meat on all other days. The two outcomes "eating meat" and "eating fish" have split into four; namely "meat on Friday," "fish on Friday, " "meat on non-Friday," and "fish on non-Friday." Of these, the second of the first pair is preferred, but the first of the second pair. The inconsistency has disappeared.

Instrumentality is violated when a decision-maker seemingly chooses an action which leads to a less desirable instead of to a more desirable outcome. Often such decisions cease to appear to be violations if we discover on closer examination that decisions have side effects, not taken into account in the outcomes. If we observe that a firm decides on a course of action which leads to smaller rather than larger net profit, we may conjecture that the decision has other less obvious concomitants. For example, public relations, potential for future growth, etc. When these are taken into account, the action may turn out to lead to the most preferred outcome.

As an example of a violation of transitivity, consider a man who has three wives, O_1, O_2, and O_3. When choosing between O_1 and O_2, he consistently prefers O_1; between O_2 and O_3, he prefers O_2. But confronted with a choice between O_1 and O_3, he chooses O_3. Here we may need to consider a certain aspect of the choice situation itself, which is not discernible in the objects compared. Suppose that O_1 is the eldest wife, secure in her seniority and above jealousy and that O_2, the next, is extremely jealous, especially of O_3, who is the youngest and prettiest. Although O_2 is jealous, she understands seniority rights, even insists on them (looking forward to the time when there will be no O_1). In her presence, therefore, the man gives preference to O_1 over her. The extreme jealousy and status consciousness of O_2 makes the preference for her over O_3 mandatory in the interest of preserving peace in the family. However, while O_2 is not looking, O_1 in her declining years has no objection to being passed over in favor of O_3. The O's can then be listed as follows in the order of preference: O'_3 (that is, O_3 when O_2 is not present) is preferred to O_1, who is preferred to O_2, who is preferred to O_3. Now transitivity has been saved but again at the cost of increasing the number of "outcomes."

We can imagine another situation in which the transitivity is violated. Suppose our decision-maker is not a single individual but a three-man committee, which makes its decisions by a majority vote. Call the members of the committee Potter, Andrews, and Fox. Let Potter prefer the outcomes (no longer wives) in the order O_1–O_2–O_3; Andrews, in the order O_2–O_3–O_1; and Fox, in the order O_3–O_1–O_2.

As an illustration imagine that the task of the committee (appointed by the governing board of a country club) is to decide on recommending an expenditure. The alternatives are O_1: to build a clubhouse with a bar; O_2: to build a clubhouse without a bar; and O_3: to build no clubhouse. Potter is a spendthrift. He prefers O_1 to O_2 and O_2 to O_3. Andrews is a teetotaler. He wants a clubhouse without a bar (O_2) but rather than having one with a bar (O_1), he would prefer having no clubhouse at all (O_3). Fox is a tightwad and a sop. He would rather spend no money at all (O_3); but if money is to be spent, he wants a bar (O_1). To him a clubhouse without a bar (O_2) is a total loss. All these preferences are shown in Table 1.

Members of Committee	Decreasing Preference $\longrightarrow$		
P	O_1	O_2	O_3
A	O_2	O_3	O_1
F	O_3	O_1	O_2

TABLE 1

We see by the table that the committee prefers O_1 over O_2 by majority vote, since Potter and Fox prefer them in that order. Also O_2 is preferred to O_3 by majority vote, since Potter and Andrews so prefer them. And also O_3 is preferred to O_1 by majority vote, since Andrews and Fox are also a majority. The committee's preference order is therefore O_1–O_2–O_3–O_1. Again the criterion of transitivity is violated.[2]

A similar situation can arise when an individual must make comparisons among objects on several "dimensions" at once. For example, O_1, O_2, and O_3 in Table 1 can be three oranges; and P, A, and F, three different bases of comparison, e.g., price, appearance, and flavor. The oranges are preferred in the order O_1–O_2–O_3 on the basis of price (O_1 being the cheapest), in the order O_2–O_3–O_1 on the basis of appearance, and in the order O_3–O_1–O_2 on the basis of flavor. If the chooser simply counts the number of aspects in which one orange rates above another, he will rank the oranges in the order O_1–O_2–O_3–O_1 and so will violate transitivity.

Thus difficulties arise even in the simplest decision problems, namely, in decisions under certainty. The most common difficulties stem from the presence of incomparable components of outcomes. They arise both in prescriptive and in descriptive theories of rational decision. Attempts to get around such difficulties constitute the so-called theory of utility. In this theory, it is assumed that all aspects of outcomes have a common scale of comparison. That is to say, *numerical* values (positive or negative) are assigned to the aspects, and it is assumed that these values can be algebraically added to ascertain the total utility of an outcome. If the orange chooser can assign such values to price, appearance, and flavor and add them, his problem reduces to that of comparing three numbers (utilities). He can then choose the orange with the largest utility. If utilities of different *people* can be added, the members of the committee can do the same. This is actually done when decisions in boxing matches or in beauty contests are made on the basis of total points assigned to contestants by the different members of a jury.

A utility theory is also indispensable on the next level of decision problems, namely, on the level of decisions under risk. We shall have more to say about it in the next chapter.

CHAPTER 3

THE OUTCOMES ARE RISKY

We now abandon our assumption that every decision leads to a single known outcome. We suppose instead that each decision may lead to one of a *specified set* of outcomes and, moreover, that the *probability* of each outcome in this set is known to the decision-maker. Such outcomes are called risky.

Clearly if the decision-maker knows only the probability with which a given decision will lead to a given outcome, he has less information than in the case where he knows the outcome with certainty. For the same reason, he seems to have less control. However, if the probabilities of the outcomes remain constant and if the decisions can be repeated, the decision-maker can expect that *in the long run* outcomes associated with his decisions will occur with known frequencies. Thus in a situation involving decision under risk, although both information and control are reduced compared to the situation involving decision under certainty, nevertheless both information and control are restored *in the long run,* if three conditions are satisfied: (1) There is a long run, that is, the situation presents itself many times. (2) The probabilities of outcomes stay put. (3) Numerical utilities are assigned to the outcomes, and these utilities can be added.

These conditions are satisfied in many types of business where risk is standardized, for example, in insurance. The long run is provided in the large volume of the business. There are millions of insured individuals. The frequency of the events against which they are insured (say, accidents) are "statistically stable," that is, the frequency does not fluctuate beyond certain limits. In business a natural measure of utility is money. Money is additive. Thus the money utility of two or more outcomes is simply the sum of the (positive or negative) amounts of money associated with them. In this way, by establishing rates of compensation and premiums, insurance companies have control over long run returns.

The long run money utility of an outcome is computed by multiplying its probability by its money utility. This is the *expected gain* of the outcome. The concept of expected gain allows an extension of the theory of rational decision to situations in which the outcomes are risky. Although the particular outcome of a particular action is not known in decisions under risk, the long run gains are reasonably certain, and so the principle of instrumentality can be applied: Choose the action which leads to the greatest expected gain.

Maximum expected gain or "moral expectation" as a principle of rational decision was proposed by the early authors of probability theory, which was first worked out in the context of gambling. It was not long, however, until a serious difficulty appeared, exemplified in the famous St. Petersburg Paradox discovered by James Bernoulli (7).*

This mathematician analyzed a game in which the player tosses a coin until it falls "tails" and collects doubling amounts with each successive "heads." Thus if the first toss is tails, he collects nothing; if the first tail is preceded by one "heads," he collects 1 unit; if the first tail is preceded by two consecutive heads, he collects $1+2=3$ units; for three successive heads he collects $1+2+4=7$ units, etc. In general, if the first tail is preceded by k heads, the tosser collects 2^k-1 units. The game is now known as the St. Petersburg Game. It can be interpreted as a bet as follows. The player bets a constant amount. His opponent bets the amount 2^k-1, this amount to be determined by k, the number of successive heads which will precede the tails. The problem is to determine the break-even bet, i.e., the constant amount that the player must bet in order to make it a fair bet. Once this constant amount is determined, the principle of moral

* Numbers in parentheses refer to bibliographical entries at the end of the volume.

expectation dictates that the tosser should be willing to bet any smaller amount per play of the game.

The surprising result is that there is no break-even bet. *Any* amount which the tosser bets gives him a positive expected gain (i.e., is to be preferred to "no bet") because the expected gain of the tosser in this game is infinite!

One way of explaining this bizarre conclusion is by invoking the "long wait." If one waits "long enough," *eventually* any losses incurred will be made up by a windfall. Nevertheless for a moderately large constant bet per play (say 10 units), the expected time of this event becomes discouragingly long. This is why the "infinite expected gain" of the St. Petersburg Game is of no practical value. Related to this explanation is the so-called gambler's ruin. It is assumed that the tosser's capital is limited. Therefore, in view of the long wait, it is very likely that he will have lost his capital and so must quit playing before his ship comes in.

Both of these explanations seem satisfactory in this context. But there are other situations in which the recommendation to accept bets with positive "moral expectation" seems dubious on other grounds. Or, equivalently, it seems rational (or prudent) to accept bets with negative expected gain. The most familiar example of the latter situation is insurance. The amount claimed multiplied by the probability of the event which justifies the claim (the moral expectation of the insured) must always be smaller than the premium for the period multiplied by the probability that no claim can be made during the period; otherwise the insurance companies are on the losing side of the bet and cannot stay in business. But then, if the expected gain criterion for accepting bets is rational, how can the buyer of insurance also be rational if he accepts the odds?

Bernoulli's concept of "utility" seems to explain both the theory of insurance and the St. Petersburg Paradox without invoking the long wait argument. It is only necessary to assume that the utility of an amount of money is not proportional to the amount but "less than proportional" to it (cf. Figure 1).

Bernoulli's theory is attractive for a number of reasons. First, as we shall presently see, it explains the paradoxes and saves the moral expectation principle. Second, it is intuitively acceptable: We feel that the same amount of money "means less" to a rich man than to a poor man. Third, the theory echoes certain findings in psychophysics: The larger the stimuli, the larger must be the differences between them to make them distinguishable.[3]

Let us now see how the theory explains insurance. First, let us compute the expected gains in money. Suppose I have a house worth

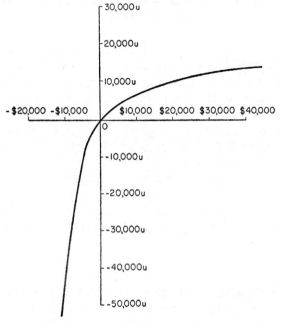

FIGURE 1. A utility scale showing a "diminishing return" utility of money.

$10,000, which I insure for $10,000, paying a premium of $1 per year. Suppose the odds against the house burning down within the year are 19,999 to 1. If a fire occurs, the insurance company repays me the value of the house, and I have lost only the premium. If no fire occurs, I still have paid the premium. My "expected gain" from this transaction is −$1. On the other hand, if I do not buy insurance, I expected to lose $10,000 with probability of one chance in 20,000 or to lose nothing with probability of 19,999 chances in 20,000. My expected loss is only 50 cents. By the principle of preferring bets with higher expected gain (or equivalently lower expected losses) I ought to reject the bet offered by the insurance company. Now let us calculate the "utiles," assuming the utility of money to be as pictured on the curve in Figure 1. The negative utility of losing $10,000 may be −50,000 utiles instead of −10,000. If this is the case, the "no insurance" bet brings −50,000×.00005 = −2.5 utiles, as against −1 utile of the insurance bet.

Such is the gist of Bernoulli's explanation of accepting "unfair bets." (The explanation of the St. Petersburg Paradox is similar.)

Let us now see how what we have said relates to formal, prescriptive, and descriptive theories of decision. Clearly, the only task of a formal theory of decision under risk is to calculate odds or expected gains. This is at times a complicated problem. In general, however, such problems yield to the tools of probability theory. Thus the formal theory, although a step removed from a mere definition of rational decision (with which it is identical when the outcomes are certain) still presents no conceptual difficulties. Prescriptive theory, we have seen, is based on the utilities assigned to the several outcomes and on the probabilities of the outcomes. These must be given or ascertained before the theory can prescribe.

Are utilities and probabilities sufficient? What about the principle of maximizing the expected (utility) gain? Is this an additional axiom of rational decision, to be added to consistency, transitivity, and instrumentality? The answer is yes, if utilities of outcomes can be determined independently of preferences of risky choices. The answer is no, if they can be determined only with reference to such choices.

To see why this is so, we must turn to the problems faced by the descriptive theory of rational decision under risk.

HOW TO DETERMINE THE UTILITY SCALE

The task of descriptive theory, we have said, is to make sense of people's decisions. For example a discovery of the following type would constitute a success of such a theory: When faced with risky outcomes, people choose actions associated with maximum expected utility gains. What would it take to verify such a rule? We should know the utilities which people assign to outcomes and the probabilities of all the possible outcomes associated with each choice of action. We are then in a position to compare the expected utility gain of the action taken with those of other actions.

But how does one go about finding out what utilities people assign to outcomes? Conceivably we could question people, but the value of their answers to such questions would be doubtful. Answers to questions about preferences are most readily given when outcomes are compared in pairs and are of similar nature. The easiest (and most predictable) answer is to the question "Which do you prefer, $1 or $2?" As the outcomes became dissimilar or complex, preferences are more difficult to establish. For example, the choice between a subway ride and a cigar is not usually clear cut. Still a preference decision between two alternatives is always possible in principle. However, such a decision does not constitute an assignment of utilities. It only determines the relative magnitudes of two utilities, i.e., positions on an ordinal scale. This is not sufficient for the calculation of expected gains. Expected utility gains are sums of products of utilities and probabilities. This means essentially that utilities must be assigned *numerical* values, not merely ordinal positions like first choice, second choice, etc.[4] If prescriptive theory is to prescribe or if descriptive theory is to describe, these numerical values must be somehow determined.

Von Neumann and Morgenstern, in writing their famous treatise on game theory (124), felt that it was necessary to put utility theory on a rigorous basis, because numerical utilities played an essential part in the theory. In terms of modern concepts of rigor, this meant that a procedure had to be specified for ascertaining a given decision maker's (player's) utility scale. In order to specify such a procedure, von Neumann and Morgenstern assumed that a preference can always be determined between any two *risky* outcomes.

To take an example, consider the choice among three sums of money, $0, $1, and $2. The accepted view is that the preference ordering will be $2 > $1 > $0. (The symbol > stands for "is preferred to.") But this does not mean that utilities 2, 1, and 0 can or should be assigned to the three amounts respectively. To determine these utilities, choices must be offered between certain and risky outcomes. First, the choice is offered between (1) \$1 and (2) a "lottery ticket," which wins \$2 with probability 0.5 or \$0 with probability 0.5. If these choices are equally attractive, then the utility "distances" between \$2 and \$1 and between \$1 and \$0 are considered equal, and so utilities 2, 1, and 0 can be assigned to these sums. But suppose \$1 is preferred to the lottery ticket? This would mean that \$1 is valued nearer to \$2 than to \$0. If so, the odds for \$2 can be raised so as to make the lottery ticket somewhat more attractive. The question is now "How much should the odds in favor of \$2 be raised in order to make the lottery ticket as attractive as \$1?" Certainly there is some point at which this happens. For suppose the "lottery ticket" guarantees \$2 with certainty. It will now certainly be preferred to \$1. Therefore at some value of the odds in favor of \$2 the choice between \$1 and the lottery ticket must have become indifferent. (If the initial preference at even odds had been for the lottery ticket, the procedure would have been reversed, i.e., the odds in favor of \$2 would have been lowered until the preference vanished.)

Suppose, then, that the point of indifference is associated with probability of 0.7 that \$2 will be paid. In this case, we say that the utility of \$1 is equal to $0.7 \times$ (utility of \$2) $+ 0.3$ (utility of \$0). Now the zero point of the utility scale, like that of temperature, is arbitrary. Let us therefore call the utility of \$0, zero. We have, then, the following result:

$$u(1) = 0.7\, u(2)$$

or

$$u(2) = 1.43\, u(1)$$

where we have designated by $u(1)$ and $u(2)$ the utilities of \$1 and \$2 respectively. Moreover, the unit of the utility scale (like that of the temperature scale and even of the money scale) is also arbitrary. Let us therefore agree to put $u(1) = 1$; i.e., the utility of \$1 shall be defined as one unit of utility (1 "utile"). Then the utility of \$2 will be 1.43 utiles. We see how this example exhibits the "diminishing returns" feature of the utility function. Although the utilities of \$0 and of \$1 are 0 and 1, respectively, the utility of \$2 is not 2 (as would be the case if utility were "linear with money") but only 1.43.

It goes without saying that our example was entirely arbitrary. There is no reason why a utility scale of some individuals should not exhibit an "increasing returns" feature, so that the 50-50 lottery ticket is preferred to $1. (In common parlance such persons would be described as fond of gambling or, perhaps, greedy.) Indeed what we have been saying has no bearing whatever on the way any real utility scale looks. We have merely described the method proposed by von Neumann and Morgenstern for determining someone's utility scale.

Is this method practical? We have already noted that it has the advantage of substituting paired choice preferences for the task of assigning numerical values directly to outcomes, although in doing so it extends the range of choices to include risky outcomes. It is assumed that choice decisions of the sort described can be obtained experimentally. If enough of these choice decisions are elicited *and if they are consistent and transitive* (a very big "if"), then, in principle a utility scale can be established for a given individual relative to some set of outcomes.

Assuming that this can be done, there is no need to add the axiom to the effect that risky outcomes with greater expected utility are preferred, because the utility scale is *defined* by just such preferences. Recall that if our hypothetical subject was indifferent between $1 and a 70-30 lottery ticket (in favor of $2), we assigned a utility value of 1.43 to $2. But this means that the *expected* utility of the lottery is equal to that of $1 (received with certainty). That is, two outcomes are equally attractive if their expected utilities are equal. In short, the maximization of expected utility value had been *built into the very definition* of utility.

A THEORY OR A CONVENTION?

From the point of view of parsimony, that is, of minimizing the number of independent assumptions upon which to build a theory of rational decision, the advantage of the von Neumann-Morgenstern definition of utility is unquestioned. The difficult task of assigning numerical values to outcomes has been replaced by a seemingly easier one of *ordering* outcomes. We must keep in mind, however, that this was done only at the cost of admitting all possible risky outcomes as objects of choice. This extension of the range of choices makes trivial the task of prescriptive theory. This is not surprising, since the proponents of the utility theory based on choices between risky outcomes were primarily interested in constructing a *formal* theory of rational decision, not a prescriptive one, least of all a descriptive one. For this reason they had to assume that everything which has to be known in a given decision problem was already known (given) so that they could proceed with the construction of *their* theory of rational decision, which was not a theory of decision under risk but a theory of decision in conflict situations. They *started* at the point where the problem of risky choice had been presumably already solved. In other words they bypassed rather than answered the question of what it is that people maximize (if anything) when they make risky choices.

In the scheme of von Neumann and Morgenstern, people are simply *assumed* to maximize something and that something is *called* "utility." The resulting utility theory is a fine starting point for the theory of games, but it is useless as a prescriptive theory of risky choice, as we shall now show.

A decision-maker is faced with a choice of two actions A and A'. Each leads to a set of possible outcomes. Suppose the decision-maker knows all the probabilities of the outcomes. He wishes to know what action to take. An "old-fashioned" utility theory man, invited as a consultant, would first try to ascertain the numerical "worths" of the outcomes. If he is given these by the decision-maker, he will compute the expected utilities associated with A and A' and will recommend the action with the greater expected utility. If asked why he recommends the particular action, he might reply somewhat like this: "I always recommend the action associated with the largest expected utility of my clients. If my clients follow this advice and stick to the principle of maximizing expected utility, then *in the long run* they will have gained almost certainly (cf. page 12) more than they would have gained had they been guided by any other policy of choosing among alternative actions." Thus the "old-fashioned" utility theorist would be doing two things to earn his consultant's fee. He would be giving advice on how to apply a general principle of choosing among alternatives (whether the advice is sound in all cases is not our concern here); and (2) he would be performing a calculation. (The triviality of this particular problem is irrelevant; in other cases calculations may well need the help of a professional.)

Now let us see what advice the "modern" utility theorist would give and whether he would be earning his consultant's fee. For him it is possible to ascertain the utilities of the outcomes only if the decision-maker answers *all* questions pertaining to choices among these risky outcomes. But the choice between A and A' is itself a choice between two risky outcomes. Therefore, the *decision-maker* will have to tell *the consultant* which of the two risky outcomes he prefers if the consultant is to estimate the decision-maker's utility scale. But this is precisely the question which the decision-maker asked the consultant in the first place, namely, whether he should prefer A or A'! Of what use is this consultant to him?

It is clear, then, that in the context of decision under risk, the von Neumann-Morgenstern utility theory is useless. It assumes as given what, according to the theory of decision under risk, is supposed to be calculated from *other* givens. If there is to be a non-trivial prescriptive theory of risky choices, utility must be defined in some other way independent of risky choices.[5] Several such definitions readily suggest themselves. One could, for example, relate utilities of outcomes to a conventional "basic scale," for example, money, or labor measured in some conventional units. In decisions made according to democratic traditions, it is usual to rank alternatives according to the numbers of votes received. This is only an ordinal ordering. But in interval scale can also be constructed, for example, by taking into account the actual numbers of votes cast for each alternative. Alternatives involving quantitatively measurable results (efficiency of operation, lives saved, degree of approach to specified goals, etc.) can also be rated numerically on conventionally established scales.

Every one of these methods is based on some agreement, namely, to take a unit of money or a vote or a percentage point of efficiency as a utile. In this context it makes no sense to ask what is the utility of a unit of money (or a vote or whatever was taken as the utile); for that is like asking "How long is a foot?"

If a utile is established by convention then a decision principle such as maximizing expected utility must somehow be rationalized. The most natural rationalization is in terms of the long run expectations. But this, in turn, involves the assumption that utilities can be *added* (or averaged), not to speak of the assumption that there is a long run. All these conventions and assumptions (accepted units, maximization of expectation, additivity, and the "long run") can be swept away by defining utility in von Neumann and Morgenstern's sense, i.e., as determined by choice preferences among risky outcomes. But if this is done, then the prescriptive theory of decision under risk reduces to a tautology. Nothing is left of it but a prescription to chose the most attractive alternative.

Thus we can have a substantive prescriptive theory of risky choice only if certain conventions can be agreed upon—the choice of a utility unit and an optimization rule. These conventions are not hypotheses to be corroborated or refuted. They are agreements to be established.

PROBABILITY

Let us now turn to the remaining ingredient involved in problems of risky choice, namely, probability, and see whether a similar situation prevails with respect to it. Probability is such a common word that its meaning is widely assumed to be clear. Now the same is true of many other words, such as "honesty," "cruelty," "difficulty," etc. It is easy to show that the clarity of meaning, often tacitly attributed to abstractions, especially abstractions involving value judgments, is illusory. What is "honesty" to one is "tactlessness" to another; what is "cruelty" to one is "firmness" to another, etc. When the haziness of these words is appreciated, little more remains to be said. We have merely pointed out that our language is not as precise as is generally imagined. With probability it is a different matter. While "honesty" is not meant to convey a precise meaning (in the sense, for example, that no numerical value is seriously attached to the degree of honesty), a "probability" is supposed to carry precise meaning, and numerical values are frequently assigned to probabilities. In such cases, there is always a danger of extrapolating the precision of a concept from an area where it is justified to other areas where it is not. Let us see how this comes about in the case of "probability."

A single die is thrown. What are the odds against a 4? Five to one, we say. Why? Because, we say, there is no more and no less reason for a 4 to come up than for any of the other five faces. This used to be called the argument of "insufficient reason" to justify the assignment of equal probabilities to events that seemed alike in every respect. Since the argument rests on ignorance, it is not without pitfalls. In the framework of "complete ignorance," we might reason as follows. Either the 4 will come up or it will not. Not having any reason to expect one result any more than the other, we might assign a probability of 0.5 to 4. To be sure, the argument seems lame, but only because we *do* know that there are six "equally probable" outcomes. But recall that it was also on the basis of ignorance that we had assumed these outcomes to be equally likely. Why is the assumption that the six faces are equally likely (in the absence of evidence to the contrary) any more justifiable than the assumption that the two outcomes "4" and "not 4" are equally likely, if we happen to be entirely ignorant of the nature of a die?

On further thought, it does not seem surprising that an argument based on ignorance is not a satisfactory argument with which to defend an assertion. We cannot with confidence assert that every face of a die is equally likely simply because we do not know why it should not be.

On still further thought, "probability" has actually nothing to do with the way the die falls. From the moment the die has left the hand of the thrower, its course is determined by its instantaneous position at that moment, its translational and rotational momenta, by the forces of air resistance and by the air currents, by the angle of impact with the surface on which it falls, etc., etc. When we speak of our ignorance of how the die will fall, we should mean our ignorance of all these factors, because if we knew them all and if we were sufficiently clever at calculations, we would not have to invoke probability. We would *know* what face was bound to come up. Now although we do not know how these factors operate, we know that they do operate. So our conjecture that the probability of each face is ⅙ means something of this sort: There is an astronomically large number of ways in which all the factors governing the fall of the die can combine to produce any of the faces; one-sixth of these unimaginably many ways will produce 4. I submit that this seemingly more sophisticated explanation does not make the assertion that the probability of 4 is ⅙ any more or any less credible than the common sense argument of "insufficient reason."

THE EXPERIMENTAL APPROACH

Perhaps there is another way. Throw the die many times in succession and observe that the more times it is thrown, the more nearly ⅙ will be the fraction of times the 4 will come up. This looks more promising, since the procedure resembles an experimental test, and we have acquired confidence in experimental verifications of assertions. Besides, this procedure seems to provide us with an operational definition[6] of probability, which has so far been absent from our discussion.

Before we rejoice at this discovery, let us note that we have abandoned precision in our expression "the more closely." There is, to be sure, a precise way to define "closer and closer" if we are willing to switch from English to mathematics. Unfortunately, our process with the die does not satisfy the conditions of the mathematical definition: The fraction of time the 4 will turn up does *not* approach ⅙ as a limit *in the mathematical sense.*[7]

Now our purpose is not to cavil. Practically speaking, the meaning of the statement that the fraction of 4's gets "closer and closer" to ⅙ is entirely clear. Suppose, then, we shrug our shoulders and declare that we are "practical men" and need the concept of probability only as a tool for making decisions; that we trust our experience which shows that when a die, whose "fairness" we have no reason to suspect, is thrown, each number comes up with approximately the same frequency in a large number of throws.

We have a perfect right to adopt this attitude. But then we must recognize that we have given up the concept of probability as something that has an independent existence, as it were, something that "resides in the events." If we are practical men, we must depend on practical definitions. If we wish to define probability practically, that is, in terms of experience, we must define it in terms of an *observed* frequency. If we are satisfied that the probability of a 4 is to be defined as ⅙ as long as the frequency of this outcome is about ⅙ in a large number of throws, then we must always keep in mind that this concept of probability derives its meaning from the observed frequency and has no other meaning outside of this context. Any extrapolations of meaning we may make, we shall be making at the risk of falling into error.

We can, of course, use the term "probability" in other senses (many words have several meanings), but when we switch the meaning, we must give notice to ourselves and to others.

DEGREE OF BELIEF

The reason we are sometimes forced to give another meaning to probability is because we do not wish to give up the privilege of assigning probabilities to events which by their nature can occur only once. Such an event, for example, is "the outbreak of a nuclear war" or, at any rate, "the outbreak of the first nuclear war." The "probability" of this event enters many discussions which are emphatically proclaimed to be "rational" (in contrast, for example, to "emotional" discussions). We are told that decisions involving the probability of the outbreak of a nuclear war are based on "calculated risks," by which term those who recommend or make decisions must imply calculations involving probabilities. Since the probability of an event such as the outbreak of a nuclear war can have nothing to do with the frequency of such events (since at this writing none has occurred, and, in all likelihood, no more than very few can occur), either the phrase "the probability of a nuclear war" has no meaning at all, in which case the notion of the "calculated risk" is only eyewash, or else "probability" has another meaning, having nothing whatsoever to do with frequency.

Now it is true that other meanings can be conferred on "probability" and that under certain conditions these meanings can even be made relatively precise. For the time being, we shall content ourselves with a rough meaning, intuitively understandable. This rough meaning of probability is a sort of "degree of belief."[8] For example, in 1952 many people believed that Eisenhower had a bigger chance to be elected president than Stevenson, and so it turned out. In 1948, many people believed that Dewey had a bigger chance than Truman, but it turned out otherwise. The elections of 1952 and 1948 were unique events, and so their probabilities could not have been related to any frequencies. Yet neither belief was entirely unfounded, whether the final outcome justified it or not.

Since we have to deal with these "degrees of belief" in studying human affairs, we cannot exclude this notion from our analysis of "rational decisions." But it will serve us well to keep in mind that there is a sharp distinction between this personal (or "subjective") definition of probability and the definition in terms of frequencies of events. It is not easy to keep this distinction in mind, because the temptation is to keep thinking that each event (whether unique or repeated) has a certain *inherent* probability, and that if the event is repeated, this probability will make itself manifest in a frequency but that even if the event is not repeated, the probability is "there" anyway, although, of course, it cannot manifest itself in a single occurrence. This is the illusion we warned against. It can easily lead to a paradox, as we will now show.

DEGREE OF BELIEF AND BETTING POLICY

Imagine that you play the following card game. The deck consists of eight cards, namely, four aces and four deuces. After shuffling, you take two cards, and your opponent takes two. After seeing your hand but before the opponent sees his, you can offer a bet, giving or asking any odds you choose that your hand beats your opponent's. Aces are high; so the highest hand is two aces, the next is ace-deuce, and two deuces is the lowest hand. Suits do not count. If the two hands tie, you lose the bet. You have just drawn an ace and a deuce. What are fair odds?

According to the standards of "rational gambling," betting policies are determined by probabilities. In this case, the relevant probabilities are those of your opponent's possessing each of the three types of hands. From your own hand you know that the remaining six cards are three aces and three deuces. It is easy to calculate the probabilities in question. That of two aces in your opponent's hand is ⅕; of two deuces, is also ⅕; and of a mixed hand, is ⅗.

It will help us appreciate the argument to follow, if we examine the reasoning by which we arrived at the figures ⅕, ⅕, ⅗. Two cards can be picked from among six in fifteen different ways. Two aces can be picked from three in three different ways. Therefore, three chances out of fifteen favor two aces. The argument for the deuces is exactly the same. The mixed hands are the remaining nine cases.

Now suppose the ace we hold is the ace of diamonds. This fact, we feel sure, is absolutely irrelevant to the arguments above. The rules of this game mention only card values, not suits; so we feel sure about the irrelevance of the suits even without going through the arguments about probabilities. Let us keep this fact in mind.

Imagine now that we have a spy working for us who informs us that *one* of our opponent's cards is a deuce. Does this knowledge change the situation? It certainly does. To fix ideas, suppose we hold the ace of diamonds and the deuce of clubs. Then before we learned about the deuce in the opponent's hand the fifteen possible hands of our opponent were:

A♠	A♠	A♣	A♠	A♠
A♥	A♣	A♥	2♠	2♦
A♠	A♣	A♣	A♣	A♥
2♥	2♠	2♦	2♥	2♠
A♥	A♥	2♠	2♠	2♦
2♦	2♥	2♦	2♥	2♥

We beat three hands out of fifteen and so have one chance in five of winning our bet.

Now if we know that the opponent holds at least one deuce, the first three hands do not come under consideration. Only twelve hands are possible, and our hand still beats three of them. Therefore, if we know that the opponent has a deuce (but do not know any more), we should estimate the probability that we shall win our bet as ¼ instead of ⅕.

Suppose now our spy tells us more about the opponent's hand. We now know that the deuce he holds is the deuce of spades. Then his only possible hands are:

A♠	A♣	A♥	2♦	2♥
2♠	2♠	2♠	2♠	2♠

five hands in all. Of these two are beatable hands. The probability that we shall win the bet becomes ⅖.

Now it is not surprising that our partial knowledge about the opponent's hand changes our estimates of the probability of what his hand may be. But it is somewhat surprising (at least to most of the people who come in contact with this problem for the first time) that *irrelevant* knowledge (namely knowledge of suit) should make a difference. Observe that if we had found out that our inference about the deuce of spades was mistaken, namely, that our opponent held the deuce of diamonds, not spades, the conclusions would still have been the same, because also two out of five hands containing the deuce of diamonds are two-deuce hands. How then does the knowledge of the deuce's suit affect the probability of the opponent's hands, although the suits are not differentiated in the calculations?

Suppose after looking at our hand $\left(\begin{array}{c} A♦ \\ 2♣ \end{array}\right)$ we have offered to bet one dollar against the opponent's four that our hand beats the opponent's. This is a "fair bet," since the odds against this event are 4:1. Suppose now that while our opponent is thinking whether to accept the bet, our spy whispers in our ear, "He has a deuce." Noting that the opponent is hesitating, we say, "You won't bet $4? All right, then $3 to our $1." This is again a fair bet in view of the changed estimate based on new knowledge. While he is still thinking it over, our spy brings a new report: "That deuce is the deuce of spades."

We again improve our offer, because now that we know the deuce's suit, we can afford two-to-three odds. We say, "How about $1.50?" Note, now, that it would have been two-to-three if our spy reported the deuce of diamonds, and it would also have been two-to-three if he had reported the deuce of hearts. In other words, no matter *what* suit the spy had reported, we would have improved our offer from one-to-three to two-to-three. But if it would have made no difference what suit was reported, what good was the report about the suit? We might just as well have ignored it. *But if there had been no report about the suit, we would have offered one-to-three, not two-to-three,* because without knowledge of the suit our odds would have been based only on the knowledge that the opponent held "a deuce." So the spy's report about the suit did and should make a difference. But if the change in odds is the same no matter what suit he reports, why should his report make a difference?

PROBABILITY AS DETERMINED BY POLICY

The paradox is resolved if we keep the connection between probability and frequency firmly in mind. The two-to-three offer was justified by a certain betting policy. If we had decided *in advance* that we would offer bets only when our spy reported to us that the opponent had some particular deuce (say the deuce of spades), then the two-to-three bets would have resulted *in the long run* in no gain, no loss for us. Any longer odds would have brought a gain. It would not have mattered *which* deuce we selected as the signal for offering a bet. *But once it has been selected*, we would have to stick to the policy of offering bets only when *that* deuce was reported. Now we see that the spy's report about the suit does make a difference. It determines whether we bet or not. It *selects* for us the betting situations in which the new odds are justified.

This reasoning breaks down if the game is played only once, because then the spy's report does not function as a selective device. If we had not decided in *advance* that we would offer a bet only when a particular deuce was reported, our knowledge of the deuce's suit would not have been relevant. It becomes relevant only when it is geared to a preformulated *policy*.

From the above discussion it follows that the question "What is the probability of an event?" has no meaning as it stands, because probability has more than one meaning. It can mean a number inferred from the observed frequency of an event in many supposedly "identical" situations. It can mean a number inferred from a ratio of "favorable" cases to the total number of possible cases, and this, in turn, depends on which "cases" are listed. It can mean a degree of belief.

Implied in this degree of belief is the circumstance that the probability of an event changes in the light of what we know. Therefore at least this kind of probability cannot reside "in the events," if we suppose that what we know about events does not influence the events. In other words, the something that we call the "probability of an event" is not, like duration or energy, an objective property of the event but depends on the way we define the context in which the event is to be considered; and this, in turn, may depend on our attitudes and policies of actions. For example, the choice of the presence of the deuce of spades in our opponent's hand as the selective principle in offering bets is not based on any "objective" property of spades. Initially, the choice of spades is arbitrary. But as a signal to bet, the deuce of spades acquires the character of a fetish. We offer bets only when we know that the opponent has that particular deuce, although any other would have done as well. Thus it is not only probability that determines betting policy (how much to bet). Betting policy (*when* to bet) determines probability. In the case of a single bet, this probability is entirely in the mind of the policy maker.

In short, arbitrary components enter all calculations of probability. This is true all the more when we have no information at all on which to base our estimates of probabilities but are forced nevertheless to assign probabilities to events. Then certainly the "probability of an event" becomes (for us) the result of something we ourselves did— a result of a *decision*. Rational decisions are based on choice preferences. In this light, probabilities which we assign to events become reflections of our preferences rather than of our knowledge.

CHAPTER 4

THE OUTCOMES ARE
PARTIALLY CONTROLLED BY ANOTHER

When decisions are made under certainty, the decision-maker has complete control of the outcome. Such situations are exceptional. Usually a choice of action can lead to a number of different outcomes. It is a matter of essential importance in decision theory to know who if any one, selects the actual outcomes from among the possible ones associated with a given action. The crucial factor in such situations is whether the "other" has also assigned utilities to the outcomes and if so what these utilities are. If the nature of the other is unknown, or if no utilities can be ascribed to him, the resulting situation is sometimes called a game against nature.

GAME AGAINST NATURE

As a simplest example of such a game, we can take the Commuter's chronic umbrella problem. Whether it is worthwhile to take an umbrella to work in the morning depends on what Nature is going to do. If Nature contemplates rain, it is definitely worthwhile; if not, not. Now the reason this game is called a game against Nature is not because rain is a natural phenomenon, but because rain, or whoever makes rain, does not care whether the Commuter takes his umbrella.

Games against nature can be schematized by means of a notation fundamental in game theory, namely the game matrix. Our Commuter has two choices, namely, to take or not to take the umbrella. Nature also has two choices: to "make it rain" or not. There are therefore four distinguishable outcomes in this game. It is these outcomes which are listed in the game matrix as shown in Matrix 1.

Nature's Choice

		Rain	Shine
Commuter's Choice	Take umbrella	Stay dry in rain	Lug umbrella in fair weather
	Leave it home	Get wet	Hands free in fair weather

MATRIX 1

The entry in each box represents the outcome resulting from the corresponding pair of choices, one the Commuter's, one Nature's.

In order to have a decision problem, utilities must be assigned to each of the outcomes. Since Nature is a disinterested party, only the Commuter's utilities are relevant. Let us suppose the Commuter can assign numerical utilities to the outcomes, as shown in Matrix 2.

	Rain	Shine
Umbrella	-2	-1
No umbrella	-5	$+3$

MATRIX 2

The interpretation is as follows. If the umbrella is left at home, and the weather turns out fine, the Commuter finds himself in the best of all possible worlds. Hence his biggest payoff is in lower right. If he takes the umbrella, and the day is fine, he is somewhat irked but not very much, because he generally feels good on a sunny day (upper right). If it rains, he feels worse (upper left), but not as bad as when he leaves the umbrella and gets wet (lower left).

This game can be turned into a decision under risk if probabilities can be assigned to rain and shine. For example, if the chances are even, the man's expected utility is $0.5(-2) + 0.5(-1) = -1.5$, if he takes the umbrella. If he leaves it home, he expects $0.5(-5) + 0.5(3) = -1$. In this case it does not pay to take the umbrella. But if the chances of rain are, say, 0.75, then taking the umbrella gives him $0.75(-2) + 0.25(-1) = -1.75$, while not taking it gives him $0.75(-5) + 0.25(3) = -3.00$. In this case, it is prudent to take it.

Suppose, however, the man has no basis on which to assign probabilities to Nature's choices. When probabilities of the "states of nature" (as Nature's choices are called) are unknown, one cannot call the situation a decision under risk. Such situations are called decisions under uncertainty, and there is an extensive theory treating such problems. The discussion of that theory is beyond the scope of this book, but we shall need some of it to introduce the ideas of game theory.

Suppose our Commuter is a pessimist. He believes that whatever decision he makes will be the wrong decision. There is a decision principle that will be in complete harmony with his temperament. The pessimist scans the two "strategies" open to him and asks, "What is the worst thing that can happen to me if I take the umbrella?" The answer is, "A rainy day." The utility of this outcome is -2. Then he asks, "What is the worst thing that can happen to me if I don't take the umbrella?" The answer is, again, "A rainy day," but this time the utility of the outcome is -5. Clearly the first "worst" outcome is better than the second. The choice of the "best of the worsts" is called the Minimax Principle.

The Minimax Principle is not the only "rational" principle governing decision under uncertainty. There is no more reason for being a pessimist than for being an optimist. If our Commuter were an optimist, he would ask, "What is the best possible outcome if I take the umbrella or if I do not take it?" Clearly this man would always choose not to take it. There are also decision principles which are blends between the pessimistic and the optimistic outlooks, and still others. The interested reader will find in (99) an excellent overview of the subject.

TWO-PERSON GAME

Let us now suppose that Nature is not neutral, that she behaves as the pessimist imagines. This would mean that Nature has an interest in the outcome and that her interests are diametrically opposed to those of the Commuter. Here we have the first genuine example of a two-person game. It turns out that the "solution" of this game is the same as the pessimist's solution of the decision problem, but this is not true of games in general. The kind of solution a game has (considered as a decision problem for two or more participants) and, indeed, whether a game has a "solution" at all depends on the kind of game it is. It turns out that the game theoretician classifies games in a way that would not immediately occur on intuitive grounds. It is essential to understand this method of classification in order to see how the theory of rational decisions extends to conflict situations and how far. Before we classify games, however, let us see what criteria must be met by a decision problem in order for it to be called a "game" at all in the technical sense of this term.

WHAT MAKES A GAME

We are now ready to define a game. We shall do so by listing certain features which a situation must exhibit in order to be described as a game.

1. *In a game we must have two or more "players" with at least partially conflicting interests.*

Note that this immediately excludes solitaires, in which there is only one player with an "interest." There is to be sure, another player, namely, Chance, whose role we shall soon discuss, but this player is disqualified as a bona fide player because she is indifferent to the outcome. Chance is only dummy player.

2. *Each of the players has a range of choices called strategies.*

This requirement excludes playing a slot machine from the class of genuine games. To be sure, when a man plays a slot machine, there is a conflict of interests, because the slot machine represents the House or a gambling syndicate. Also the slot machine makes "choices." The fact that the choices are random does not matter. As we shall see, randomization of strategy choices is actually itself a rational strategy choice in many cases. So the slot machine is a bona fide player. But the man is not. He is the dummy, because he has no choices. He can do only one thing, namely, put a coin in the slot and pull the lever.

3. *A play of the game consists of a single simultaneous choice of a strategy by each of the players.*

This extremely important point requires elucidation. Ordinarily we think of games as *successions* of choices, for example, the moves which the players make, each move being a response to a move of the other. However, it is possible (in principle) to conceive of a decision which encompasses specific responses to all possible move sequences of the other player.

A simple example will serve to illustrate how moves are "collapsed" into strategies. Consider a game in which the first move is made by the first player, who has two choices. The second player, after learning the first player's choice, now also has two choices. Call the choices of each player 1 and 2. The first player has two strategies, each corresponding to a choice. The second player also has two choices, when his turn comes, but he has *four strategies,* namely:

1. Choose 1 regardless of what the other does.
2. Choose 1 if the other chooses 1; otherwise, choose 2.
3. Choose 2 if the other chooses 1; otherwise, choose 1.
4. Choose 2 regardless of what the other chooses.

Note that these strategies provide for all possible contingencies. Thus although an advance commitment to a *choice* by the second player does not give him all the flexibility that the situation allows, an advance commitment to a *strategy* does, since all contingencies which can arise are already included in the decision. The advantage of the concept of strategy is that it enables the game theoretician to lump everything that is known to the players into one category and everything that is unknown into another. What is known in any game is the complete set of all available strategies, one's own and the opponent's. What is unknown is the (single) choice of a particular strategy, which will constitute the player's "part" in the particular play of the game.

4. *When each of the players has chosen his strategy, the outcome of the game is determined.*

This is a direct consequence of the definition of strategy. The definition allows the two-person game to be represented as a matrix. The rows are the strategies open to one player; the columns are the strategies open to the other. When each has chosen a strategy, an outcome is determined. The outcomes are the "boxes" of the matrix. A game represented in this way is said to be "in normal form."

5. *Associated with each outcome is a set of payoffs, one to each player.*

The payoff sets are the entries in the strategy matrix, one payoff to each player. The payoffs are expressed in utiles. It is assumed that if the outcome of a game is not certain (e.g., when chance devices are used in the course of the play) the expected utility of the outcome can be computed by multiplying the utilities of the various outcomes by the respective probabilities of occurrence and adding the products. The resulting expected utility figures in strategic calculations just as any other utility.

These five requirements constitute the scope of situations which can in principle be represented as games. Let us now compare these requirements with those ordinarily ascribed to games in common parlance. We shall find that in many ways the technical requirements correspond to those commonly assumed. In other respects, however, there are important differences. Thus many situations ordinarily thought of as amenable to treatment by "game theory" (as it is popularly conceived) do not really meet the requirements, while other situations, on the contrary, commonly thought of as falling outside the scope of game theory, can be (in principle) included.

The most obvious feature of a game is a set of rules. In real games, rules are established by agreement among the players. Or one could say that when the players have agreed to play the game, they have implicitly agreed to abide by the rules. The games examined in game theory are, of course, also based on definite rules. Thus the denotation of the rule criterion is the same in game theory and in common parlance. Here, however, the difference between everyday language and the language of game theory becomes important. The meanings of the terms in purely formal language are strictly circumscribed. They carry no penumbras of connotation. In everyday language, on the contrary, connotations are unavoidable. Thus the term "rule," especially "rule of a game," reminds us ordinarily of voluntary agreements. Accordingly, if a situation is incompatible with such agreements, it may appear that such a situation does not fall within the scope of those subsumed under "games." One such situation comes readily to mind, namely, war. It is sometimes argued that game theory cannot be of assistance in the solution of strategic military problems because wars are not fought according to rules, or, in any case, are no longer fought this way. As we shall see, the applications of game theory to the conduct of wars are indeed extremely limited, but not primarily for the reason offered. For the term "rule of the game," as it is used in game theory, is free of all the connotations conferred upon it by everyday language. A rule of the game need not be an expression of any agreement, and the reliability of the rule need not depend on the good will or the honesty of the "players." The essential meaning of "rules of the game," as the phrase is used in game theory, resides in the circumstance that the totality of rules determines precisely all the situations that can occur in the course of a play of the game, and that the totality of the situations plus a termination rule determine, in turn, all the possible outcomes. Now when a game has been represented in normal form, the situations which can occur in the course of the play have already been abstracted out. Therefore the specific rules have become immaterial. The important things are the outcomes, or rather, the payoffs associated with the outcomes. Hence any situation can be represented as a game in normal form, provided only that

1. The finite set of single choices (decisions) can be listed for each player; and
2. A pair of payoffs can be assigned to each pair of choices.

How these alternatives are put into effect, whether as explicitly stated complete strategies or in some other way, i.e., as a set of roughly specified courses of action, does not matter.

Moreover, the payoffs need not be associated with determinate results. They can well be expected utilities associated with a range of results, each characterized by a probability. Such situations sometimes occur in military or in business life. A commander may at some point in a campaign have at his disposal just so many "plans." And he may be aware of the range of plans available to the enemy. A business firm may at a given time have a choice of just so many policies and also information concerning the range of policies from which a rival firm must choose. The details of carrying out the plan or the policy chosen may be irrelevant to the essential results. The essential results are the outcomes which obtain when the respective plans or policies are put into effect. Thus situations of this sort may be represented by games in normal form even if the detailed rules of the game are not specified or do not exist.

TAXONOMY OF GAMES

The principle achievement of game theory, as it was formulated by von Neumann and Morgenstern (124), was a profoundly discerning taxonomy of games, that is, of situations involving conflicts of interests.

To see the basis of this taxonomy, let us begin by examining the ordinary ways of classifying games which may occur to anyone. Asked to classify games, the proverbial man-in-the-street may, for example, start by dividing them into indoor games and outdoor games. Upon more careful reflection, if he is asked to concentrate on the essential elements of the game itself instead of on its recreational function, our man may abandon distinctions like indoor versus outdoor games in favor of, one, say, between games of chance and games of skill. Among the latter, he may distinguish card games from board games; he may place games like post office or charades in another class; he may create a category of "children's games," to include hopscotch, marbles, tic-tack-toe, etc.

After still more deliberation, he may admit that tic-tack-toe, simple as it is, is in a way more like chess than like hopscotch. He may recognize that chance is a frequent feature in some games of skill, e.g., bridge and poker; but he may not be sure to what extent skill enters some games of chance as craps. In this way, the attention of our man-in-the-street can be gradually focused on the "essentials" of games.

By the "essentials" of games we mean those features which remain after all the incidental features have been eliminated. These incidental features are the reasons for playing the games, social attitudes toward them, their effects on the characters of the players, the apparatus used, etc.

In game theory, even the specific rules of a game are usually removed from scrutiny. This is indeed climbing high on the ladder of abstraction, since the rules of the game are certainly thought of as essential features. But game theory, going still further in its abstracting process, has succeeded in reaching a vantage point from which the logic of strategy appears with dazzling clarity.

The mathematical theory of games distinguishes first of all between games involving two players and games involving more than two players. Our concern in this book will be only with two-person games.

Among the latter, there is a most important distinction between zero-sum games and non-zero-sum games. The name "zero-sum" derives from the fact that the sum of the payoffs accruing to the players is zero regardless of what the outcome of the game is. It follows that in two-person zero-sum games, what one player wins, the other necessarily loses. The same is essentially true in "constant-sum" games, where the sum of the payoffs is the same in all outcomes. Whether this sum is zero or not is irrelevant because the zero point of the utility scale on which the payoffs are determined is arbitrary anyway. In our discussion we shall be referring to both zero-sum and constant-sum games as zero-sum, since this term enjoys the broadest usage.[9]

Both zero-sum and non-zero-sum games can be further subdivided. We shall treat a selection of such subclasses which are relevant to the principal theme of this book. As in the case of the decision problems, we shall discuss the various classes of two-person games in the order of increasing complexity.

Here we must point out that we shall judge the "complexity" of a game by standards which may seem strange at first sight. "Complexity," in our way of speaking, will have next to nothing to do with the difficulty of mastering a game or with the range of its strategic potentialities. By ordinary standards, chess is an enormously complex game, while matching pennies is a ridiculously simple one. But according to game-theoretical taxonomy, chess is in the same class with tic-tack-toe, i.e., among the very simplest games, while matching pennies belongs to a "higher class." If this classification seems bizarre, this is largely due to the difficulty of discarding the notion that the theory of games is or ought to be concerned with the analysis of specific games (perhaps with a view of discovering how to play them cleverly). But game theory is not at all concerned with know-how. It is concerned with the logic which underlies the "know-how" of strategy. The difference between a game theorist and a game virtuoso (say, a chess master or a military genius) is, in a way, analogous to the difference between a physicist and an engineer. The physicist knows the principles on which the engineer's skills are based, but he may not be able to design an engine that will work. The difference between the linguist and the polyglot is of the same sort. The linguist knows the structure of many languages; yet he may not be able to speak any of them. The polyglot may speak a dozen languages fluently without being able to state correctly a single grammatical rule.

A taxonomy of games reveals not the way specific games should be played but how to *look* for the best ways of playing them and what to expect from the search. For example, game theory tells us that *there is* a way of playing chess which, if once found, will guarantee the best possible outcome to the player who plays that way, and moreover that the player need not ever vary this best strategy. But the situation in matching pennies is quite different. There is *no* pattern of choices that will always insure the best outcome to the player who makes them.[10] The best way of playing matching pennies is to randomize one's choices, preferably in such a way that the player himself does not know what choice he will make next. Thus the principles of playing chess and of playing matching pennies are entirely different. The former game requires the greatest possible awareness and discrimination; the latter game, on the contrary, is best played in complete ignorance of what one is doing!

In the next chapter we shall be concerned with the two principal types of zero-sum games, while in Chapters 6 and 7 we shall take up the problems associated with non-zero-sum games.

CHAPTER 5

ZERO-SUM GAMES

~~~~~~

From the point of view of seeking an optimal strategy, there are just two classes of two-person zero-sum games: those with a saddle point and those without. (The meaning of a "saddle point" will be explained below.) The first class can be further subdivided into three subclasses:

1. Games in which both players have a dominating strategy
2. Games in which only one player has a dominating strategy
3. Games in which neither player has a dominating strategy

These categories are listed in the order of increasing complexity of the reasoning which leads to the optimal strategy. Games without saddle points are the most complex. The following examples will make these distinctions clear.

BOTH PLAYERS HAVE A DOMINATING STRATEGY

Consider the game represented by Matrix 3.

	B_1	B_2	B_3
A_1	4, -4	-1, 1	3, -3
A_2	0, 0	-2, 2	2, -2
A_3	0, 0	-3, 3	1, -1

MATRIX 3

The first payoff in each box is to the row chooser; the second to the column chooser.

Comparing the available strategies, A_1, A_2, and A_3, player A should see the perfectly obvious choice, namely, A_1. No matter which strategy player B decides upon, A is at least as well off and sometimes better off with A_1 than with either of the other strategies. Player B is in the same position. No matter which strategy is chosen by A, B is better off with B_2. Note that in the decision problem, each player can arrive at this decision *without taking account of the character of the adversary*. If instead of player B, Nature chose among the columns, A's best choice would still be A_1. Also it does not matter to A whether B is clever or stupid. B's choice need not be taken into account by A, since A_1 is best for A regardless of how B chooses. The situation is the same from B's point of view.

A strategy which is best (or at least as good as any) regardless of what happens is called a *dominating* strategy. In general, one strategy will be said to dominate another if all of its outcomes are better than or at least as good as the *corresponding* outcomes of the other strategy (i.e., no matter what happens). The choice of a dominating strategy is sometimes referred to as an application of the "sure-thing principle" (99, p. 21).

ONLY ONE HAS A DOMINATING STRATEGY

Let us now introduce a minor change in the matrix and obtain the following game (Matrix 4):

	B_1	B_2	B_3
A_1	4, −4	−1, 1	3, −3
A_2	−3, 3	−2, 2	2, −2
A_3	0, 0	−3, 3	1, −1

MATRIX 4

We see that A_1 still dominates A_2 and A_3. But B_2 no longer dominates B_1. For should A choose A_2, B would be better off with B_1. Thus, although A can still act as promptly as in the preceding case,

B has to go one step further in his reasoning. He can no longer say, "B_2 is best for me no matter what A does." All he can say now is, "B_2 is best for me unless A chooses A_2." Then he must inquire whether there is a chance that A may, in fact, choose A_2. Thus B, in contrast to A, must now take into account what the other player *may* do. Accordingly, he looks the matrix over and decides that A will *not* choose A_2 since there is no inducement whatever for him to do so. In coming to this decision, player B need not ascribe to A any "reasoning power" —only the ability to discriminate payoffs and to act on the sure thing principle. Certainly this is the minimal assumptions one can make about the rationality of the other. In short, when one of the players has a dominating strategy, while the other does not, the former can still act without assuming anything about the other's rationality, but the latter must make the *minimal* assumption about the former's rationality, namely, that the former knows enough to choose according to the sure thing principle.

NEITHER HAS A DOMINATING STRATEGY

Our next step, which the reader may already have anticipated, is to deprive both players of the dominating strategy and so of the sure thing principle. This has been done in Matrix 5.

	B_1	B_2	B_3
A_1	5, -5	-1, 1	4, -4
A_2	-3, 3	-2, 2	5, -5
A_3	10, -10	-3 3	-20, 20

MATRIX 5

Here neither player has a dominating strategy. A_1 fails to dominate A_2, and vice versa, because A_1 is better in the first column but worse in the third; A_1 does not dominate A_3, nor is dominated by it, because A_1 is better in the third column but worse in the first. A_2 fails to dominate A_3 because A_3 is better in the first column; but neither is

A_2 dominated by A_3, because A_2 is better in the second column. Similar comparisons will establish the fact that none of the column strategies dominates any other.

In a game of this type it is not possible for either player to arrive at a rational decision without taking into account the other player's decision process. Moreover, the "taking into account of the other player's decision process" means in this case not only taking into account the other's choice preferences but also taking into account the other's taking into account one's own choice preferences, as well as one's own taking into account of the other's taking into account, etc., ad infinitum.

Although this reasoning goes on ad infinitum, it leads to a perfectly definite conclusion, provided the game has a saddle point. A saddle point is an outcome in which the payoffs to both players are the "best of the worst." We see that in Matrix 5 the outcome in the first row, second column, is of this sort. The row player's payoff, -1, is the worst in that row, but it is better than the other two worst payoffs, namely, -3 (in row 2) and -20 (in row 3). B's payoff, $+1$, is the worst in that column, but it is better than either of the other two worst outcomes. A saddle point is also known as a minimax. The meaning of minimax is the same here as in the game against Nature discussed on page 33.

We shall now show that in a game with a saddle point, both players should choose strategies containing a saddle point. The outcome of such a game will be the minimax payoff to each player.

Suppose A decides to choose the row containing the minimax (row 1 in Matrix 5) as the "safest" choice. He asks himself, "If B knew that I chose this row, which column would he choose?" The answer is, obviously, the column containing the minimax (column 2), for that is B's best reply to A's choice. "Now knowing that B will choose column 2 (since he assumes I will choose row 1) can I improve the outcome for myself?" asks A. The answer is no. "Can B improve his outcome, knowing that I will choose row 1?" Again no. Therefore the minimax outcome is a sort of stable equilibrium. Neither player can get more than it gives unless the other acts foolishly, and a rational player does not expect another rational player to act foolishly.

Examining the simpler games with dominating strategies (Matrices 3 and 4), we see that they too have saddle points. In fact, the Commuter's game against Nature (Matrix 2) turns out to be of the type in which only one player has a dominating strategy (in this case Nature). We see also that the pessimistic Commuter chooses the strategy with the saddle point. We would expect this, because pessimism in this context is tantamount to attributing malevolent intentions (opposite interests) to Nature.

Now let us change the Commuter's personality somewhat. Assume that he is not very adversely affected by rainy weather as such (although he still dislikes getting wet). Let his upper-left payoff be +2. Assume also that Nature is indeed malevolent, so that the decision problem is a genuine two-person zero-sum game. Now Nature's payoffs are those of the Commuter with opposite signs, and we need to show only the Commuter's payoffs. The resulting game is shown in Matrix 6.

	Rain	Shine
Take umbrella	+2	−1
Leave it	−5	+3

MATRIX 6

Observe that this game has no saddle point. For the Commuter's minimax is −1, at upper right, while Nature's minimax, −2, is at upper left. Let us see where the Commuter's reasoning now gets him if he tries to figure out what (malevolent) Nature is likely to do. Beginning with his own minimax, he tentatively decides to take the umbrella. If Nature "knows" of this decision, the weather will be fine (so as to give the Commuter −1, not 2). But if Nature decides to shine, clearly the Commuter should leave the umbrella home and take advantage of +3 at lower right. But Nature, being intelligent as well as malevolent, is expected to be aware of *this* decision of the Commuter. Therefore, concludes the Commuter, it will rain. But if it rains, he should take the umbrella. But Nature is up to *that* too. . . . We see that the ad infinitum reasoning process has here a literal meaning. And if instead of Nature, we had a real opponent, he, too, would be going around in circles.

The principal result in the theory of the two-person zero-sum game shows a way out of this impasse. The Commuter can *randomize* his choices in such a way as to guarantee for himself the maximum *expected* payoff, regardless of what Nature does. This will happen if the Commuter takes the umbrella on eight days out of eleven. His expected payoff will be $+\frac{1}{11}$ utiles. Nature, as the opponent, can make sure that the Commuter gets *no more* than $+\frac{1}{11}$ by making rain on 4 days out of 11 and fair weather on 7.[11]

To be absolutely sure of these results, each player must completely randomize his choices. That is, he must leave the choice on any particular play of the game to some chance device appropriately constructed so that each alternative results with the assigned probability. Such a choice is called a mixed strategy. The game-theoretical result mentioned above proves that every two-person zero-sum game representable in normal form has a solution, i.e., a prescribed mixed strategy to each player. That is to say, each player computes a certain optimal probability with which to choose his own available strategies. (Some of the probabilities may be zero, that is to say, the corresponding strategies are never to be chosen. In case the game has a saddle point, probability 1 is assigned to the strategy which contains it.[12])

The spirit of the mathematical theory of games can be clearly appreciated from the implications of this result. We are not told how to play any specific game. But we are told what an "optimal strategy" *means* in the two main classes of zero-sum games. In games with saddle points, there is *a* best strategy for each player (there may be several, but they all lead to the same payoffs). Once such a strategy is found, it can *always* be used. There is no point in keeping such a strategy secret (assuming of course, that the other player is also rational, that is, that he too can figure out both optimal strategies). In fact, there is no point in playing such a game at all, once it has been solved, because the outcome is known in advance. Tic-tack-toe has been solved, and that is why adults do not play this game. Chess is also known to be a game with a saddle point, but this game has not been solved. That is why the victory goes sometimes to White, sometimes to Black, and sometimes to neither. If the game were solved, the results of all chess games would be the same.

With games without saddle points, it is a somewhat different matter.

Optimal strategies in these games are mixed strategies, and so the results of each play of the game may be different even if the players are rational. But the long term results (if the payoffs can be added or averaged) will be the same. Poker is a game without a saddle point. Like chess, it has never been solved [although some simplified forms of poker are solved in von Neumann and Morgenstern's treatise (124)].

The notion of mixed strategy was known, of course, to players of games long before the advent of game theory. In poker, mixed strategy is involved in bluffing and in raising. The experienced poker player does not bet in accordance with the strength of his hand, since this would give away his hand. Occasionally he raises by a large amount when his hand is weak (bluffs), and occasionally raises only by small amounts when his hand is quite strong (in order not to scare away the other players). If someone took the trouble to solve poker, each player would know just how to *randomize* his bets, depending on his hand. No player could do better (in the long run) than with this optimal strategy. The results of each play would still be different, but in the long run each player would come out without gains or losses, since poker is a game in which each player's expected gain is zero.

Mixed strategies can, in principle, be applied in military tactics provided a situation can be depicted as a zero-sum game. The commander of each side lets *chance* decide for him which of the available plans to choose (assuming that the opponent is aware of all the possibilities). The commander only fixes the probabilities with which the various plans are to be chosen. These *probabilities* need not, in fact cannot be, kept secret from a rational enemy even though the particular plan chosen on a specific occasion must be kept secret.

Thus there is a definitive procedure recommended by game theory for every solved two-person zero-sum game. It is in this sense that the theory of such games is called complete, and it is in this sense that it can be called normative.

CHAPTER 6

PRISONER'S DILEMMA

Prisoner's dilemma is the best known example of a non-zero-sum game which illustrates the dramatic failure of zero-sum methods in the new context. The name of the game derives from an anecdote which was originally used to illustrate it.[13] We shall use another illustration closer to the main theme of this book.

The players are two nations, A and B. Each has a range of defense policies, i.e., levels of armaments, deployment of weapon systems, etc. For simplicity we shall assume that only two policies are under consideration by each government, namely, Policy C: total disarmament; and Policy D: high level of armaments. To continue to keep the problem simple, we shall also assume that A and B are the only nations whose military potential needs to be considered, and that when both are fully armed, a "balance of power" obtains, that is, each nation has reasonable assurance that the other will not attack it. When both countries are disarmed, we shall assume that each is likewise secure from attack. However, *unilateral* disarmament (we shall suppose) is highly disadvantageous to the disarmed nation, and advantageous to the nation that has remained armed (or, say, has rearmed while the other has remained disarmed).

Besides safety there are also costs to take into account. High levels of armament, it is generally conceded, are more costly than low levels. Thus, the degrees of safety in both the bilaterally armed and the bilaterally disarmed state being the same, we must assign a lower utility to the bilaterally armed than to the bilaterally disarmed state. Let us assign the value $+5$ to the latter state and the value of -5 to the former. Since being disarmed alone is worse than being armed (even if the other is) we shall assign −10 to this state. Similarly, the advantage of being the only armed nation shall be represented by +10. The resulting game is represented by Matrix 7.

	C	D
C	5, 5	−10, 10
D	10, −10	−5, −5

MATRIX 7

Now the principal feature of this game is the fact that strategy D dominates strategy C for both players. On the face of it, therefore, we seem to be confronted with the simplest type of two-person game, namely, one in which each player has a clearly dominating strategy, one that is sure to be better than the other no matter what the other player does (cf. page 42). In fact, if B is armed, this is the strongest of reasons for A to remain armed. If B disarms, A is still better off armed, because it is then the only armed one. In the case of the zero-sum game, the choice of a dominating strategy, if such exists, is the only rational choice. Observe, however, that in the game now before us, this is no longer the case. If both players choose the dominating strategy (remain armed), they both do worse than they would have done if they had both chosen the dominated strategy (to disarm).

An obvious way out of the dilemma is for the players to get together and to agree to disarm. But this raises a host of questions. For example, what does it mean to "agree"? The concept has not been used heretofore except in the context of agreeing to abide by the rules of the game. But here the meaning of "to agree" is clearly different. Agreement refers here not to something that occurs before the game (and so need not be considered again) but to something that takes place *during* the game. Is agreement a "move"? But games schematized in matrix form do not have "moves." Is an agreement a new rule set up while the game is progressing? Whatever the nature of this "agreement," the following question is interesting in its own right. What if the rules of the game explicitly prohibit communication (or the nature of the situation makes it impossible)? Can one speak of "agreement" in that case?

CAN THE COOPERATIVE CHOICE BE RATIONALIZED?

The dilemma results from a bifurcation of the idea of rationality. If one asks, "With which strategy am I better off?" the answer is unequivocally, "With strategy D." The choice of strategy C is dictated by collective interest. If one asks, "Where are we both better off?" the answer is, "With strategy C." Thus, strategy D is dictated by self-interest while strategy C is dictated by collective interest. Nevertheless the choice between C and D is not quite a choice between altruism and selfishness. In choosing C, a player does not necessarily serve collective interest *at the expense* of his self-interest as does, say, a man who suffers discomforts or faces danger to promote the welfare of others. The motivation for choosing C is cooperation, not self-sacrifice. But the player who chooses C does not control the outcome by himself. The outcome depends on what the other player does. If the other chooses D, the attempt to induce cooperation fails. The defector benefits at the cooperator's expense, but it was not intended this way. The cooperator assumed that the other would cooperate, not defect. If he had cooperated, *both* would have benefited. Therefore the choice of C is not an act of self-sacrifice but rather an act of trust. But trust is not enough, because even convincing evidence that the other will choose C need not induce C.[14] Not only must one be trusting; one must also be trustworthy; that is, one must resist the temptation to betray the other's trust.

Is it "rational" to be trusting and trustworthy? Here the common usage of the term "rational" sometimes intrudes and beclouds the issue. The usual sense of this question is, "Is it safe to trust people?" But put in this way, the question is clearly an empirical one, to be answered by examining the behavior of a given sample of people in given circumstances. It is not the justification of a policy on the basis of empirical evidence that makes the policy rational but rather the consistency of the policy with certain axiomatically stated principles. Clearly to be "trusting" in a prisoner's dilemma game means to assume that the other will not choose a dominating strategy, i.e., to deny "rationality" to the other. On the other hand to be "trustworthy" means to discard the dominating strategy in favor of a dominated one, which is not "rational."

To be sure, one could defend trustworthiness, at least in response to the other's trust, on the basis of insuring the other's trust the *next* time. This is clearly advantageous and is reflected in the business dictum "Honesty is the best policy." However, such pragmatic arguments do not apply if there is no next time, if the game is played only once. In this case, there is only one good reason to choose C, namely in order to remain at peace with one's conscience.

It appears that we have now brought in a concept totally alien to the notion of rational decision. The notion of conscience is sometimes gotten around by invoking the idea of "hidden utility." The man who chooses C, it is argued, must assign greater utilities to the associated outcomes than are indicated in the game matrix. (In other words, if we observe that someone chooses C, we conclude that the game he is playing is not prisoner's dilemma.) Such an argument cannot be refuted, because it reduces the question of motivation to a tautology. Whatever is chosen guarantees *ipso facto* the greater utility. But we have seen how such a reduction makes trivial the very notion of utility and with it of motivation. We learn nothing if we always redefine utilities in such a way that the choices come out "right." But we may learn a great deal if we observe how people choose when the motivations dictating the choices conflict, e.g., when desire for gain indicates one choice while other considerations prescribe another.

Whatever "conscience" is, considerations having to do with it are not instrumental. One does not obey one's conscience in order to gain some other end, but simply in order to appease it. In other words, obeying one's conscience is an end in itself like escaping from pain.

Actually we encounter situations of this sort already in those decisions under risk where one must gamble on unique events. Suppose the decision-maker must choose between two acts, each involving a risky outcome, knowing that the situation will never recur. The prevailing opinion is that he should choose the risk with the greater expected gain. But why? If the situation were to be repeated many times, the choice could be rationalized on the grounds that the expected gains will in the long run become *actual* gains, so that the gambler will be simply choosing a larger gain over a smaller one (supposing that the utilities accruing successively can be added). But clearly this argument does not hold for the single case.

There is no getting around the fact that the decision-maker who chooses the gamble with the greater "expected value" cannot rationalize his choice on the basis of comparing the actual returns. What he compares are *expectations* i.e., his own states of mind associated with each of the choices. If there is no long run, the expectation remains an expectation, that is, only a mental state like conscience. In the last analysis, one chooses the gamble with the greater expectation simply because "it is the right thing to do."

If the choice of strategy C in a *single* play of prisoner's dilemma can be rationalized at all, it must be rationalized on similar grounds. The player who chooses C does so because he feels it is the proper thing to do. He feels that he ought to behave as he would like the other to behave. He knows that if they both behave as he expects, both will benefit. I submit that these are pretty compelling reasons for choosing C. However, they are not strategic reasons. Indeed they contradict the "rational" strategic principle, which dictates D unconditionally.

The strategic superiority of D ceases to be unconditional if the game is repeated. We shall analyze this situation by representing a repeated prisoner's dilemma as a supergame, in which the successive plays become the moves. The supergame too can be collapsed into normal form. We shall do this and then examine the properties of the resulting matrix.

Since the number of available strategies grows very rapidly with the number of moves, it will be impractical to consider even a moderately large number of repeated plays. Fortunately, the principle we wish to illustrate comes out clearly, even in a two-move supergame.

PRISONER'S DILEMMA PLAYED TWICE

Imagine a game with two moves. Each of the moves, made by the players simultaneously, is a play of an ordinary prisoner's dilemma game (cf. Matrix 7). The result of the first move is announced to the players before they make the second (final) move.

In this game, each player has eight strategies (compared with two in the simple game). A's strategies are shown in Table 2.

Strategy	On First Move Play	If B Played C on First Move, on Second Move Play	If B Played D on First Move, on Second Move Play
1	C	C	C
2	C	C	D
3	C	D	C
4	C	D	D
5	D	C	C
6	D	C	D
7	D	D	C
8	D	D	D

TABLE 2

B's strategies are, of course, entirely analogous. In normal form, this game is represented by Matrix 8.

	B_1	B_2	B_3	B_4	B_5	B_6	B_7	B_8
A_1	10, 10	10, 10	−5, 15	−5, 15	−5, 15	−5, 15	−20, 20	−20, 20
A_2	10, 10	10, 10	−5, 15	−5, 15	0, 0	0, 0	−15, 5	−15, 5
A_3	15, −5	0, 0	0, 0	0, 0	−5, 15	−5, 15	−20, 20	−20, 20
A_4	15, −5	15, −5	0, 0	0, 0	0, 0	0, 0	−15, 5	−15, 5
A_5	15, −5	0, 0	15, −5	0, 0	0, 0	−15, 5	0, 0	−15, 5
A_6	15, −5	0, 0	15, −5	0, 0	15, −5	−10, −10	15, −5	−10, −10
A_7	20, −20	5, −15	20, −20	5, −15	0, 0	−15, 5	0, 0	−15, 5
A_8	20, −20	5, −15	20, −20	5, −15	5, −15	10, −10	5, −15	−10, −10

MATRIX 8

We shall henceforth refer to the ordinary prisoner's dilemma game as PD and to the two-move game as PD^2. From the matrix we learn that strategy 8, the totally uncooperative strategy, analogous to strategy D in the simple game, is still an *equilibrium* (minimax) strategy for each player. If one of the players holds on to this strategy, the other must also, since none of the other strategies are better against it, and all but one are actually worse. In this sense the new two-move game is no different from the simple game. However, in PD^2 it is no longer true that strategy 8, the totally uncooperative strategy, *dominates* every other (the way strategy D dominates strategy C in PD). For instance, we see from Matrix 8 that against B's strategy 2, A's strategy 4 is better than strategy 8.

Therefore, we can no longer say that it is to each player's *unconditional* advantage (even strategically speaking) to choose the totally uncooperative strategy 8. It is still true, however, that neither player has any reason to suppose that the other will play anything but the totally uncooperative strategy. This strategy (being the minimax) remains "the most prudent," just as strategy D had been in PD. However, while the knowledge of what the other was going to do was irrelevant in PD (cf. page 49) it is no longer irrelevant in PD^2. Hence the reasons for choosing strategy 8 are not as *compelling* as the reasons for choosing strategy D had been in the simple prisoner's dilemma game. To rationalize strategy 8 it is no longer enough to point out that it is obviously superior against *any* opponent, friendly or hostile. The rationalization now requires an argument based on the assumed nature of the opponent, namely, that he is a "prudent man" rather than a "just man with an initial reservoir of good will," for the latter is what we might call a player who chooses strategy 2 in PD^2, as we shall see in a moment.

Strategy 2 could properly be called an "initially trusting tit-for-tat strategy." Stated in words, the strategy says: "I shall play cooperatively on the first move; on the second move, I shall play the way the other has played on the first." Against this strategy, the other player will do better to cooperate, at least on the first move. Even if he cooperates on both moves, he does better than with the totally uncooperative strategy 8. However, his "best" answer (from the point of view of self-interest) is to cooperate on the first play and to defect on the second, which is strategy 4.

But in order to be safe in playing strategy 4, B needs to be assured that A will indeed play strategy 2, rather than strategy 8. To be sure, it is to A's advantage to play strategy 2 (against which B will play strategy 4 if he is rational), but this will happen only if B *knows* that A has chosen strategy 2 (rather than, say, 8). Now in the game under consideration, there is no way for A to communicate to B that he is in fact choosing strategy 2 (which is of advantage to both). This may seem like an artificial restriction. If a real life situation resembles PD², why should not one player inform the other that he will use strategy 2, which is of advantage to both? In our formalized game, the rules do not allow it (as for example, the rules of bridge do not allow communication between partners which would be of advantage to both). But in real life cannot one of the parties take things into his own hands?

To this there are at least three answers.

One answer is on the basis of an assumption that there are rules governing communication, for example, a rule that states who communicates first. Note that this does not contradict the assumption that a player "takes matters into his own hands." If he is in a *position* to do this, this means that the situation makes this possible. Recall that the source of the rules is not specified in game theory. The rules need not be agreements; they may be in the nature of the situation itself. If this is so, then the choices of acts under the constraints of the rules, in particular choices of communicative acts *which are not simultaneous,* constitute *moves* (not strategies) in a still larger supergame. It is that game which we must now represent in normal form. Once we have done this, we are again faced with a situation where strategies are chosen simultaneously and only one choice (by both players) determines the outcome.

The second answer is on the basis of the assumption that there are no rules. That is, the constraints are not known. If so, a player can make no "plans" as to what he will communicate. The timing of the communication may be an essential element in its effect. This is especially true in pre-empted communications like irreversible threats, of which we shall have more to say in later chapters. An irreversible threat is effective only if it arrives before the opponent has sent *his* irreversible threat. If there are no rules one cannot be sure that one can beat the other to the punch. If the irreversible threats arrive simultaneously, the effect of "taking things into one's own hands" may be not at all the intended one.

The third answer is also on the assumption that there are no rules. If so, there is no rule governing the credibility of the communication. In fact "to believe or not to believe" is a choice open to the receiver of communication and can itself be considered a move of a game.

Formally speaking, a "game" can in principle be constructed from any of these situations, if we allow for indeterminate outcomes, for example, if the question of whose communication arrives first is a matter of chance (in case there are no rules governing the sequence of communications). But this is *another* game and must be analyzed in its own context. Whatever the game is, we arrive at the same sort of situation when we have reduced it to normal form. If the game in normal form has a dilemma in it, one does not resolve the dilemma of *that game* by introducing communication moves. If one does this, one is considering another game.

THE DILEMMA HAS NOT BEEN RESOLVED

It appears we have again arrived at an obstacle, the same obstacle we faced every time when a definition of "rational decision," which had been sufficient to provide optimal choices in previous decision problems, ceased to be sufficient in a new problem. Previously, when faced with such situations, we extended the range of concepts needed to define rational decision, successively adding utility, probability, awareness of others' interests, mixed strategy, etc.

In the original formulation of game theory (124), the decision problem generated by the non-zero-sum game is solved in the extended context of *enforceable agreement* between the players. Such agreements were not assumed as a factor in the zero-sum game; and indeed there is no point to such agreements, since in those games the interests of the players are diametrically opposed. In the context of the non-zero-sum game, an enforceable agreement can be a crucial factor. This can be seen immediately if we assume that the two players of prisoner's dilemma can make a pact (collusion, coalition) to effect the mutually advantageous outcome (CC). But a pact implies concepts not considered hitherto. The prospective partners must have a common language. They must also either profess allegiance or render obedience to a common authority, either coercive, like a police force, or internalized, like conscience. That is to say, pacts must be enforceable. Observe that if a non-enforceable agreement to choose C is made by the two players of PD, the question "Should I *keep* the pact?" induces another game exactly like PD: of the two available strategies, namely C′ (to keep the pact) and D′ (to break the pact), D′ is the dominating strategy. (It is more advantageous to break the pact regardless of whether the other keeps his.) The assumption that agreements are enforceable is therefore vital if coalitions and collusions are to be included as factors in rational decisions.

CHAPTER 7

BARGAINING AND ARBITRATION

~~~~~~

We have seen that the introduction of enforceable agreement can solve the prisoner's dilemma. But it is not true that every non-zero-sum game can be solved with finality by the same expedient. Suppose B wishes to buy a house; A wishes to sell it. Usually there is a minimum amount of money for which A will be willing to sell. Let the bottom price be $20,000. Similarly there will be a top price above which B will not buy, say $26,000. We can say that the house has for A the same utility as $20,000 and for B the same as $26,000. There-fore, if the house is sold for, say, $22,000, A gains two utiles (1 $u=$ $1,000), and B gains 4 utiles. And in general, if the house is sold for $(20 + x)$ thousand dollars. A gains x utiles, and B gains $6 - x$ utiles.

We should also keep in mind the important and in many cases quite likely outcome—no sale. To this outcome, let us assign the payoffs $(0, 0)$.

The situation can now be depicted as a simple bargaining game. Such games are conveniently represented by diagrams drawn in the "payoff space." Let the seller's utilities be marked off on the horizontal axis and the buyer's on the vertical. All possible outcomes are repre-sented by points inside and on the boundary of the triangle shown in Figure 2.

If A and B are "rational" in the business sense, they need to con-sider only the outcomes along the "northeast" boundary, since they can *both* do better at some point of the boundary than at any point within the triangle. The sort of dilemma we considered in the last chapter does not plague them here, because we are now supposing that the two can strike a bargain. It is, to be sure, true, that even in such situations people are sometimes unable to come to a mutually beneficial agreement, but this is because extraneous factors are operating, for example, expectations to do better with another buyer (or seller) or psychological inhibitions not taken into account in the utilities. And so the problem is to decide where on the "northeast" boundary of the outcome space the bargain will be struck.

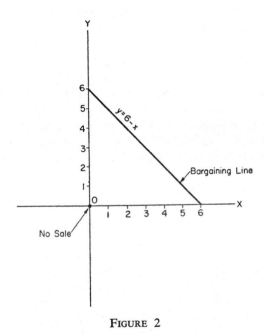

FIGURE 2

Nash (81) has proposed the following solution. Let the *product* of the utility gains of the two parties relative to No Sale be maximized. In a moment we shall see the rationale for this solution. First let us see what it means in the present case.

If the seller's utility gain relative to No Sale is x, then the buyer's gain, we have seen, will be $y = 6 - x$. The problem reduces to finding the value of x such that the product $x(6 - x)$ shall be a maximum.

This problem is easily soved by elementary calculus.[15] The quantity $x(6 - x)$ attains its maximum when $x = 3$, that is to say, the house should be sold for $23,000.

Now this result may seem obvious. It does no more than split the difference between what the seller will accept and what the buyer will give. This advice could have been given without any knowledge of either bargaining theory or of the calculus. In reality, however, this result is based on much deeper considerations than just splitting the difference. We shall see what they are if we inquire into the reasoning which leads to the rule of maximizing the product of the utility gains.

The task which Nash set for himself was to find a "rational" solution to the bargaining problem. So the first thing is to define "rationality" in this context. He proposed the following criteria for rationality.

1. If the game is symmetric with regard to the players, equal utilities should be awarded to both. That is to say, if the bargaining opportunities are the same for both, there should be no way of distinguishing between the players.

2. Whatever the utilities awarded, the players ought not to be in a position to improve upon them *jointly* within the constraint of the game, since they would have taken advantage of this opportunity in the first place if they are rational.

3. If certain feasible outcomes are added to the bargaining problem (No Sale remaining the same), then the original outcome either remains the same or is among the added outcomes. That is, available outcomes which will not obtain (except possibly No Sale) should not have any bearing on the outcome which will obtain.

4. If the utility scales of either or both players suffer a linear transformation, this should not affect the outcome.

The criterion which is not obvious is 4. Why should the result be invariant if the utilities are subjected to a linear transformation? This is because utilities must be specified on an *interval* scale (cf. note 4). If all the utilities of one player are multiplied by the same factor, this should not effect the solution of the game. Also, if the same number is added to all the utilities of one player, this should not affect the solution of the game. In our case, this means that if instead of the numbers which we have used for A's utilities, we used another set of numbers obtained from the former by multiplying them by a constant and by adding another constant, the solution of the bargaining game should not be affected, and similarly for B.

Nash proved that his solution satisfies all four criteria listed above (81). However, he obtained also a much stronger result. He showed that his solution (maximizing the product of the utility gains) is the *only* one that satisfies the four criteria.

To a mathematician it is a source of satisfaction to find a unique solution which satisfies certain prescribed criteria. But people interested in bargaining will hardly be satisfied with just these formal properties. They will feel (and rightly so) that a great deal more is involved in bargaining. Where is bargaining skill? Where is bargaining strategy which takes advantage of the weaknesses of the other side by the use of feints, threats (to leave him with No Sale), etc.?

These "realistic" demands actually concern two kinds of factors. Bargaining skills may involve attempts to "propagandize" the opponent, to induce him to see the situation not as it actually is; for example, to convince the buyer that the house is worth to him more than $26,000. These factors Nash deliberately ignores on the grounds that rational bargainers will see through these ploys. But there may also be a real difference in the "objective" *bargaining positions* of the two parties. These are taken into account in Nash's model.

To illustrate the use of the method in a more complex situation, we shall suppose that the outcome space is inside and on the boundary of the region bounded by the coordinate axes and a parabola, whose equation is $y = \sqrt{2 - x}$.
This space is shown in Figure 3.

Roughly speaking, the meaning of this situation is the following. The conflict of interest is still there, because along the parabola (the essential portion of the outcome space) y decreases as x increases, and vice versa. But the rate of decrease of y is uneven. When x is near zero, y decreases slowly relative to x; but when x is near its upper limit (which is 2), y decreases very rapidly relative to x. Psychologically, this means that the buyer yields easily when the seller gets small utilities and gets progressively tighter as the seller gets large utilities. The seller's bargaining behavior is similar vis-à-vis the buyer.

The situation depicted is thus psychologically plausible. Moreover, there is another asymmetry between the two. The seller is not quite so tight a bargainer near his asking price as the buyer is near his offer. This is reflected in the slopes of the parabola at the extremes: practically vertical near the horizontal axis, but not perfectly flat at

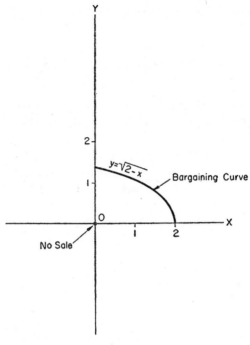

FIGURE 3

the vertical axis. Yet we cannot conclude that the buyer is "a tighter bargainer" than the seller. Consider the point at which the increase of utility of one is exactly offset by the decrease of utility of the other. This occurs at the point where the parabola has a slope of -1. This point is farther along the seller's axis than the buyer's (cf. Figure 3). This means that the buyer becomes tighter than the seller only when the seller has already got pretty much his way, but then he really gets tight.

It appears, then, that there is no lack of richness in this model. All these features are reflected in the solution, which is mathematically exact to the extent that the conditions are described with mathematical exactness.

If we solve this bargaining problem by Nash's method we obtain $x = 1.33$, $y = 0.81$, approximately.[16] We note that the seller gets two-thirds of his maximal utility. The buyer gets about 54 per cent of his maximal utility. To translate this result into the money settlement we must know more, namely, the way money maps on the utility functions of the bargainers. We were not told this but only how the utilities were related to each other.

Nash's method of solving the simple bargaining problem has been extended by him to any two-person non-zero-sum game in which the players can negotiate enforceable agreements. I shall call such games *negotiable*. Games in which enforceable agreements cannot be made I shall call non-negotiable.[17]

In discussing negotiable games, Harsanyi (51) emphasizes the difference between bargaining solutions and arbitration solutions. In the former, only the relative bargaining positions of the players are reflected. In the simple bargaining problem, these positions depend on what the threat of No Sale (the result of a failure to agree) means to each player in terms of his utilities. In more general non-zero-sum games, a number of such "threats" may be open to each player. Characteristically, each threat, if carried out, involves a cost to the threatening party as well. The strategic problem is then to find the most efficient threat, a sort of compromise between the cost of the threat (if carried out) to other and to self.

In arbitration, in addition to the relative bargaining positions of players some *equity* principle is invoked. Frequently the invocation of such an equity principle neglects some of the threat potentials, which the players might use in a bargaining situation. To illustrate both bargaining and arbitration solutions, we shall use the following game.[18]

THE BATTLE OF THE SEXES

A man and a woman would like to spend their vacation together. He prefers roughing it, while she prefers a fashionable resort. Their desire for each other's company is stronger than their preferences of vacation sites, and so their payoffs, if they go together, are higher than if they go separately. However, the strengths of preferences are different, and the relative intensities of their chagrin (should they go separately) are also different. All this is represented in the payoffs (cf. Matrix 9).

Woman

		Resort	Camping
	Resort	0, 5	−2, −2
Man	Camping	−3, −1	3, 1

MATRIX 9

Let us see what these payoffs represent. Upper left and lower right are easily interpreted. If both go to the resort, the man is indifferent (0), but the woman is delighted (+5). If both go camping, the man is pleased (+3), but the woman is only mildly satisfied (+1). Lower left represents the man's and the woman's chagrin if they go their separate ways. Upper right on first thought makes no sense, since we would not expect both of them to go to places they dislike. However, we include this outcome for completeness, and besides it is not inconceivable, if each stubbornly insists on making a "sacrifice." Note that if this happens, the man feels somewhat better (-2) than if he had gone camping alone (-3), possibly because there are other women at the resort; while the woman feels somewhat worse camping alone (-2) than at the resort without the man (-1), possibly for analogous reasons.

The outcome space is represented in Figure 4.

The equation of the negotiation set line is $4x + 3y = 15$. Let now lower left represent the threat that each can use in the bargaining. *This* outcome is now taken as the No Sale point. Since the man's gain over No Sale on the negotiation line is $x + 3$, while the woman's gain is $y + 1 = 6 - \frac{4}{3} x$, we must now maximize the expression $(x + 3)$ $(6 - \frac{4}{3} x)$. Proceeding exactly as before, we have the bargaining solution of the game, namely $x = \frac{3}{4}$; $y = 4$.

To translate this solution into a decision, we note that the point (¾, 4) is one fourth of the way from (0, 5) to (3, 1). (Cf. Figure 4). The couple can toss two pennies and agree to go camping if the result of the toss is two heads. This gives the man one chance in four. His expected utility is ¼ × 3 + ¾ × 0 = ¾, as required. The woman's expected utility is ¼ × 1 + ¾ × 5 = 4, as required. If the situation presents itself annually, the couple can agree to go

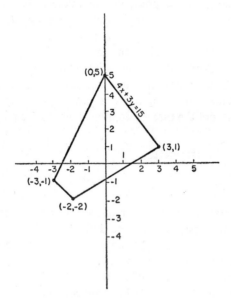

FIGURE 4. The outcome space of the Battle of the Sexes.

camping once in four vacations (provided the utilities remain the same).

ARBITRATION SOLUTION I

As Harsanyi has noted, arbitration schemes are those which introduce some notion of equity into the negotiations. An equity principle proposed by Shapley (106) is one where the No Sale point is determined by the *security levels* of the players. Let the couple play the game as if it were a zero-sum game, where each is concerned only with his (her) own maximin[19] mixed strategy. For the man, this mixed strategy turns out to be ¾ for resort, and ¼ for camping. It guarantees him a minimum expected payoff of $-¾$ utiles. For the woman, the maximin mixed strategy is ⅓ for resort and ⅔ for camping, and this guarantees her ⅓ utiles.[20] If now the point $(-¾, ⅓)$ is taken as the No Sale point of the induced bargaining problem (which, in this context, Harsanyi would call an arbitration problem), the solution turns out to be $x = 11⅛; y = 1⅝$.

We see that arbitration gives the man a better break than bargaining. We would expect this result since the equity principle in this arbitration scheme takes into account only what each player can actually guarantee for himself by a properly chosen strategy as a reference point, not the threat potentials open to the players.

ARBITRATION SOLUTION II

Another arbitration scheme proposed by Raiffa (90) takes into account the relative advantages that the players have over each other in the various outcomes. These relative advantages are the algebraic differences of their payoffs. If these differences are entered into a new matrix, we get a zero-sum game, since the two differences are negatives of each other. The couple can now play the zero-sum game for relative advantage. Since the solution of the zero-sum game is unique, the question of relative advantage can be decided. Once it is decided, both can then *jointly* improve their payoffs until they get the maximum possible under the constraints of the game, preserving the relative advantage of one over the other. Let us see how this comes about.

Taking the man's point of view (in solidarity with the weaker party), we enter his relative advantages (of which only one is positive) into Matrix 10.

The zero-sum game represented by Matrix 10 has a saddle point at lower left. Hence its solution is a relative advantage of $+2$ for the woman. Accordingly, we write $y = x + 2$. This is a straight line with positive slope equal to 1 in the outcome space. If we follow this line "northeast," we will reach the negotiation line at the point $x = ⁹⁄₇$,

		Woman Resort	Camping
Man	Resort	−5	0
	Camping	−2	2

MATRIX 10

$y = 23/7$. This is not so good for the man as the Shapley solution but better than the bargaining solution.

However, the above solution has one very serious drawback. It is meaningful only if the numbers representing the utilities are the actual utilities of the players, not just particular representations of the utilities. Recall that in game theory the latter is assumed. That is to say, the utilities of each player could just as well be multiplied by some constant or increased by some constant or both without changing the situation. If we preserve this assumption, the arbitration method we have just described is meaningless, because it will give a different solution if the utilities of one or both players are subjected to a linear transformation. Obviously this will not do if an arbitration procedure is to lead to a unique solution. Evidently we need an equity principle that would give us some standard scale on which the utilities of both parties should be measured.

Raiffa (90) proposed one such scale. Let the highest utility accruing to each player in the game be denoted by 1 and the lowest by 0, and let the other utilities be placed on the interval (0, 1) so that the ratios of the intervals equal the original ratios. This makes the man's utilities 1, $1/2$, $1/6$, and 0; while the woman's utilities become 1, $3/7$, $1/7$, 0. The game now becomes as is shown in Matrix 11.

		Woman Resort	Camping
Man	Resort	$1/2$, 1	$1/6$, 0
	Camping	0, $1/7$	1, $3/7$

MATRIX 11

The game of relative advantage (from the man's point of view) becomes that shown in Matrix 12.

Woman

$-\frac{1}{2}$	$\frac{1}{6}$
$-\frac{1}{7}$	$\frac{4}{7}$

Man

MATRIX 12

The saddle point is, of course, preserved (as it should be under a linear transformation). But now the line of relative advantage is $y = x + \frac{1}{7}$. The negotiation set line also has a different equation, namely, $8x + 7y = 11$.

Solving these equations simultaneously, we get $x = \frac{2}{3}$; $y = \frac{17}{21}$. Translated into our original notation, this gives the man 1 utile and the woman $11\frac{1}{3}$. Under this arrangement, the man gets his way one-third of the time. Raiffa's arbitration scheme gives the man less than Shapley's scheme (the woman's advantage carries a greater weight in the former) but it gives him more than the straight bargaining scheme.[21]

ASSUMPTIONS UNDERLYING THE VARIOUS SOLUTIONS

The models just presented by no means exhaust the proposed approaches to a formal theory of negotiable games. Another approach [also due to Nash (82)] amounts to constructing a "metagame," whose moves would be bargaining acts, that is, predominately offers, counteroffers, threats, counterthreats, etc. Nash's aim is essentially to reduce the negotiable game to a non-negotiable one. It should be noted that reducing a negotiable game to a non-negotiable one does not mean denying the players the opportunities of negotiation but rather making explicit the non-negotiable features *of the negotiation itself*. These features are the *negotiation strategies*. It is from these that Nash proposes to construct the new non-negotiable game. Nash considers such games as "basic."

It is interesting to inquire why non-negotiable games appear more basic to some game theoreticians than negotiable ones. I suspect that this feeling derives from the fundamental result proved by Nash to the effect that every non-zero-sum game has at least one "equilibrium point" (82). The equilibrium point is a set of strategies (pure or mixed), one chosen by each player (i.e., a pair in the case of the two-person game). Each of these strategies has the property that if a player departs from it while the others stick to theirs, the player in question will not improve his payoff and, in general, will worsen it. Thus no "rational" player being motivated to depart from the equilibrium point strategy, every player will remain at the equilibrium point. This gives the equilibrium point the character of a "solution." If there are several such equilibrium points, it is possible to state a way of choosing among them consistent with certain plausible criteria of rationality (52). In this way, a unique solution can be found for every non-zero-sum non-negotiable game. We have already seen that no such unique solutions exist for negotiable games because of the multiplicity of solution methods. But if every negotiable game is reduced to a non-negotiable one (by depicting the negotiations as a sequence of moves), uniqueness can be achieved for negotiable games also. In this way the theory of non-zero-sum games can be made as complete as that of the zero-sum game.

As far as formal theory is concerned, the argument seems convincing to me. The formal theory of non-negotiable games is mathematically "clean." Also it requires no other assumptions of rationality than those already postulated in classical (zero-sum) game theory. But to my way of thinking, this philosophy of rational decision plays havoc with the normative theory. For the DD outcome of the prisoner's dilemma game (cf. page 49) is a Nash equilibrium point. If the equilibrium point is proposed as a *normative* solution of prisoner's dilemma, the dilemma disappears, but at a cost which I find unacceptable: The payoffs acheived by two "rational" players are smaller than the payoffs accruing to two "irrational" ones. It seems to me that the equilibrium solution bypasses the dilemma; it does not resolve it.[22]

We have already argued that the rationality postulates of classical game theory do not suffice for a normative theory of non-negotiable non-zero-sum games. In view of the multiplicity of arbitration solutions of negotiable games, we see that no arbitration scheme is compelling. Harsanyi seems to agree with this conclusion with regard to arbitration solutions (here he admits the necessity of introducing an equity principle) but not with regard to bargaining solutions, for which, he argues, only the perception of each other's rationally is required, as in the zero-sum game.

I am inclined to accept Harsanyi's argument as it applies to the simple bargaining game, in which the utilities of the No Sale outcome are *given*. But where the No Sale point must be established in the process of the negotiation, I do not agree that it can be established uniquely and obviously. The determination of the No Sale point involves evaluation of threats, hence psychological characteristics of the players, for example, propensities for risk-taking (which Harsanyi himself has pointed out). Consideration of these propensities and also how they would be affected in the negotiation process (since rational players are aware of the way their propensities affect the outcomes!) would take us far beyond axiomatically established criteria of rationality. The conclusion appears inescapable that the non-zero-sum game cannot be treated within the formal framework of normative rational decision theory without disregarding some of the most important features of these games.

CHAPTER 8

RESUMÉ OF PART I

We shall now review the empirical requirements of a theory of rational decision. A formal theory, by definition, requires no data. A descriptive theory of behavior can be based on whatever data are available. If a descriptive theory purports to be a theory of rational decision, its task is to define the criteria which seem to be criteria of rationality (so-called "as if" criteria), so that people's behavior appears consistent (therefore "rational") if it is in accord with those criteria. This can always be done, of course, but if the criteria of rationality so defined do not conform to any of our intuitive notions of what rationality is like (at least approximately), the theory will be a trivial (*ad hoc*) one. The most stringent requirements are those which must be imposed upon a normative theory. For a normative theory demands *specific* data. If such data are not available, there can be no prescriptive decisions, hence no normative theory that can be used.

DECISION UNDER CERTAINTY

A normative theory requires that the decision-maker "know his mind," i.e., that he be able to rank-order the outcomes by preference. He must also know the correspondence between choices of action and outcomes. The latter requirement, however, falls outside of the scope of decision theory.

Do people know their own minds? Sometimes, to be sure, they do, but often they do not. Here the appropriate descriptive theory is of interest, namely, the theory of preferences. Various experiments have been designed in order to see to what extent people are consistent in their preferences. The paired comparison test is a useful technique in this context. From a number of objects (or options), people are presented with selected pairs and asked to indicate their preference. Inconsistencies are revealed when choices turn out to be intransitive, for example, when A is preferred to B when paired with it, B to C, and C to A. These intransitivities do not cripple a descriptive theory of rational preference, because in principle a utility scale could be constructed in which utilities of the objects (or options) could be reflected in the frequencies with which they are preferred when paired with other objects (73, 74). Such attempts quickly lead into abstruse and complex mathematical models. A discussion of the literature on the subject is beyond the scope of this book, but it can be safely said that no *compelling* theory exists which enables us to construct even an ordinal utility scale for an arbitrary set of objects or options (5). If the decision-maker is a group (or a population) the problem of constructing a consistent rank order perference becomes still more difficult. Since such a scale is essential before a normative decision theory can be developed, we are forced to the conclusion that even in the context of decision under certainty, we have nothing approaching a usable and general normative theory of rational decision: Preferences cannot in general be unambiguously deduced from actual choices.

DECISION UNDER RISK

A normative theory requires (1) utilities of outcomes on an interval scale and (2) probabilities assigned to the different possible outcomes associated with each of the available courses of action. It is generally assumed in a theory of decision under risk that a rational decision maximizes expected utility. This is a tautology if utilities are so *defined* that the action with maximum expected utility is always preferred. Therefore, if a normative theory of risky decisions is not to be vacuous, utilities must be defined independently of the choices made in the context examined. If this is done, the principle of maximizing expected utility becomes an *additional* criterion of rationality. If the situation is repeated many times *and* if the payoffs of the individual outcome can be meaningfully added together, maximization of expected gain can be rationalized, since in the long run the expected gains become practically identical with actual gains. However, in the case of a single decision, this argument does not hold. Here maximization of expected gain becomes simply a definition of rational decision. One makes the proper choice because one feels that this is the "right thing to do." The "rightness" cannot be supported by any obvious principle of preference. It is simply the result of an extrapolation of what one would do if there were a long run and if the utilities of the successive outcomes could be added.

We have seen that in addition to the difficulty of assigning utilities on a interval scale, there are formidable conceptual difficulties in assigning definitive probabilities to unique events. In such cases, the assigned probabilities prove in the last analysis to be "subjective," i.e., dependent on choice rather than on knowledge. Therefore, non-rational factors must perforce enter decision theory at this point.

There is a large literature dealing with descriptive theories of risk behavior, mostly based on results of laboratory experiments. If the utilities and the subjective probabilities are assumed as given (a very strong assumption), the object of such experiments is usually to ascertain whether people actually maximize expected gains or, perhaps, use some other decision principle (25, 26). Usually, however, experiments on risk behavior are designed with a view to ascertaining the utility scales of subjects with respect to the prizes (assuming that the objective probabilities of the outcomes are "accepted" by the subjects) (74) or else with a view to ascertaining the subjective probabilities of the outcomes (given independently established utilities) (39). With respect to either of these, the "rationality" of human subjects leaves a great deal to be desired. This in itself does not refute a normative theory of rational decision (it merely establishes the fact that people do not behave as the theory prescribes). But the results do indicate that a rational decision theory based on an assumption that *others* follow rational principles of risky decisions could be extremely misleading.

DECISION UNDER UNCERTAINTY

This theory comprises the so-called games against nature where the probabilities of the states of nature are unknown. The theory requires a choice of a decision principle, e.g., equal probabilities assigned to all possible states on the basis of ignorance, or a minimax (pessimistic) principle, or a maximax (optimistic) principle, or whatever. Here, clearly, the decision-maker himself decides what will constitute a rational decision.

DECISION UNDER STRICT CONFLICT OF INTEREST

This theory comprises the theory of zero-sum games. We have seen that a zero-sum game with a saddle point requires the assignment of utilities on a ordinal scale and an assumption that the other prefers the outcomes in the reverse order. The rational choice of strategy in this case involves no risk. However, the *outcomes themselves* may be risky (with regard to states of nature, not the other's choice of strategy). In this case, the problem of assigning utilities to such risky outcomes is of the sort discussed above. Zero-sum games without saddle points require the assignment of utilities on an interval scale and the principle of maximizing expected utility.

The assumption of the "rationality" of the other is inherent in the theory of the zero-sum game. Failure to make this assumption exposes the decision-maker to the risk of being seduced into choosing a strategy deviating from the minimax. On the other hand, if the other is assumed "rational" but is not, the minimax strategy may fail to take advantage of the other's "irrationality." But this irrationality can be determined only by means of an effective descriptive theory. Thus if a normative theory of the zero-sum game is to be useful in practice (i.e., against real, live opponents), it must be linked with a descriptive theory of decision.

Experimental investigations of behavior in zero-sum games have established some interesting findings. For the most part, the minimax solution is beyond the knowledge of subjects ignorant of game theory (71). In some cases, it has been demonstrated that when plays of the same game are repeated, the subject's behavior is more consistently explained by a stochastic learning theory rather than by game theory (117, 44). The results of the two theories are at variance with each other.

DECISION UNDER CONFLICT WITH MIXED MOTIVES

Here we are in the realm of the non-zero-sum game. It is our contention that in this context no definition of rationality can be given which would remain intuitively satisfactory in all contexts. One cannot, therefore, speak of a normative theory in this context unless one invokes specific extra-game-theoretical considerations. Frequently, these considerations belong to the realm of ethics. Not only does a normative theory demand a knowledge of the other's ethical prescripts but it frequently must prescribe ethical principles to the decision-maker from whose point of view the problem is seen. Failure to understand this point cripples the theory of non-zero-sum games in applications.

The interlacing of a normative theory of mixed-motive games with ethical prescripts makes its application fundamentally dependent on a successful descriptive theory of decision. Experiments on mixed-motive games are presently being vigorously pursued (9, 34, 76, 80, 93, 105, 114, 117). Some of them, performed in the author's laboratory, will be described in Chapter 14.

Our conclusion is that a normative theory of rational decision cannot be based on a few rigorously defined postulates; nor can such a theory be successfully applied except in certain very special situations (e.g., where utilities, probabilities, ranges of strategy, etc., are unambiguously defined). For the most part, decisions depend on the ethical orientations of the decision-makers themselves. The rationales of choices so determined may be obvious to those with similar ethical orientations but may appear to be only rationalizations to others. Therefore, in most contexts, decisions cannot be defended on purely objective grounds. A normative theory of decision which claims to be "realistic," i.e., purports to derive its prescripts exclusively from "objective reality" is likely to lead to delusion.

Part II. Hazards and Pitfalls of Strategic Thinking

CHAPTER 9

EXPANDING HORIZONS

In Part I we sketched the various theoretical approaches to problems of rational decision. In Part II we shall make an appraisal of the uses and misuses of these approaches.

A theory can be useful in two ways, as a basis of a technology and as a focal point of conceptual organization. In our society the first of these roles is easy to explain; the second, very difficult. This is because in our society science is respected primarily for its role as a basis of a technology.

The technological advances spurred on by science since the Renaissance have been dramatic and conspicuous. It is doubtful, however, whether our technological civilization could ever have blossomed if man's conception of his environment did not at the same time undergo profound changes. It takes certain attitudes and motivations to acquire knowledge. Such attitudes and motivations favorable for the growth of technology were concomitant to the second role played out by science, namely broadening man's perspective and at the same time keeping his speculations anchored in reality. As technology was matching fairy tale magic, it was also undermining the basis for believing in fairy tale magic.

It is instructive to recall that some of the most important principles which have served as the foundations of our scientific theories were statements of impossibility. For example, the most general and important physical laws are the so-called conservation laws. These laws typically state what cannot be done. The first law to be so formulated was Newton's conservation-of-momentum law. The law states roughly that the total momentum of a mechnical system cannot be changed by forces within the system. Later, the law of conservation of matter was discovered. It says that matter can be neither created nor destroyed. The law of conservation of energy became established when it was observed that changes of mechanical energy of an isolated system were always accompanied by equal and opposite changes in its heat content and, consequently, that the total energy of the system could be neither increased nor decreased. This law put an end to the dream of constructing a perpetual motion machine. Briefly another dream flickered, namely, the possibility of converting heat totally into work in a cyclic operation. This dream was shattered by the stern second law of thermodynamics. And so it went.

Seen in this way, it would seem that scientific theory should have served to discourage rather than to encourage man's striving for power. But the meaning of scientific laws is not confined to their negative aspects. By pointing out what cannot be done, a scientific law suggests what can be done and, moreover, provides a sober outlook on the nature of the problem. When it became clear that mechanical perpetual motion machines were impossible, man turned his attention to the problem of converting heat into work. The result of this insight was the Industrial Revolution. Although the second law of thermodynamics put an end to the hope of unrestricted conversion of heat into work, it provided a profound understanding of chemical reactions. The law of the chemical immutability of elements dissipated the alchemists' ambitions of turning base metals into gold but opened the way to the fathoming of atomic structure until the (physical) mutability of the elements and the duality of matter-energy were discovered. Thus knowledge of what is impossible has its creative, positive side.

Knowledge of impossibilities is not confined to natural science. The great leaps foward in mathematics were instigated by discoveries that certain problems cannot be solved. In destroying the hope of solving age-old problems, modern mathematics rendered a much more important positive service. It showed *why* it is impossible to solve them, and this knowledge is much more far-reaching in the sense of imparting mathematical sophistication than a positive solution of the problems would have been. For example, the knowledge that it is impossible to solve by radicals the general equation of degree higher than four (and why) is much more important than the solution of such equations (if this were possible) would have been. Even the shattering theorem of Goedel, to the effect that no self-consistent mathematical system can be complete, carried an impetus of constructive development in the wake of its pessimistic conclusion.

In general, then, discoveries of what cannot be done contributed to the maturity of the sciences.

Now, it is natural for technologically oriented seekers of "solutions" to resist the idea that certain problems are not solvable. It is never pleasant to be told that one's searches are futile. Moreover, some grave pronouncements of technological impossibility have been on occasion dramatically refuted. Finally, it is not easy to abandon one's accustomed methods, especially if these methods had been successful within the spheres of their legitimate applications. Nevertheless, in spite of these sources of resistance, verdicts of impossibility in the natural sciences and in mathematics eventually had to be accepted, because the evidence on which such verdicts are based is, as a rule, compelling. The die-hards remain only on the fringes: self-taught mathematically semiliterate eccentrics, who continue to send papers on squaring the circle to mathematical journals; antirelativity physicists, who persist in repeating the Michelson-Morley experiment and interpret experimental errors as positive results; anti-intellectual thinkers, often extremely talented ones, like Russia's T. D. Lysenko, who continue doggedly in their attempts to disprove the laws of genetics, etc.

Let us now see how matters stand in decision theory. Consider the decision problems in the order in which they were presented in Part I. Each new "level" of decision problems originates in the realization that the methods which had sufficed on the preceding level suffice no longer. Hence each level might be properly introduced by a declaration of impossibility.

For example, the simplest decision problem concerns the choice among alternatives, each of which leads with certainty to an outcome. Knowledge of which alternative leads to which outcome and an ordering of outcomes according to preference suffices to determine the "best" alternative, namely, the one which leads to the most preferred outcome. In this context, the knowledge one needs is the knowledge obtainable through classical scientific investigation—the investigation of causes and effects operating in the environment. Once this problem is solved and preferences have been established, the decision problem becomes trivial.

The matter looks quite different when decisions are made under risk. An investigation of the environment can establish at best the probability with which each of the possible outcomes is likely to result from each of the alternative actions. Here we cannot answer the question "Which is the 'best' alternative?" without further expanding the notion of what we mean by "best," because some of the possible outcomes associated with a given course of action are better than other outcomes associated with another course, but some are worse. Note also that the very notion of "probability" is a new notion that did not figure in the simpler problem of decision under certainty. Therefore when we redefine "best alternative" in the context of risk, "best" acquires a new meaning constructed from more abstract notions, such as "maximizing expected utility gains."

As we pass to decision problems in conflict situations, still other concepts enter our repertoire, and the old methods of finding the "best alternative" work no longer. For example, in a zero-sum game without a saddle point, we can no longer speak even of *the* expected-utility-maximizing strategy. For we are no longer facing Nature, who unconcernedly mixes her strategies but still allows us to choose the best counterstrategy against her mixture. In a zero-sum game we face a rational opponent, who will discern the strategy we choose against his mixture. Consequently, we must mix our own strategies in order to confound *him*. This amounts to abdicating our decision-making prerogative and leaving the choice of strategy to chance. We retain only the control of the probabilities with which our strategies are to be chosen.

Up to this point, no matter how farfetched and abstract the notion of optimization becomes, as we move to the more complex decision situations, we can still define what we mean by an optimal solution of a decision problem. But we have seen that even this principle goes by the wayside as we pass from the realm of two-person zero-sum games to non-zero-sum games. We have seen, for example, how the very notion of rationality becomes ambiguous in the prisoner's dilemma game, how it bifurcates into individual and collective rationality and how the dictates of the two conflict.

To many the minimax solution of the prisoner's dilemma already seems intuitively unacceptable. And if it is argued that this dis-satisfaction must be suppressed as a prejudice bacuse the logic of the dominating strategy is irrefutable, the argument no longer holds in the case of prisoner's dilemma played twice. For although in that case the totally uncooperative strategy is still the minimax (or equilibrium) strategy, it is no longer dominating. Evidently, the notion of an equilibrium strategy is more complex than that of a dominating strategy.

Now when the theory we have outlined is pursued as an abstract discipline, its lessons are clear. Thorough analysis provides opportunities for insights into the nature of rational decisions, and an appreciation of the impossibility principle provides the leverage for expanding our understanding. Unfortunately, decision theory has been cast into another role, namely, that of a prop for *rationalizing* decisions arrived at by processes far from rational. We shall attempt to show that in this role rational decision theory can become a source of dangerous fixations and delusions.

CHAPTER 10

PRESSURE FOR SIMPLIFICATION: UTILITIES AND PROBABILITIES

~~~~~~

The strategist, like the engineer and like the operations analyst, assumes that decision problems have rationally defensible solutions. Our intent in Part I has been to show that "rationality" is not a simple, straightforward notion, that as the environment becomes more and more complex, more and more sophisticated concepts enter into the definition of rationality. With increasing complexity controversial features begin to appear, as is shown in the analysis of non-zero-sum games.

The strategist's commitment, however, is to the solution of "strategic problems." Unlike the mathematician who before undertaking to solve a problem usually inquires whether a solution to a given problem exists at all, the strategist tends to assume that *his* problems *have* solutions. There must be (he tacitly assumes) some optimal level of nuclear weaponry, an optimal allocation, an optimal schedule of threats and counterthreats, etc.

Now whether a problem has a solution or not depends on how the problem is put. For problems are not given to us by Nature. Nature presents us with situations, which we *formulate* as problems. Someone who is professionally committed to getting definitive answers to decision problems will be understandably under pressure to formulate his problems in terms of paradigms that yield to the techniques he commands.

The strategist is not alone in this respect. Every translation of a situation into a problem involves simplifications, sometimes extremely drastic ones. The history of physics, the most rigorous of the natural sciences, is a history of fortunate simplifications which have enabled the physicists to fit a wide sector of phenomena into a grandiose theoretical scheme. However, the physicist is usually aware of the limitations which his simplified models impose on the range of validity of his conclusions. In order to construct a theory of behavior of gases, for example, it was necessary to begin with a theory of an idealized "perfect gas." But no physicist would apply such a theory to, say, the behavior of carbon dioxide near its critical point. The behavior of carbon dioxide, which is very different from that of a "perfect gas," has also been explained, and the corresponding explanation was evolved from the more primitive one, but between the two there are several intermediate theories of increasing complexity. These theories could not have been developed by simply progressively complicating the original model, because the modifications could have gone in several directions. What made the modern complex theory of gases posssible was a continuous interplay of theory and experiment. At each step, experimental data suggested to the theoretician the direction of theoretical development. Each step in the development of the theory, in turn, suggested relevant and illuminating experiments. Thus while it is perfectly true that in natural science simplification has been a powerful tool for gaining real knowledge, it was continual comparison of model with reality which insured the selection of the most essential features of the phenomena studied and allowed the scientist to ignore the relatively inessential ones.

Aside from certain simulation techniques (to be discussed in Chapter 13), the strategist has no experiments to guide him in his theoretical development. Moreover, he works in an atmosphere of "applied science," that is, he is expected to come up fairly soon with fairly usable results. Accordingly he simplifies not in order to build a science from the bottom up but in order to get answers. The answers he gets are answers to the problems he poses, not necessarily, not even usually, to the problems with which the world we have made confronts us with.

We have seen that even in the simplest type of decision (decision under certainty) the problem of assigning utilities to outcomes still looms large when the outcomes are not directly comparable. On the other hand, when the outcomes can be associated with a single-dimensional scale, utilities can be naturally assigned if the scale represents a quantity of which one cannot have too much—a "pure good." The pressure toward simplification, accordingly, brings out precisely those aspects of the situation in which the "pure good" can be clearly pointed out.

The most prominent examples of such pressure are seen in the arguments made in favor of civil defense. A standard argument in favor of civil defense is the lifesaving potential of this program. Given certain assumptions about the magnitude of a nuclear attack, the distribution of targets, and so on, the number of lives lost can be estimated from the physical characteristics of the attack, e.g., the range of the blasts, spread of fire storms, areas affected by fallout, etc. These calculations usually stop with the dissipation of the fallout (given a single attack). Thereafter, the estimates become progressively more vague, because the ultimate survival ratio depends to an increasing degree on higher-order effects, e.g., famines resulting from disrupted transport, epidemics resulting from the breakdown of sanitation and medical facilities, crime resulting from a paralysis of law enforcement apparatus, etc. In some studies, these "higher-order" calculations are carried out, but their reliability quickly decreases as the time span of prognosis increases, because the farther the calculations go, the more they depend on assumptions piled on one another. However, the reliability of the calculations is not the issue for the present. We are examining the basic, often tacit, assumptions, namely, that a civil defense program that "saves" more lives is better than one that saves fewer lives. In particular, therefore, any civil defense program, according to this assumption, is better than none, if it can only be shown that some lives can be saved by implementing it. The proponents of civil defense seldom, if ever, put it this way, but the conclusion just cited is a logical consequence of the basic underlying assumption that in the context of civil defense the number of lives saved is a "pure good."

Now it is easy to show that "lives saved" is certainly not a "pure good" in our society.

At present we kill about 40,000 persons per year on the highways. Doubtless the figures would have been still higher if certain measures had not been taken over the years: improving the highways, the vehicles, traffic law enforcement, safety education, etc. The fact that more lives are not saved indicates one of two circumstances: Either nothing else can be done to reduce fatalities further or the marginal utility of human life has dropped below the marginal costs under the present conditions. In the opinion of experts, the first conclusion is unlikely. The second sounds harsh, but it is hardly avoidable. If, then, one continues to reason within the framework of utility calculations, then one could conceivably calculate the present marginal utility of human life in dollars (based, say, on the present cost of saving an additional human life on the highways, a cost which is *not* met by our society) and see how extensive a civil defense program is justified on this basis. To my knowledge such calculations have not been carried out.

It should be clear that our purpose here is not to propose a "more rational" decision procedure for choosing a civil defense program which would give the biggest returns (in utiles, not lives) per dollar invested. Rather our purpose is to point up the absurdity of such calculations. On the other hand, if such calculations are not made, for instance, if human life is valued above any material costs involved in saving it, then there are simpler ways than civil defense of saving lives, for example, by preventing war altogether, even if this means unilateral disarmament or "surrender." But these are precisely the alternatives which are never seriously considered by the strategists.

The problem of estimating the value of human life in political utiles is put by Herman Kahn in the opening chapter of *On Thermonuclear War* (58, p. 29): "If 180 million dead is too high a price to pay for punishing the Soviets for their aggression, what price would we be willing to pay?"

Having formulated the problem, he undertakes to solve it (58, p. 30): "I have discussed this question with many Americans, and after about fifteen minutes of discussion, their estimates of an acceptable price generally fall between 10 and 60 million, clustering toward the upper number."

The nature of the hypothetical aggression will be discussed below (cf. page 106). The sources of the answers to the question are, however, not specified, while the phrasing of the question would scandalize anyone in the least familiar with the problem of assessing public opinion. Nevertheless, the question and answer imply that some objective assessment of a "socially accepted" valuation of human life has been made, and so one is entitled to proceed with the analysis on the basis of the established utility scale.

The glaring social fact is, of course, that the marginal utility of human life varies tremendously with the context. While the public remains relatively indifferent to the loss of tens of thousands of lives in traffic accidents, six trapped miners throw the entire country into anguish and utmost efforts are exerted to save them without regard for material expense. The difference between the two situations is immediately apparent. The prospective victims of traffic accidents are anonymous. The trapped miners are individuals with identities and with whom we can consequently identify.

However, the identity or anonymity of individuals is by no means the only factor which makes for huge disparities in the valuation of human life. Consider the following situation, presented here as hypothetical, but which is possibly taken from real life.

NOT THE CHANCE OF DEATH BUT WHO METES IT OUT

In World War II at a certain bomber base in the South Pacific a flier's chances of surviving his quota of thirty missions were rated at 25 per cent. The young men lived the life of the doomed. Then a way was found to improve the situation. It was calculated that if the bombers carried bigger payloads, that is, more bombs per plane, the missions could be accomplished at the same rate with half the number of planes. The only way to increase the payload of the planes was to reduce the amount of gasoline carried. This could be done if the planes went on *one-way missions*. In other words, if the fliers agreed to sacrifice their lives with certainty instead of accepting one chance in four for survival, only half of them would need to perish instead of three-quarters. The new procedure would require a flier to draw lots with a 50 per cent chance of success. If from a box containing two balls, he drew a white ball, he would be rotated to the States, if a black ball, he would have to go on the one-way mission. This arrangement would give each flier twice as large a chance to survive than the previous one.[23]

As the reader may have guessed, the one-way-mission system was never put into effect. Clearly lives could have been saved if it were adopted. Therefore the cost of saving these lives must have been too high. But where was this cost reflected? Before we undertake to answer this question, let us consider some other examples.

Our next case, although purely hypothetical, is nevertheless instructive because it serves to bring out the otherwise hidden considerations which often govern our preferences. Suppose it were possible to reduce traffic fatalities by 10,000 lives per year, provided 5,000 persons were selected every year by lot to be killed, the victims being unaware of their fate until the very last moment. Is it reasonable to suppose that such a scheme would be adopted in our society?

Next, consider the lifesaving value of drugs or vaccines. Suppose a vaccine is discovered which immunizes children against leukemia, but is lethal to a certain percentage of the children. How low would this mortality have to be for the vaccine to be accepted? We conjecture that it would have to be much lower than the mortality of leukemia, perhaps only one-tenth of the latter. In other words, the purely arithmetical lifesaving potential of a vaccine would not be sufficient to induce its acceptance.

Finally consider the choice sometimes offered to mothers of sons held as hostages. If, for example, two sons were in custody, the mother would be told that one of them was to be shot and that she was to name which one. If she failed to name one, both would be shot. We guess that under these conditions, many a mother would refuse to make the choice, thus failing to take advantage of the opportunity to save the life of one of her sons.

In all of these examples, we feel we can "justify" a decision which opts for saving fewer lives than more lives, even though no material costs are associated with saving more lives. Undoubtedly there are other costs associated with the saving of lives, costs which are evidently too high, if they are not met. What are they?

In the case of the fliers, one might conclude that the cost is that of *knowing* that one is going on a suicide mission; perhaps also that of knowing that someone else, not self, has to go to his certain death while self has been saved. Among men facing death together this situation is frequently more agonizing than the prospect of certain death itself.

But this cannot be the only factor, because it is not present in the second example. Here the prospective victims would remain to the end as anonymous as the traffic victims. If our conjecture is correct that the proposed scheme would not be acceptable, it can be only because the death of 5,000 "by lot" is felt to be worse in some way than the death of 10,000 "by accident." Perhaps many of us nurture the thought in the back of our minds that victims of accidents are at least partly responsible for their deaths. The comfort of this thought is denied to us if the victims are chosen by lot.

But this explanation does not suffice either, as is seen in the next example. Here guilt cannot be ascribed either to the victims of the disease or to the victims of the vaccine. Both kinds of death stem from similar "causes," a more-than-average susceptibility to the disease, on the one hand, a more-than-normal susceptibility to the vaccine, on the other. One would think, therefore, that here the "other things" are indeed "equal," and so the number of lives should be the only consideration in choosing between deaths caused by the disease and deaths caused by the innoculation. But very many, quite likely a majority, would not accept this conclusion.

The difference in the valuation placed on human life must be related to our sense of "responsibility" for it. A death for which we feel responsible is harder to bear than one which is attributed to powers beyond our control. The death of a flier at the hands of the enemy is one thing. His death on a suicide mission is quite another. This death has been *prearranged*. Even though chance decides who goes, the manner of going is prepared by the man's associates. It is *they* who fill his gasoline tank only half full. The child who dies of leukemia is killed by the disease. The child who dies of a vaccine is killed in part by the pharmacists who prepared the vaccine, by the nurse who injected it, and by the parent who arranged for the injection.

The parable of the hostages illustrates this principle more dramatically. The mother cannot bring herself to save one of her own sons, because she feels *she* is killing the other to do it. If she is silent, it is the enemy who kills her sons. If she names one, she shares the guilt.

Unless these psychological factors are taken into account, the assignment of rank orders to outcomes become little more than a ritual. But the assignment has to be made if the decision problem is to be formulated. The strategists' expertness comes out to best advantage in the calculations of tangibles. These people are usually at home with physics, logistics, and ballistics. They can make estimates about how many megatons how deployed will cause how many megadeaths, and how many shelters dug how deep will postpone how many megadeaths by how many weeks. In these calculations their professional prowess is invested and in them they see the focus of the problem. The problem of assigning utilities to outcomes is not within their competence or concern. For this reason, they tend to bypass or to ignore this problem. The easiest way to ignore it is to assign utilities in the crudest possible way: the fewer megadeaths (or say megadeaths per ton of concrete) on our side and the more on the other side, the better. In this way, strategic thinking with its built-in pressures for simplification builds its elaborate theoretical edifices on vulgar or naive assumptions.

Although many examples of the sort of thinking just described can be pointed out, it is not true that all the writings of the strategists are on the same level. In fact, for every example of strategic thinking at its crudest, the defenders of the method can point to examples which are more sophisticated in the sense that they show more appreciation of the difficulties inherent in decision problems. There is, indeed, a considerable range of insight exhibited by the strategists. Our contention is that the range is not sufficient to enable the strategists to cope with the important issues of our day. The range is limited by the scope of strategic thinking itself. This limitation exists on all the levels of decision problems considered by the strategists. It generates pressures to reduce these problems to a tractable level.

EXPECTED UTILITY

What frequently happens is this. A decision problem is seen to be more complex than it had been represented. Accordingly a more complex level of analysis is proposed. This gives the impression that the problem has been put into proper perspective.

As an example, consider the methodological argument by J. David Singer (109, pp. 23 ff.). Singer is a thoughtful and severe critic of prevailing strategically oriented policies. But he has set for himself the task of criticizing these policies entirely within the framework of strategic thinking. He points out that it is insufficient to rank-order possible outcomes on the basis of their utilities alone (as one does in decision under certainty) or on the basis of their probabilities alone but that one must combine the two criteria so as to rank the outcomes according to expected utility. And this is indeed done by Snyder in his theoretical discussion (113, p. 270).

Snyder represents the state of international affairs by the following matrix:

		Soviet Union		
		No Attack	Nuclear Attack on U. S.	Ground Attack on Europe
	Probabilities	.60	.10	.30
United States	No response	0	−500	−100
	Massive response	0	−400	−400
	Ground force response	0	0	−150

MATRIX 13 (*after Snyder*)

The Soviet Union, it appears, has three options: to attack the United States by nuclear weapons, to attack Western Europe by ground forces, or to do nothing. The United States has three options: massive response (retaliatory nuclear attack), ground response, or no response. The negative numbers in the matrix are presumably the estimated costs to the United States in utiles of the associated outcomes. Observe, however, that at least some of the zero entries cannot be meant to represent such payoffs. For example, the zero entry in the box which represents a ground force response to a nuclear attack cannot mean that the cost of that eventuality to the United States is zero. Nor is it clear why a "massive response" by the United States to *no attack* (can this mean a pre-emptive attack?) should be rated zero, i.e., the same as "no response to no attack." We can only conclude that the zeros have been entered into the boxes which represent outcomes left out of consideration. From Snyder's discussion it appears that a policy has *already* been chosen, namely, to respond massively to a nuclear attack and not to respond at all to a ground attack. The "expected cost" of this policy is obtained by multiplying the relevant costs by the associated probabilities and adding the results together with the preparedness cost required. If the latter is say 50 units, the total cost (negative utility) of this commitment turns out to be $(-400) \ (0.10) \ + \ (-100) \ (0.30) \ + \ (-50) \ = \ -120$.

Next, Snyder compares two alternative strategies: (1) to prepare better for massive retaliation, thus reducing both the probability and the cost to the United States of a Soviet attack and (2) to prepare better for a ground response, which reduces the probability and costs of a ground attack but leaves the probability and cost of a nuclear attack the same.

It turns out that if the numbers invented by Snyder represent actual costs and actual probabilities, the decision to bolster ground troops rather than massive retaliatory capability is to be favored, since it reduces the "expected costs" by a greater amount.

In presenting such schemes (there are many such examples) Snyder makes clear that they are examples only and that they are by no means to be taken seriously as realistic models of actual situations. Nevertheless the examples do direct thinking along certain lines. The schema of the "game against nature" (for this is the way the situation is depicted) is to some degree firmed in the reader sympathetic to the strategic approach. Above all, the impression remains that even though the numbers suggested in the example are fictitious, somewhere there *are* numbers of this sort which represent "reality," that if we could get at them, we could solve problems of this type by "calculating risks." In this way, while avoiding the gross error pointed out by Singer (neglecting the "two-dimensionality" of expected utility) the strategist is likely to fall into the next trap set for him by his method, namely, depicting situations controlled by *antagonists* as games against nature in which the probabilities of Nature's strategies are independent of one's own.[24]

The crassest example of this fallacy is again provided by the arguments for civil defense, perhaps the greatest collection of *non sequiturs* derived from unwarranted assumptions in the entire strategic enterprise. The situation depicted by civil defense arguments is invariably depicted as a game against nature. If it were depicted as a genuine two-person game, the arguments for civil defense would be revealed as incredibly naive. But the proponents of civil defense prefer to make the arguments of their opponents seem ludicrous. And this can be easily done if the situation is viewed as a game against nature.

Kahn (59, pp. 88–89) quotes with approval the following letter to the editor of the *Harvard Crimson* (published October 30, 1961), purporting to reduce to absurdity the objections against a civil defense program.

It has been brought to our attention that certain elements among the passengers and crew favor the installation of "lifeboats" on this ship. These elements have advanced the excuse that such action would save lives in the event of a maritime disaster such as the ship striking an iceberg. Although we share their concern, we remain unalterably opposed to any considerations of their course of action for the following reasons:

1. This program would lull you into a false sense of security.

2. It would cause undue alarm and destroy your desire to continue your voyage on this ship.

3. It demonstrates a lack of faith in our Captain.

4. The apparent security which "lifeboats" offer will make our navigators reckless.

5. These proposals will distract our attention from more important things, i.e., building unsinkable ships. They may even lead our builders to false economies and the building of ships that are actually unsafe.

6. In the event of being struck by an iceberg (we will never strike first!) the "lifeboats" would certainly sink along with the ship.

7. If they do not sink, you will only be saved for a worse fate, inevitable death on the open sea.

8. If you should be washed ashore on a desert island, you will be unaccustomed to the hostile environment and will surely die of exposure.

9. If you should be rescued by a passing vessel, you would spend a life of remorse mourning over your lost loved ones.

10. The panic engendered by a collision with an iceberg would destroy all vestiges of civilized human behavior. We shudder at the vision of one man shooting another for the possession of a "lifeboat."

11. Such a catastrophe is too horrible to contemplate. Anyone who does contemplate it obviously advocates it.

Now satire, of course, can cut both ways, and I cannot resist the temptation to tell the fable about the town near a high cliff, from which view-loving tourists frequently fell. The town councilors split into two factions, those who favored a railing on the top of the cliff and those who favored an ambulance below. After much haggling, the ambulance faction won out when they made the incontrovertible argument that it is not the *start* of the fall that hurts the victims, but the *end* of it down below, so that is where the countermeasure belongs.

The civil defense enthusiasts among the strategists will, of course, insist that they favor both the railing and the ambulance. This seems reasonable if it can be shown that the two are compatible. And they do seem compatible if civil defense measures are compared to precautions against a *natural* disaster. The enemy (in this context alone!) is pictured as an indifferent iceberg which we will never strike first. The situation looks different if the "iceberg" is endowed with receptors and reflexes and if the ship is equipped not only with lifeboats but also with guns trained on the "iceberg." The point is that if (by chance) the iceberg is also convinced that it will not strike first, it might wonder if this is a good idea as it watches the lifeboat drills upon the approaching armed ship.

Let us return to the calculation of utilities.

THE SINGLE UTILITY SCALE

The background of the strategist is frequently the world of engineering, business, economics, operations research, and the like, areas in which the assignment of quantitative utilities is frequently given by the nature of the problem itself. The engineer deals with efficiency factors, safety factors, etc. The businessman deals with trade volumes, costs, profits, shares of the market, and the like. The designer of weapons deals with indexes of accuracy and of destructive power. In problems faced by these professional people, these quantities are naturally interpreted as utilities (positive or negative), and so a rational decision is seen as one which either maximizes or minimizes one of those quantities or some mathematical combination of them.

An essential complication arises when the quantities are scaled on different dimensions.

Kissinger, for example, writes (65, p. 13):

> The technological race is not between weapons which have the same mission; rather it is between offensive and defensive capabilities. And because the offensive and defensive weapons systems have different characteristics, one of the most important problems of strategy is to decide on the relative emphasis to be given to each and to the "mix" which will provide the greatest security and flexibility.

The pressure to reduce security and flexibility to a single index is unmistakable. In practice this leads to the calculations for which the paper warriors have become notorious: How many of our lives can be traded for how many of theirs; what is the level of risk to us that is amply compensated by a threat to them. Stalin's famous question, "How many divisions has the Vatican?" has become a proverbial example of cynical reductionism. The strategist who has taken "intangibles" into account is more likely to ask a more sophisticated question. "The Vatican's influence in world politics is equivalent to how many divisions?"

Now this is not to say that the strategists do not know that in many situations the "mix" is an absurd solution. For example, they see the falseness of the argument that the ideal American home should be designed for 2.31 children, the "expected" number. But in this instance it is possible to replace the "mix" by a rational policy, namely, to build so many homes for one-child families, so many for two-child families, etc. But there can be only one weapons procurement policy at a time. The "mix" may give the best "expected value" but it may be absurd nevertheless, because what will occur will certainly not fit the "mix." And one cannot convincingly argue that "in the long run" the actual expected value will be realized. There is not likely to be a long run in this sense.

It is easy to see where the "mix" idea comes from: It is the military counterpart of the investment portfolio, where one reduces the total risk by spreading one's investment bets. But the analogy makes sense only if the expected gains compensate for the expected losses. Such compensations occur only in the mind of the strategist who has reduced the insanities of war to entries on a financial sheet or on a score board.

ASSIGNING PROBABILITIES

Now let us recall that throughout this discussion we assumed that the objective probabilities of events are known. Estimates of such probabilities can always be made on the basis of observed frequencies of the events in question among events of an inclusive class. The more numerous the events and the more constant the environment in which they occur, the more reliable are the estimates of the probabilities. Gambling games provide the best-known context for decisions based on objectively estimated probabilities. The devices used in such games (cards, dice, roulette wheels, etc.) are especially designed to approximate the conditions of repeated "identical" events. In real life, such conditions can sometimes be assumed with varying degrees of justification. Actuarial work is based on assumptions according to which all individuals of a certain class (e.g., all native born, male, white collar workers 33–35 years of age) are equated with respect to a propensity for some characteristic of interest (e.g., mortality, marital status, etc.). Accuracy of such estimates ought to increase as the individuals constituting a class are defined by a larger number of features in common. For example, the class just mentioned can be further refined by specifying the locality in which those men live or their income bracket.

But the process of successive refinement with a view to getting more accurate estimates of certain probabilities is ultimately self-defeating. For the more characteristics we list, the narrower the class becomes. Finally, we may list so many characteristics that only one individual remains in the class (for example, a red-haired bank teller in Detroit, Michigan, born on August 1, 1928, who plays the oboe, drives a Rambler, and has two daughters named Susan and Daisy). When the class is reduced to a single member, the "propensities" (which had been defined in terms of observed frequencies) lose all operational meaning.[25] Now we cannot say anything about the "probability" that our bank teller will within a year develop glaucoma or abscond with the cash or what not. Either he will or he won't.

Does this mean that probability has no meaning except with reference to a frequency? Some would have it this way, but others disagree and defend the notion of a "personal" or "subjective" probability. We must make clear what it means to "defend" a notion in this context. The fact that an "idea" of personal probability exists cannot be denied. We are all aware of degrees of beliefs which we assign to events, including unique events. The question is whether the notion of personal probability can be made precise, so that at least in principle it is possible to determine what probability a given person assigns to a given event. It turns out that such a procedure can indeed be indicated and carried out "in principle." It is possible to say what to do to determine a personal probability scale but it is by no means certain that the procedure will yield definitive results (cf. the remarks concerning the determination of personal utility scales on page 21).

In spite of all these difficulties, let us grant that a personal probability assigned to a given (unique) event can be determined. Now let us ask the next question. Is there any way to test the *accuracy* of such an assignment? There is not. As we have said, the unique event will either occur or it will not; therefore in neither case will the assigned probability be put to a test. In order to justify an assigned probability by some objective evidence, we must put the event into a class of events, so that its (repeated) occurrence can give an estimate of its frequency among the events *in that class*. But which class shall we take?

Returning to our red-haired bank teller, we can see him from several different angles. He belongs to the class of red-haired people, and to the class of Detroiters, to the class of amateur musicians and to that of bank tellers and of fathers of daughters named Susan and Daisy. Suppose some event of interest (say, an automobile accident) has a well-defined frequency in every one of the classes we can define as including our man, and suppose these frequencies are all different. Which class is the *relevant* class? We do not know. It seems the safe thing to do would be to take the *intersection* of all of these classes.[26] But we have already seen that the intersection may become too small, may even reduce to our single member, in which case we cannot estimate any frequency.

The question of relevance is often lost sight of because the relevance of the class into which we put our individual in order to estimate some frequency that interests us sometimes seems self-evident. For example, if the event in question is absconding with $30,000, then the relevant class is "bank teller," not "father of girls named Susan or Daisy." But the matter is not always so clear.

And so a "check" on personal probability can be made only if we agree on the class into which we shall put our unique event. The reader will recall that this was precisely the crux of the paradox in the ace-deuce game we described on page 28. *If* we are at liberty to decide when to bet and *if* we confine our bets to the times when our opponent has the deuce of spades, then we shall come out with larger winnings at the same odds than if we bet every time he gets just any deuce. *Now* the probability can be translated into a frequency and is verifiable by observation. But in the individual case, this difference of probabilities reflects nothing but our state of mind, i.e., the class of events into which we have chosen to put the event in question.

Now let us look at the problem of assigning to an event a probability on the basis of which a policy is to be formulated. Say we are asked to assign a probability to the outbreak of a nuclear war under certain conditions. In the discussions of columnists and news commentators probabilities of such events are often tacitly assumed to be as well defined as the probability of filling an inside straight. On the basis of what we have said, we could justifiably dismiss such talk outright as crass nonsense. Nevertheless, although the question of how to assign probabilities to events whose frequencies have never been observed cannot be decided, it can certainly be argued. The man who argues for assigning a greater probability to the outbreak of a nuclear war will list all the ways in which such a war could start accidentally, will place much weight on certain self-perpetuating processes instigated by the compulsions under which the decision-makers of each side are operating, etc. The man holding the opposite opinion will mention safeguards presumably operating to prevent accidental war, the face-saving "outs" available to crises, etc. In arguing this way, both men will be *selecting from the environment* those factors which support their respective points of view. The argument, then, is not about "what is" but about *what one ought to pay attention to*. Such arguments are not and cannot be supported by lines of proof. They are supported by bids for attention to certain matters in preference to others. That is to say, such arguments are essentially pleas.

Pleas are unavoidable in discussions where values are involved. The present book is a plea to pay more attention to matters which strategic thinking habits have de-emphasized or have excluded from consideration altogether. The arguments for weapons development, counterforce strategy, continued deterrence on the basis of a balance of terror, and the rest, which pervade the writings of the strategists, are also pleas.

For instance, when a strategist says (65, p. 77), "Perhaps a long period of peace would alter the Soviet regime. But we cannot give up the Middle East to purchase it," he is pleading that the Middle East is worth more than the prospect of a long period of peace (and incidentally assuming that the Middle East belongs to us, which is also a plea, not a statement of fact, for possession is a state of mind).

Again, when a strategist says, "War is terrible, but so is peace," he is telling us to hate war less than we do or else to love peace less than we do or both. Some of us may feel that such a plea may stem from morbid impulses or, perhaps, is a pose struck for the sake of a quotable *mot* or a symptom of a lack of imagination. But at least such a statement does not pose as a recommendation of a rational policy. But when a decision is recommended as based on rational analysis, supposedly derived from a "calculated risk," in which utilities and probabilities are multiplied and the products compared, we have to do with either fraud or a gross misconception of what the notions of utility and probability refer to. Actually, the recommendations of such a decision are no less a plea than an outright appeal to assume certain attitudes toward certain events. In this case, the plea is simply to prefer one alternative to another. The assignment of "probability" and "utility" is made in such manner as to make the recommended alternative the more attractive one.

We see, thus, that much more choice is involved in arriving at so-called rational decisions than the name warrants. The connotation of a rational decision is such that we *believe* it to be somehow a compelling decision, in the sense that mathematical theorems are compelling. It should be clear that the assumptions on which action decisions are made contain a large measure of arbitrary choice. Certainly utilities do not exist in nature to be "observed." Utilities reflect our preferences. We choose them. With regard to probabilities, an argument can be made on partially rational grounds for assigning a certain *range* of probabilities to a unique event. But the latitude of this range is very great, and the smaller the mean probability of that range, the greater the relative range and so the less meaningful the notion of calculated risk. Let us see how this comes about.

DIFFERENCES BETWEEN SMALL PROBABILITIES ARE BIG DIFFERENCES

We have said that the ambiguity of assigning a probability to a unique event stems from the fact that the comprising class of events can be defined in different ways. We also said that in some cases there is little question that one of such classes is more relevant than another. At other times, the perceived relevance of the classes is a reflection of our attitudes and so points up the basis of the subjectivity of "relevance."

Suppose we wish to assign a probability to the statement "Country A will (or will not) honor its obligations under treaty X." If the probability we assign is only a measure of the degree of our confidence in Country A, we are under no obligation to support our estimate of it. However, if we claim some sort of "validity" for our estimate, we must indicate facts in support of it. These facts or allegations may be of different kinds. The following are some examples.

1. During the past 100 years Country A has complied with the provisions of so many treaties and has reneged on so many.

2. Country A has a regime of a certain type. Taking all countries with similar regimes as our universe of discourse, we observe that

in the past ten years so many treaties have been honored and so many broken.

3. Our own government would under such and such circumstances honor (or break) a similar treaty.

4. The treaty in question belongs to a given type of treaties. Taking the class of such treaties as a universe of discourse, we observe that such and such fraction have been honored (broken).

Depending on which universe of discourse we select, we will come up with a different estimate of our probability. The historian may take pains to record every treaty to which Country A has been a signatory for the past 100 years. The political scientist may be more interested in the way countries with different types of regimes honor or fail to honor the treaties they make or else make distinctions between types of treaties. A sociologist, on the other hand, may not be as interested in the "type of regime" as in the type of social organization characteristic of Country A and may make his estimate on the basis of pressures which he expects will develop within a society so organized. The psychologist may have still other ideas about how to relate the situation in question to other "relevant" situations (relevant to the psychologist, that is.)

We see, then, that although "facts" can always be marshalled in support of probabilities to be assigned to unique events, we are at liberty to select those facts, and select them we must, because we must establish a universe of discourse before we can make arguments to support an estimate of a probability.

In the last analysis, then, arguments in support of probabilities assigned to events are pleas to pay attention to some facts more than to others. A change in our attitude brings up a different set of facts as the relevant set and changes our perceived probability of the event in question.

So much for supporting our probability assignments by facts. For the most part, even such support is not attempted. Probabilities are often simply "estimated," and the estimates are solemnly offered as if they were estimates of next week's price of wheat. These estimates lose all significance when we are dealing with events which are extremely improbable. In the middle range it is not so bad. At least the probabilities can reflect roughly our degree of belief. When we are most uncertain whether an event will occur, we assign to it a probability of 0.5. A shift of one-half of this fraction, e.g., to 0.75 or to 0.25, reflects a moderate change of our estimate. But now suppose we assign a probability of 0.0001 (one chance in ten thousand) to an event. A shift by a factor of ten either way makes little difference in reflecting our "degrees of belief." In this range it does not matter whether we call the probability of a very unlikely event 0.001, 0.0001 or 0.00001, if the "probability" is no more than a reflection of our belief. But if we "calculate" risk on the basis of these probabilities the actual magnitude may make all the difference in the world.

Consider the choice of action in one of the persistently recurring crises, as it might have been presented to a head of state in the garb of "decision under risk." There are two choices of action, namely D: stand firm; and C: give in. There are also two "states of nature," namely D: the other party stands firm; C: the other party gives in. We know, of course, that C and D are not states of neutral nature at all, but a pair of strategies open to another *player,* which is a very different thing. However, the pressure for simplification often forces the strategist to reduce the decision problem to the simpler context (thus bypassing the thorny problem of determining the other's utility scale). And so the problem reduces to that of estimating the probabilities of the two "states of nature." First, however, the decision-maker must enter his own utilities into the decision matrix. The outcomes are shown in Table 3.

Own Choice	State of Nature	Outcome
C	C	Moderate gain for both
C	D	A large loss (of face) to the first player
D	C	A triumph resulting from standing firm
D	D	Disaster (showdown) followed by war

TABLE 3

We shall assume a realistic estimate, in which the anticipated loss associated with war outweighs the loss resulting from backing down (although, of course, many in positions of influence argue as if the opposite evaluation were self-evident). The resulting game is shown in Matrix 14. Only one set of payoffs is shown, because the opponent's payoffs are not considered. (The opponent's strategies are treated as "states of nature."[27])

	C	D
C	10	−100
D	100	−20,000

MATRIX 14

Observe now that if we estimate as one in a thousand the chance that the other will be as stubborn as we are, the "expected gain" (whatever it may mean in the present context) of standing firm is greater than that of giving in. But if we estimate that there is one chance in a hundred that the other will stand firm, then the "expected gain" of giving in is greater. In this way either decision can be easily rationalized. There is no way to distinguish a probability of 0.01 from that of 0.001 in a situation like this one, where some of the events in question can by their very nature occur only once.

In general, then, the notion of "calculated risk," which plays a vital part in rational decisions wherever the context permits a clearcut definition of risk (in terms of probabilities and utilities), becomes no more than a figure of speech in other contexts where no such definitions can be made. Frequently the pressure for simplification induces the strategists to carry over the concept of calculated risk into situations where it is inappropriate.

CHAPTER 11

PRESSURE FOR SIMPLIFICATION: THE ZERO-SUM TRAP

The most pervasive and pernicious result of the pressure for simplification in strategic thinking is the tendency to represent conflicts as zero-sum games.

This pressure stems from the difficulty or impossibility of determining the utilities assigned to outcomes by the other. The assumption that a game is zero-sum obviates this necessity.[28] One needs, to be sure, to assign one's own utilities to outcomes. This task, we have seen, if taken seriously, is already a formidable one. Discovering the other's utility assignments is incomparably more difficult. To be able to do so, one should know the other's values, the other's prognoses and estimates, the other's hopes and fears. Presumably, systematic investigations of these matters is the business of social scientists. The mammoth research organizations which serve the military do employ social scientists. There is little evidence, however, that either the empirical findings or the insights of social scientists find important applications in strategic thinking.

For example, in an ambitious attempt to simulate[29] global conflict (95) the designers and programmers solemnly inserted "ideological sub-models" into the process in which the propensities for action on the part of Soviet leaders were assumed to be governed by "Marxist-Leninist ideology." In other words, the calculators have assumed that this ideology can be translated into a "program" and that they can estimate the appropriate parameters!

By and large, however, such attempts are eschewed, especially in discussions of purely military strategy. The simplest assumption is that whatever one player can do to hurt the other he will do. This is essentially the underlying assumption of the zero-sum game.

Naturally the emphasis is always on the *other's* ruthlessness.

Kauffman writes (61, p. 4): "The ideology of Marx, Engels, and Lenin, with its emphasis on expansion and revolution, still stands as the formal model governing Communist analysis and behavior. The whole culture of Bolshevism works to create the expectation that competition will be the way of international life; it stresses the philosophy of kill or be killed, and exalts the utility of force and fraud in political action."

Kissinger writes (65, p. 14): ". . . the first charge on our resources must be the capability for waging all-out war, because without it we would be at the mercy of Soviet rulers."

Knorr writes (66, p. 75): "The time is drawing close, if it has not already come when the Soviet Union will be capable of inflicting massive destruction in all-out nuclear war. . . . The case for preparing all kinds of defenses against air attack must receive full and genuine hearing."

The theory of deterrence rests squarely on the assumption that the all-consuming passion of the Enemy is to destroy us and that only the realization of his own vulnerability prevents him from doing so. In the strategists' view this axiom is not doubted. The only genuine problems revolve around the question of how much deterrence is enough, i.e., how much the Enemy is willing to pay to wipe us off the map.

Snyder writes (113, p. 57): "Perhaps the most uncertain factor, for the United States, is the degree of prospective damage which would be sufficient to deter the Soviet Union from attacking. Would the Soviets be deterred by the prospect of losing ten cities? Or two cities? Or fifty cities? No one knows, although one might intuitively guess that the threshold is closer to ten than to either two or fifty."

Kahn asks an analogous question, namely, how much is it worth to *us* to punish Soviet aggression. In order to present our attack on the Soviet Union in acceptable terms, Kahn supposes that "the Soviets have dropped bombs on London, Berlin, Rome, Paris and Bonn. . . . simply to demonstrate their strength and resolve." This is the situation which gives rise to the problem we discussed above (cf. page

87). How many American lives is it worth to us to punish this demonstration of strength? (Kahn's answer: about 60 million.)

It must be emphasized that I am not planning a categorical refutation of this and similar assumptions made by the nuclear strategists. It may very well be that the Russian counterparts of Kahn, Snyder, *et al.* are making analogous computations, and it is possible that these computations enter into the design of Soviet military strategy. It is also possible that once these options are *considered,* they may be implemented, since they have a built-in self-propelled logic: He may, therefore I ought, therefore he will, therefore I must.[30] My critique is intended to be more basic than a critique of a particular policy or strategy. It is directed rather at strategic thinking itself. For although the strategists repeat often and with great emphasis that a nuclear war would spell a loss for both, they nevertheless fall into a conceptual trap of their own making. Recall that although prisoner's dilemma is a non-zero-sum game and is readily perceived as such, it is *strategically* indistinguishable from a zero-sum game in which both players have a dominating strategy (cf. page 41). This is the zero-sum trap. Strategic thinking seals this trap, because it seeks one strategic "solution," but there is no strategic escape from the trap.

Now with respect to choosing between alternative *actions* in the conduct of the Cold War, the strategists do not uniformly advocate courses calculated simply to hurt the opponent (in the short run). To begin with, such recommendations would at times clash too harshly with sensibilities even in the present climate. The zero-sum-game assumption is most pronounced in the fact that we attribute to the *other* preferences for those courses of action which are most devastating to ourselves. The fact that the other does not as a rule carry those actions out is attributed almost exclusively to the effectiveness of deterrence.

The most important of the Enemy's potential choices is, of course, the nuclear surprise attack.[31] In the writings of the strategists the "successful" nuclear surprise attack is represented as a winning move of a game.[32] The analogy is obvious. A winning move ends the game because the loser has no moves left. The winning of the game is the ultimate objective in the conduct of the Game. All other considerations are related *to* it. To question the value of winning the Game is senseless in the context of playing the Game. If we did not strive to win, we would not be playing the Game seriously in the first place.

There is no doubt about the seriousness with which the strategists are doing their job. A tremendous amount of work goes into calculations of war potentials and the very investment of talent, energy, and money into these calculations makes the assumption of their importance mandatory. To question the relevance of this work means to bring into view the possibility that this magnificent intellectual effort was wasted—an awful possibility to contemplate.

This sort of *ex post facto* justification is quite common in human behavior. Consider the man who has ordered too much in a restaurant. He strains his will and eats his plate clean. Why does he do it? "I hate to see food go to waste," is the frequent reply. When we make our children do it, we sometimes add a moral lesson and mention Asia's starving millions. But the food left on the plate will go into the garbage can, not to Asia. If the leftovers go to feed animals or the destitute (as sometimes happens) then it would be *less* wasteful to leave them on the plate than to eat them, for certainly excessive eating does not benefit the eater. What then is the sense of straining to eat the plate clean? It is this: "If I eat it all, it will appear *as if* the food was not wasted." But if no one is watching? Then eating up unwanted food is reassuring to *self* that one has not wasted food. By this purely symbolic act the impression of waste is removed, and so it seems that there has been no waste. This is manifest self-deception, but it is widely practiced.

The term "vested interests" has been much abused. It brings to mind oversimplified explanations of complex events. Thus World War I has been at times blamed entirely on the connivance of munitions makers. Economic stagnation has been blamed exclusively on monopolistic practices, etc. Ever since the profit motive came into prominence as a sociological determinant (largely thanks to Marx's penetrating analyses), there has been a tendency, especially among the Marxists, to view in it the only prime mover of capitalist society.

I submit that vested profit interest is only a special case of a more general principle. An individual or a group can have a vested interest not only in stocks and bonds but also in self-esteem, in social status, in the amount of effort expended along certain lines. One does not only throw "good money after bad." One does not only get trapped in trying to win back gambling losses. One also makes intellectual commitments, which will color one's outlook when these commitments have to be rationalized.

The strategists have made their commitment. Most of them may have made it with the best intentions: It seemed to them to be a commitment to rational analysis, to self-discipline, to resisting the seductions of passion. It turns out, however, that seduction lurks also in the mental habit of rational analysis. For this analysis requires detachment. While detachment is a source of supreme strength in the investigation of nature, it may be debilitating if it is carried over bodily from natural science to areas purporting to deal with human behavior. For what in natural science has been an emancipation from anthropomorphism becomes in the formalism of strategic thinking simply an obtuseness in psychological matters. It ought to be a truism that if it is inappropriate to attribute human characteristics to inanimate matter or to lower animals, it is equally inappropriate to ignore human characteristics when dealing with human beings.

CHAPTER 12

ATTEMPTS TO ESCAPE
FROM THE ZERO-SUM TRAP

We have seen how preoccupation with strategy leads into the zero-sum trap, the closed system of thought in which the only reality is a struggle between participants with diametrically opposed interests. This is the most natural strategic model, since it offers no conceptual difficulties and has ample realization in the familiar worlds of business and power diplomacy. In business at a given time there is just so much market. And even if the market can be expanded to the benefit of all competitors, they can shift the struggle for the *share* of the market. Whether the market expands or not, all the "shares" must add up to 100 per cent, and so the game once more becomes zero-sum. This is eminently true of a power struggle. Power is a conservative quantity par excellence.[33] Following Machiavelli, Clausewitz, and Stalin, self-styled realists view politics as primarily a struggle for power, and judge the realism of political theory by how convincingly the theory reduces political acts to bids for power. It is not surprising, therefore, that the zero-sum game model enjoys hegemony in this field also.[34]

Since the late 1950's, however, that is, since the demise of American nuclear monopoly, the non-zero-sum aspects of the global struggle have forced themselves on the strategists. Statements to the effect that no one can win a nuclear war appear in practically all the writings of the past five years or so, even in the writings purporting to show how such a war can be won. But this is not to say that all the strategists have drawn appropriate conclusions.

Hart writes (53, p. 95): "It would be better if [tactical atomic weapons] had never been introduced. Not only have they increased the risk of local conflicts developing into total war, but they may even turn to our disadvantage—*now that the Russians have also got them* [emphasis added]. But since the Russians have got the tactical atomic weapon, the Western forces can hardly discard it."

Translate this into prisoner's dilemma terms to read: "It was a mistake to defect from CC to DC (gaining temporary advantage), since this induced the other to defect also, resulting in DD. But now that we are in DD, we dare not leave it. DD is, after all, the minimax."

Here again is the zero-sum trap in its essence: the hypnotic fascination with the minimax "solution" prescribed by the *normative* game theory.

However, not all strategists bow to the inevitable consequences of following the normative prescriptions of zero-sum game theory. In particular, T. C. Schelling was one of the first to point out its limitations.

Schelling writes (101, p. 5):

Thus, strategy—in the sense in which I am using it here—is not concerned with the efficient *application* of force. It is concerned not just with enemies who dislike each other but with partners who distrust or disagree with each other. It is concerned not just with the division of gains and losses between two claimants but with the possibility that certain outcomes are worse (better) for *both* claimants. In the terminology of game theory, most interesting international conflicts are not "constant sum games" [here called zero-sum games—A.R.] but "variable sum games" [here called non-zero-sum games—A.R.], the sum of the gains of the participants involved is not fixed so that more for one means less for the other. There is a common interest in reaching outcomes that are mutually advantageous.

An excellent beginning.

But Schelling is a professional strategist. Accordingly, he could not be satisfied with merely pointing out the limitations of a normative theory of decision in mixed motive situations (e.g., non-zero-sum games). He set for himself the task of "reconstructing" game theory with a view to removing these limitations, in other words with a view to including a theory of non-zero-sum games in the strategist's tool box.

THE THEORY OF PROMINENCE

The psychological component of Schelling's formulation comes out most clearly in his concept of *prominence*. This concept becomes of prime importance when the interests of the players coincide (as they sometimes do in non-zero-sum games), but the players have no way of coordinating their choices in order to realize their common interests.

Suppose, for instance, two people independently are to write down either "blue" or "green," with the understanding that if they write the same color, both will win a dollar; otherwise both will lose a dollar. Clearly, there is a coincidence of interests but no way to choose between "blue" and "green." Suppose, next, that the choice is between "blue" and "red." This may make a difference. It is sometimes observed that red is the color most frequently named in response to a request to name a color. Therefore, it seems more likely that coincidence will be achieved if red is chosen. Moreover, the fact that one has a *notion* that red has a better chance of being matched leads one to believe that the other possibly has the same notion and also the notion that the other has the notion, etc. The bias, may be *objectively* small (i.e., only a small plurality may choose "red" spontaneously), yet the very existence of the bias, however small, amplifies the propensity of people to make use of it if they are seeking *a focal point of tacit agreement*.

This focal point of tacit agreement becomes a principal theme in Schelling's discussion. In various pilot studies he demonstrated that people match each other's choices if there exists a "prominent" choice which can serve as an anchor of tacit agreement. Asked to choose between heads and tails (with the understanding that coincident choices will be rewarded) people prefer heads because most people *believe* that heads are preferred. Asked to name a large sum of money, people tend to name $1 million. If one is to meet a friend in New York City at an unspecified place at an unspecified time of day, one will do well to go to the information desk of the Grand Central Station at noon, etc., etc. (101, p. 56).

Seen in these contexts, the "prominent choice" is a psychological phenomenon. Game theory, being largely a formal theory and at most a normative one, is not equipped to deal with psychological matters. Therefore, when Schelling calls for an *extension* of game theory to include such matters, one can take issue with the proposal on the grounds that such an extension cannot be made within the framework of the game-theoretical method. As for combining the method of psychology with that of game theory, this program is easier to propose than to carry out. The two disciplines do not mix well. Scientific psychology, still very largely empirical, does not possess a rigorous theoretical framework and so is not readily cast into a formal deductive scheme. Game theory, on the other hand, being a branch of mathematics, is entirely formalized and so pursues its results without regard for concrete realization or practical applications.

Thus the gap between demonstrable strategic psychology and formal strategic theory is still enormous. However, consider the idea of the prominent choice divorced from the concrete interpretations used by Schelling in order to illustrate the idea in a simple scheme. Two players are asked to name independently of each other any sum of money. If the sum of the amounts they name does not exceed one dollar, each gets the amount he named. If the sum exceeds one dollar, neither gets anything. For simplicity, let the choice of amounts to be named be limited to 25 cents, 50 cents, and 75 cents. The game just proposed is shown in Matrix 15.

	25	50	75
25	25, 25	25, 50	25, 75
50	50, 25	50, 50	0, 0
75	75, 25	0, 0	0, 0

MATRIX 15

Now intuitively we feel that the outcome (50, 50) ought to obtain. (Experimentally, it is found that this outcome does obtain most frequently). Let us try to rationalize this outcome. It is not a minimax for either player. The most compelling rationalization of (50, 50) is its *prominence*. There are only three symmetric outcomes, namely (25, 25), and (50, 50), and (0, 0); and of the three the outcome (50, 50) is clearly the most preferred.

We have rationalized a strategic choice on the basis of prominence, which, we had said, was a psychological principle; yet we have not appealed to the specific psychologies of the players (such as their knowledge of the conventional rendezvous point in New York or the like). Therefore, there is an aspect of prominent choice which seems to fit into purely strategic analysis, and so this approach is not to be entirely discarded as a prospective extension of game theory, in spite of its psychological flavor. On the contrary, the prominent choice idea may be instrumental in bringing psychology into game theory by degrees, as it were. In what follows, we shall pursue this idea.

Let us change two of the payoffs in Matrix 15 so as to obtain Matrix 16.

	25	50	75
25	25, 25	50, 25	75, 75
50	50, 25	50, 50	−25. 75
75	75, 25	75, −25	0, 0

MATRIX 16

This game also has a single prominent choice, namely the same outcome (50, 50). According to Schelling's theory, then, we ought to expect (50, 50) to be chosen by two rational players. Now let us remove the top row and the left-hand column from Matrix 16 and obtain Matrix 17.

The prominent choice is still there. It can still be identified as the preferred outcome of the only two symmetrical outcomes. However, the game represented in Matrix 17 is our old friend prisoner's

	C	D
C	50, 50	−25, 75
D	75, −25	0, 0

MATRIX 17

dilemma! It turns out, therefore, that prisoner's dilemma also has a prominent choice, namely CC. If prominence is advanced as a rational principle of choice, ought it not at least compete with dominance, where the two principles clash? For the dominance principle dictates the choice of D (the dominant strategy), while Schelling's prominence principle dictates the choice of C (the prominent strategy). We bring this point up because the game-theoretical prescription (if such is attempted) in the case of prisoner's dilemma is, in the absence of communication, D not C. (It is, of course, C if explicit collusion between the two players can be effected).

The choice C has been recommended on ethical grounds but never, to my knowledge, on strategic ones. But Schelling's prominence principle was not proposed in any ethical garb. It was proposed as a means of *implementing tacit agreements among players with at least partially coincident interests in situations where explicit agreements are impossible.* The prominence principle can therefore be viewed as a strategic principle. And so it appears at first sight that prisoner's dilemma does not necessarily involve a conflict between a strategic principle (do the best you can for yourself) and an ethical one (do what you would wish the other to do) but between two rival strategic principles.

Seen in another way, however, the prominence principle is not at all strategic. It is rather a principle which allows players of a non-zero-sum game to achieve an outcome which (we may suppose) would have been the result of an arbitration. However, aside from the principle of prominence, the strategists, including Schelling himself, characteristically ignore the theory of arbitration.[35] And even the prominence principle has been proposed as an illustration of how the victims of impasses which occur in certain non-zero-sum games can escape from the impasses in the *absence* of arbitration procedures.

Bargaining, as distinguished from arbitration, does appear in the strategists' formulations; but it appears in a characteristically strategic garb. The simplest and the most typical example is the idea of pre-emption in the game of chicken, which is the dominant theme in Herman Kahn's *On Thermonuclear War*. The essentials of this game are represented by Matrix 18.

	W	S
W	1, 1	-10, 10
S	10, -10	-1000, -1000

MATRIX 18

The designations W and S refer to weak and strong strategies, respectively, for this is the way the corresponding Cold War strategies are conventionally described. Note that chicken is not strategically isomorphic to PD or to PD^2. Unlike PD, chicken does not present either player with a dominating strategy. Unlike PD^2 chicken prescribes the non-accommodating strategy, S, as the best answer to the accommodating strategy, W.

In chicken, as in PD^2, it is to each player's advantage to announce his strategy, rather than to keep it secret. But whereas in PD^2 it was more advantageous to announce an accommodating strategy like 2 (cf. page 53) than a "harsh" one like 8, in chicken it is more advantageous to announce the non-accommodating strategy, S, than the accommodating one, W. As in PD^2, the problem of establishing credibility enters here. But in the context of PD^2 "to believe the other" meant to *trust* him, while in the context of chicken "to believe the other" means to *fear* him, that is, to believe that his threat is real, that he would rather perish than not have his way.

In the context of the real game of chicken (the balance of terror) the strategists have made various proposals for establishing such "credibility." The most drastic one (although it is an open question how seriously it was offered) involves the Doomsday Machine. This is an imaginary device set to blow up the planet if certain signals impinge on its sensory apparatus. These signals could, for example, be triggered by nuclear explosions on the territory of the nation which keeps the Doomsday Machine. The function of the Doomsday Machine is presumably to prevent the Enemy from attacking.

The fundamental feature of the machine is the fact that no one, including its possessor, can disconnect it. This helplessness makes the possessor of the Doomsday Machine immune to blackmail by the Enemy. In the same way, ignorance of the combination to the vault makes the bank employee immune to the bank robber's threats, provided, of course, that the robber *believes* that the employee does not know the combination.

The announcement that the Doomsday Machine has been set must be made credible to the extent of permanently inhibiting any temptation to put that statement to a test. But there is another requirement which must be met if this maneuver is to "succeed." The announcement that the Doomsday Machine has been set and the key thrown away must come as a complete surprise. Otherwise, the Enemy may be driven to present an ultimatum to *discontinue the construction* of the machine (backed up by sufficiently credible threats of his own.) Also, the Enemy may be driven to "pre-empt" the construction of the Doomsday Machine itself, i.e., to build one sooner, equipped with an equally irreversible detonating device, which will be activated by the *announcement* that a Doomsday Machine has been set on the territory of the original builder. There is no logically compelling reason why this argument cannot go on ad infinitum. On the other hand, if one invokes a "practical" argument, based on physical and human limitations, there is no reason to suppose that one of the competing parties (i.e., "our" side) will win rather than the other. So much for the "credible threat" solution of the game of chicken.

Some strategists are entirely aware of these considerations. Kahn, discussing the Doomsday Machine as one possible deterrent, says that it is physically feasible and not prohibitively expensive. (Since he is a specialist in such matters, there is no reason to disbelieve him.) He also says that it is not a good idea to invest defense efforts into a Doomsday Machine., essentially in view of the considerations just presented. *But he does mention it.* His avowed task is to make the unthinkable thinkable on the assumption that it does not hurt to think seriously about anything, apparently because thinking about something does not obligate one to do anything about it. I will come to grips with this argument in Chapter 16. Meanwhile, I will point out that although the Doomsday Machine is still a fantasy, the strategic principle on which it is based is quite operative in practice. In practice the principle is known as brinkmanship.

STRATEGY AND COMMUNICATION

After devoting about one-third of his book (101) to exploring the opportunities offered by the "prominent solution," Schelling devotes the rest of the volume to features of the non-zero-sum game which game theory has neglected.

He writes (101, p. 119): "By abstracting from communication and enforcement systems and by treating perfect symmetry between players as the general case rather than the special one, game theory may have overshot the level at which the most fruitful work could be done and may have defined away some of the essential ingredients of typical non-zero-sum games. Preoccupied with the solution to *the* zero-sum game, game theory has not done justice to some typical game situations or game models and to the 'moves' that are peculiar to non-zero-sum games of strategy."

What, then, are the "typical" situations as they appear to Schelling? Here they are (101, p. 120): "A shepherd who has chased a wolf into a corner, where it has no choice but to fight, the shepherd unwilling to turn his back on the beast; a pursuer armed only with a hand grenade who inadvertently gets too close to his victim and dares not use his weapon; two neighbors, each controlling dynamite in the other's basement, trying to find mutual security through some arrangement of electric switches and detonators."

Schelling goes on to say, "If we can analyze the structure of these games and develop a working acquaintance with standard models, we may provide insight into real problems by the use of theory."

The crux of Schelling's idea, as I see it, is to examine the role of *communication superimposed on a game*. He begins with the game in normal form, that is, schematized as a matrix of outcomes, each the result of *simultaneous* strategy choices by the players. It is *about* this game that communication is supposed to take place.

Before we look at Schelling's specific contributions, we must briefly review the possible roles which communication can play if it is in this way superimposed on a given game. The principles to be stated are direct consequences of the structures of the games themselves, which have been analyzed in Part I.

If a game is in normal form, there is *by definition* no communication between the players. Any communication that does take place in the course of the actual game (i.e., the succession of moves) has already been incorporated in the definition of strategy. Therefore, when all the possible choices open to a player in the course of the game have been collapsed into a *single* choice among the strategies open to the player, it is necessary to view these choices as independent of each other, because if there are still sequential choices to be made, they too can be collapsed. Schelling, however, raises the question (among others) of what happens if one player tells the other which strategy he will employ. If he does this, the choices of strategy cease to be independent, and the game ceases to be in normal form.[36] From the point of view of formal game theory, therefore, nothing is added when a communication strategy is superimposed on a game. Such an "extension" merely substitutes one game for another. But let us ignore this purely technical argument, and let us consider the communication aspect for its own sake. This, I believe, is the correct formulation of Schelling's problem.

It is now instructive to see how the role of communication (or of information that is communicated) changes as we pass from one type of game to another.

In games with perfect information, everything that has already transpired is known to both players. But a player's *future* (contemplated) moves are presumably hidden from his opponent. Hence the opponent's (single) choice of strategy remains secret when the game is cast into normal form. One might now surmise that a strategic advantage could be gained if one had access to the opponent's strategic deliberations. This conjecture is both correct and mistaken, and it is highly enlightening to see in what sense it is correct and in what sense mistaken. The conjecture can be *theoretically* refuted. Every game of perfect information, we have seen, has a saddle point. The rules of the game determine the strategy matrix. Thus the strategy (or strategies) containing a saddle point are known to both players from a sufficiently complete analysis of the game, and there is nothing they can gain from knowing each other's deliberations. In fact, theoretically every outcome of a game of perfect information is determined in advance in the sense that matters, namely, in the sense of the associated payoffs. *Theoretically* there is no point even in playing such games, and this futility is actually appreciated in the case of completely analyzed games of perfect information, such as tic-tack-toe or nim.

In another sense, however, there is an advantage in having access to the opponent's reasoning. In practice, human powers of analysis are severely limited. The fact that games of perfect information (chess, go) continue to fascinate brilliant minds attests to the difficulty of achieving an exhausting analysis of such games. In view of this difficulty, access to the opponent's deliberations is not so much like a discovery of a military secret (we shall take this matter up separately in a moment) as like an extension of one's own power of analysis. One could have gotten this information oneself, but it may be "cheaper" to tune in on the other's thought processes if this is feasible.[37]

There is another sense in which the reading of an opponent's mind may be advantageous. Since real players are fallible, it may happen that a player will decide on a strategy which does *not* contain a saddle point. If this is known, the opponent can take advantage of it. As an example, suppose B mistakenly chooses B_1 in the game shown in Matrix 5. If A finds this out, he can take advantage of B's mistake by choosing A_3. But if a player plays a minimax strategy in a game with perfect information,[38] knowledge of this fact is of no value to the opponent. In fact, the opponent, who is himself rational and attributes rationality to the other, *already* assumes this will be the case.[39]

Here, then, is a matter to which Schelling's remarks concerning the importance of the asymmetry of the players is pertinent, namely, in the zero-sum case. The matter has to do with taking advantage of the opponent's weaknesses, as, when in playing chess, one often makes unsound moves when facing a weaker player in the hope that he will not be able to take advantage of their unsoundness.[40]

The matter stands differently in the case of games without perfect information, which, as a rule, do not have saddle points. In such games, it is vital to conceal from the opponent the particular strategy chosen on a particular play. For instance, if a convoy of ships can travel to its destination by three different routes, the actual route chosen on a particular voyage is kept secret. The use of the three routes may be randomized (mixed strategy), and the proportions in the mix may be calculated according to the minimax principle (provided utilities can be assigned to all possible outcomes). Here we have indeed a paradigm of a military secret in its proper sense. But the secret refers to something which is impossible to ascertain by analysis, for example, the result of a chance move, not to something which is difficult to determine because of the complexity of analysis.

In mixed strategy zero-sum games, then, it is generally advantageous to obtain knowledge of the other's intentions (or hidden moves) and disadvantageous to make your own intentions known to him.

As we pass to non-zero-sum games like the prisoner's dilemma, the situation again changes. Consider prisoner's dilemma played once. From the purely strategic point of view, it seems neither advantageous nor disadvantageous to let the other know one's own choice of strategy. Whatever strategy one announces, the other will serve his interest better by choosing the non-cooperative strategy D. On the other hand, if one does not announce one's strategy, one does not thereby increase the likelihood that the other will choose C. From the strategic point of view, the other will choose D whether one announces one's strategy or not and regardless of which strategy is announced.[41]

This is not the case if prisoner's dilemma is played twice, i.e., if each play is considered as a move in a supergame. In this supergame (described above on page 53), we have seen that against A's tit-for-tat strategy 2, B's best response is not strategy 8 but strategy 4. However, if B does not know that A has decided on the tit-for-tat strategy, he may still decide on the minimax strategy 8, thus hurting himself as well as A. It is therefore to A's advantage to announce a tit-for-tat strategy.

While in the repeated prisoner's dilemma, the announcement of strategy may be of advantage both to the announcer and to the recipient, in the game of chicken (cf. page 116) played once, the announcement of the reckless strategy (pre-emption) benefits the announcer but hurts the recipient.

This, incidentally, is the case which finds extensive treatment in the writings of the strategists. The case is the paradigm for the Doomsday Machine and all the other forms of "automated response." The idea there is to make sure that *your* communication reaches the opponent but that *his* cannot reach you (for example, to insure this you can cut all your telephone lines, destroy all your radio receivers, and puncture your ear drums).

Commitment includes maneuvers that leave one in such a position that the option of non-fulfillment no longer exists (as when one intimidates the other car by driving too fast to stop in time. . . . as when authority to punish is deliberately given to sadists or when one shifts his claims and liabilities to an insurance company) (101, p. 128).

The credibility of an irrational response may be increased if the deterrer can appear to commit himself to this response by some device which removes or reduces his freedom of choice. Such "automation" is itself rational, even though paradoxically the response is not (113, p. 24).

It appears, therefore, that an act of communication can confer an advantage on either the communicator or the recipient or on both; or, on the contrary, can put either of them at a disadvantage in a strategic conflict situation.

In bringing in communication acts, whether formally, as Schelling does, or otherwise, the strategists frequently call attention to *psychological* aspects of such acts. That is to say, while in the case of the conventional moves of a game there is no problem of interpretation, there is such a problem associated with the so-called communication moves. For example, should one or should one not *believe* a communication of the opponent? Note that we are not talking about legalized bluffing as it appears in certain games. Bluffing too can be considered a "communication move," but it is a communication move already built into the game. In poker, for example, one does not ask oneself whether one ought to "believe" a bluff. One only considers what to *do* in response to a bluff, for example, whether to see or to raise or to fold. But the communication acts with which Schelling and other strategists are concerned are not bona fide moves in the game. True, they can be redefined as such (turning the game into a different one), but they are not treated as such. They are, as we have already said, *superimposed* on the game. They are statements by players *about* the game. Therefore, also, the choice to believe a communication or not to believe it is a choice outside the game context. Questions with regard to such choices are at least as much psychological questions as strategic ones.

Now some of the more sophisticated strategists (I believe Schelling, in particular) would readily agree that advances in psychology are sorely needed in order to utilize game theory as an applied strategic science. However, the paucity of psychological knowledge among strategic thinkers is appalling, and quite understandably so if they model life after the maxims of Clausewitz and quantify values in terms of megabucks, megatons, and megadeaths. I am doing my best to avoid the deeper psychological issues connected with compulsive pre-occupation with coercion and destruction which is the most conspicuous theme in strategic literature. Let me, however, raise just one genuinely psychological question.

Consider two games: PD^2 (cf. Matrix 8, page 53) and chicken (Matrix 18, page 116). In both the pre-emption of communication benefits the pre-emptor. However, in PD^2 the recipient of communication *also* benefits, i.e., gets more than if the communication had not been given, while in chicken, the recipient of communication is intimidated (cowed into choosing the lesser of two evils). One would think, therefore, that in the first case, the recipient of communication will react positively to the communication (and to the sender) while in the second case, he will react with resentment to the communication (and almost certainly to the sender, who, in this case, is not merely the bearer but also the maker of bad news). One would think it might be important to find out to what extent decision-makers share such human predilections with the rest of us. Overwhelmingly, however, strategic analysis postulates "actors" whose only psychological traits are those which the strategist finds convenient to endow them with or those which the strategists, in their professional involvement, imagine themselves to possess. Nowhere in strategic literature does one find searching questions concerning the role of real psychological factors. In their place, one finds mostly formalized assumptions or standard clichés. It seems, therefore, that the strategist's wistful longing for psychological know-how will not be fulfilled. At best, he may get some idea about the reliability or unreliability of the human link in his weapons systems and such matters which relate to operations. The strategist will not get the sort of knowledge he wants because he does nothing to inquire into its underpinnings, namely, the deep commitments of people, their concepts of equity, their real hierarchies of values (which do not necessarily fit into unidimensional "utility scales"), and their noble and ignoble impulses, which may invalidate the strategist's entire conceptual system.[42] The strategist will not get the right answers in matters beyond his system of thought because he does not ask the right questions. He cannot ask the right questions because his libidinal commitment (I will permit myself just this one depth-psychological term) is to power *over* the other, not to knowledge *of* the other.

The strategist defends nightmare images of the world as a "realistic" vision, forgetting that any vision of the world is compounded of elements which one has selected for observation. The strategist sees what he has selected to see.

CHAPTER 13

SIMULATION

~~~~~~

Simulation is a technique which allows us to study replicas of phenomena or systems which normally cannot or must not be tampered with. The oldest and most familiar examples of simulation are ordinary physical models used in the crafts. The seamstress has her dress form, the apprentice barber his dummy head. The infantry soldier, unable to stick his bayonet into real people until the proper time, practices his art on simulated human torsos.

All these are used in the acquisition of operative skills. Quite complex simulated systems can also be useful in obtaining complex knowledge. The construction of an efficient flying machine requires a knowledge of how its shape will determine the distribution of forces acting on it during flight. Since shapes of airplanes are very complicated, the problem of determining the distribution of forces is not often solved on the basis of general principles of aerodynamics. On the other hand, it is out of the question to test experimentally designed machines in real flight. Accordingly, aerial engineers use a wind tunnel in which the airplane is suspended. The readings of instruments attached to different points give the required information.

The laws of physics are sufficiently reliable and control of them can be sufficiently complete to allow an extrapolation of the results obtained in simulation of purely physical conditions to expectations in real life.

The wind tunnel simulates physical conditions directly. But simulation can be used in another way, namely, to obtain specific numerical answers to mathematical equations which are supposed to represent some process but which are too difficult to solve in their general form.

As an example, consider an epidemic. The passing of a disease from an infected individual to another depends on many factors: in the first place, of course, on the two individuals coming into contact. Next, if they do come into contact, whether the disease will be transmitted will probably depend on the state of infectiousness of the infected individual (which may vary with the duration of the infected state), the susceptibility of the uninfected individual, the duration and the intimacy of the contact, etc. All of these factors can be treated as the independent variables, i.e., the "causes." An epidemiologist is interested in the relations between these and the "effects." Among these effects may be the rate of spread of the disease, the total expected number of cases, the expected time of the peak, the geographical distribution, etc. Another interesting variable is the threshold of an epidemic. Many communicable diseases are always present in the population. But as long as the density of the infected individuals does not exceed some critical value, an epidemic will not occur. This critical value (the threshold density) is of obvious interest.

Now mathematics provides a way of developing a theory of such processes from a set of probalilities. There is a certain average probability that any two persons in a population will come in contact within a given interval of time. If they do, there is a certain probability that the disease will be transmitted, etc. These probabilities can be conceived in a gross manner (lumping all individuals, localities, etc.) or in a more or less refined manner, in which individuals and events are classified in some relevant way (cf. page 98). The more conditions are specified, i.e., the more specifically the corresponding probabilities are defined, the more accurate will be the resulting model of the phenomenon. As has already been pointed out (cf. page 99) there is a price to pay for slicing the classes of events too fine, namely, the probabilities are more difficult to get at even if they are estimated from observed frequencies (because the statistical fluctuations become more severe as the classes of events become smaller). Another price that one has to pay for listing too much detail is that the mathematics becomes progressively less manageable. Indeed none but the simplest epidemic problems have ever been solved by a formula in which the dependent and the independent variables are related by a specific mathematical function. Such formula, if obtained, constitutes a complete solution of the theoretical problem. If the underlying assumptions about how the probabilities are related are reasonably correct (nothing is said at this point about the actual *values* of the probabilities) then the formula, being strictly mathematically derived, is also correct. Now only the empirical problem remains, namely, to determine the numerical values of the independent variables in question. If these can somehow be obtained, they can be "plugged into" the equation, which then yields the values of the dependent variables. Or else, the problem can be turned around. The erstwhile dependent variables can be treated as independent ones: Plugging in *the observed* quantities associated with an epidemic, one can infer the factors contributing to it (susceptibilities, infectiousness, etc.). Whereas the former direct problem is of interest in applying the theory of epidemics, the latter inverse problem is of interest in developing the theory further.

The power and value of the mathematico-deductive approach is severely limited by the range of problems that can be solved in this way. The equations referred to are, typically, non-linear differential equations, for which no general method of solution exists to this day. Before the advent of mathematical technology mathematicians did the best they could by developing ingenious approximation methods, algorithms of computation, etc. For the most part, problems which led to equations too ugly to look at were simply left alone.

COMPUTERS AS SIMULATORS

High speed computers changed all this. Equations which refused to yield to general analytic methods were ground down by frontal attack, i.e., simply by numerical computations, made possible by the prowess of the calculating idiots (the computers). Specific numerical solutions can be obtained, to be sure, only if numerical values of the relevant variables are available. However, computers have come into use not only as calculators but also as simulators. Not knowing what values to give the principal factors of the process, the investigator can plug in any set of guessed values. The computer grinds out the results. The mathematical model simulates a *hypothetical* situation. From the results so obtained one can see how a real system *would* behave if it were characterized by the values assigned to its parameters. That is to say, simulation becomes a matter of testing different values of the hidden factors to see which of them would yield results reasonably close to what is observed in real life.

The example of epidemics is only one of many. Any large scale process governed by probabilities of large numbers of "small" events can be simulated. At present, simulation is coming into its own in traffic engineering. If traffic engineers want to decide whether a traffic light or a four-way stop sign will be more efficient at a given intersection; if they want to know whether a prohibition of left turns will alleviate jams or make them worse; if they want to know the optimum duration of red and green lights for each of two or more intersecting thoroughfares; if they want to know the optimal speed to be imposed on vehicles going through a tunnel, there is no need to tamper with the system directly, using the motorists and the pedestrians as guinea pigs, provided the system can be reasonably simulated. A good simulation depends on singling out the important factors and getting accurate estimates of their values.

In comparatively simple situations under comparatively constant or predictably varying conditions (of which traffic flow is a good example) simulation is a useful and efficient tool for seeking out optimal designs.

SIMULATED DIPLO-MILITARY SYSTEMS

In recent years simulations of diplo-military systems have become common in the United States. One of the chief aims of this development is, evidently, to provide some substitute for controlled experiment for the science of strategy, which purports to deal with such systems. Since the links between the simulated and the real process are missing, there is little hope of making simulation of diplo-military procedures a useful tool for arriving at strategic decisions.[43] It must be pointed out, however, that the enthusiasts of simulation are well aware of this difficulty and that they evaluate the positive contributions of this method from an entirely different point of view. Before we examine these arguments, let us look at the method more closely.

Guetzkow (49), Brody (15), and others distinguish between three types of simulation, namely (1) all-computer, (2) computer and human beings, (3) all human beings.

Actually it is not the physical presence of the computer but its function which determines the character of the simulations in which computers are used. In principle it would be possible to replace the computers with human beings, but this would not change the character of the procedure. I prefer, therefore, to classify simulations as follows: (1) those in which both the assessments of situations and the decisions are made in accordance with completely explicit rules; (2) those in which the assessments are made in accordance with explicit rules, but the decisions are made freely by human beings; (3) those in which assessments are made freely by human beings, but the decisions are made by rigid rules; (4) those in which both the assessments and the decisions are made by human beings.

In the literature "simulations and gaming" are usually discussed together. But a useful distinction can be made between the two and also between them and a third class, which the strategists call "scenarios."

The term "simulation," in my opinion, ought to be reserved to refer to procedures in which both the assessment of the situation and the decisions are carried out in accordance with formal rules. Since the decision rules are often complex and, also, assessments require a great deal of calculation, the computer takes over both these functions; but they could also, in principle, be performed by human beings instructed to follow the rules of assessment and decision to the letter.

"Gaming," on the other hand, is an appropriate term for simulated situations in which either assessment or decisions but not both are made more or less freely by human beings. The term "scenario," introduced by some strategists to denote imagined sequences of events, represents situations in which both the assessment and the decisions are improvised. We shall use this term in the same way.

Assessment is the determination of what has happened and of what could happen in a given situation during the course of the simulated process. In simulations and in gaming of type 2, assessment is made in accordance with strictly specified rules. For instance, in chess, assessment means the determination of the position and of all its immediate potentialities. This is not a matter of human choice. The position in chess is completely defined by where the pieces stand, and the potentialities are all possible next positions. These matters are strict consequences of the rules of the game; they had been programmed in advance. The decision, however, is the player's choice.[44] Chess becomes a simulation when the decisions too are made in accordance with strict (decision) rules. This is the way computers "play" chess.

In a scenario, the "rules" according to which the events become consequences of each other are not specified exactly. This is left to the imagination of the participants in the scenario. There may be several participants, each taking a role; or there may be just one author-actor-producer. In all cases of scenarios, there may be a special player called Nature who makes assessments. According to our distinction, if Nature makes her assessments in accordance with preprogrammed rules (which may involve chance events with preset probabilities), we are dealing with simulation or gaming. If, on the other hand, Nature may improvise developments on the spot, we have a scenario.[45]

Let us now examine an example of each type.

A SIMULATION

An example of such a genuine simulation is the "simple diplomatic game" designed by Oliver Benson.[46] In this game there are nine players, the big and medium powers, namely the United States, the Soviet Union, Britain, France, Western Germany, Italy, India, China, and Japan. There are also nine "target areas," selected at the time the game was designed as possible scenes of diplo-military moves by the powers, namely, Indonesia, Iran, Vietnam, Formosa, Guatemala, Egypt, Hungary, Lebanon, and Korea. Besides, there are nine "levels of action," all hostile, representing a gradation of intensity in moves and countermoves by the powers. In the program these are simply scaled from 0.100 to 0.900, but they are also named to suggest "reality":

.100 Diplomatic protest
.200 United Nations action (presumably a censuring one, not conciliatory)
.300 Severing diplomatic relations
.400 Propaganda subversion campaign

.500 Boycott and/or reprisals
.600 Troop movements
.700 Full mobilization
.800 Limited war
.900 All-out war

Each of the powers has a certain war potential, a combination of eight quantified variables: manpower, transportation, gross national product, gross national product per capita, energy production, steel production, literacy, and atomic capability. At a given time the power calculated from these indexes may be distributed among the actor nations in various ways. For example if two coalitions between them control over 90 per cent of the total power, this distribution is called "tight bipolar"; if two coalitions control about 75 per cent of the total power, the distribution is designated as "loose bipolar"; if no two coalitions control as much as 75 per cent of the power, this is designated as a "balance of power" situation (presumably because the remaining states can exert influence by their potential contribution to the one or the other coalition). Finally the situation is influenced at each stage by a degree of involvement of one state with another (this degree being, in turn, determined by the amount of "trade, coalition membership, presence or absence of military bases of the actor in the target area, and geographic proximity") and by the propensity of a state to act (or react).

This "propensity to act" is a probability, computed from certain indexes characterizing a nation, which Benson selects following Quincy Wright's theory of such determinants: aggressiveness, militarism, flexibility, tension, stability, violence, defensiveness, frustration, and internationalism.

The game begins with one of the actor states (powers) perpetrating an act (all acts, we recall, are hostile but in varying degrees) against a "target" (a small state, i.e., a pawn in the power game). Now the computer goes to work and decides in accordance with the programmed decision rules for each of the other eight actor states what it ought to do, after taking stock of the existing power distributions. After all the states have acted a new situation results and also a new power distribution. This in turn determines the next round of acts.

Since probabilities (propensities to act) are built into the rules, the process is a "stochastic" one. That is to say, the course of action is not strictly determined; different sequences of situations may result, even though they start with the same initial condition.[47]

Thus, both the assessments and the decisions are "untouched by human minds" except to the extent that human minds have designed the decision rules to start with.

FORMALIZED ASSESSMENTS, INTUITIVE DECISIONS

A large international relations gaming project is the subject of a book by Harold Guetzkow and several co-authors (49). The actors are several states, as in the preceding example, but now the roles are assumed by people. Moreover, roles are differentiated also within nations. There is a Central Decision Maker, an External Decision Maker, who communicates with his opposite numbers of the other states, and even an Aspiring Decision Maker, waiting to take over when the Central Decision Maker is removed from office by an election or a revolution. There are also Validators, whose role is played by a computer (or equivalent). The state of the Validators (their degree of satisfaction with the way things are going) has a bearing on the Central Decision Maker's tenure of office.

The States dispose of certain "basic capabilities," which they can increase (or lose) and which they allocate to military and civilian channels. The Validator's satisfaction depends in part on the availability of consumers' goods, in part on "security"; and these, in turn, depend on the respective allocations of basic capabilities.

The States enter into agreements with each other, engage in trade, (and even in aid) negotiate, compete, and fight wars. The scope of this simulation, as is evident, is much larger than Benson's, and the situations are presumably more realistic. The interactions between the states are not confined to hostile ones, as in the previous example, but range over a wide spectrum. The States hold world conferences, organize international credit systems, etc. Actually there is nothing in the way the game is set up to prevent the States from disarming, devoting all their resources to peaceful development, and cooperating in a prosperous world. But this can happen only if they all do it together. Unilateral disarmament is made difficult by the fact that the disarming nation would find itself in a strategically disadvantageous position, which displeases the Validators and makes a change of administration likely. The Aspiring Central Decision Maker may have other ideas. Also the temptation to "take over" the disarmed nation is always there. The role-playing participants evidently cannot get away from the conventional view of world politics, nor from the game atmosphere. After all, games are played to win.

In short, the existing view of international relations is simulated faithfully and in detail in this game with the exception of war. The latter is a highly formalized affair requiring an official declaration (with a "red flag" attached to the communication), specific commitments of resources (Decision Maker's choice), and formally decided outcomes (calculated from probabilities which depend on the resources committed).[48]

The results of such runs are essentially case studies. They make fascinating reading, rich in detail and quite convincing as facsimiles of international affairs. However, because of the vast numbers of variables involved, it is out of the question to view the results of these runs as outcomes of "experiments" in the accepted sense. Even the numerically specified variables are useless in this context. There are five States, each with a different level of basic capability, a different level of force capability, and a different range of decision latitude (meaning the range of decisions which the Validators will tolerate). To relate the outcomes to these values, each would have to be varied in turn, which would make the experimental design enormously unwieldy. Obviously these games were designed not for experimental but for demonstration purposes, and this is made clear by the authors. As such, they present considerable interest.

INTUITIVE ASSESSMENTS, FORMALIZED DECISIONS

This type of gaming is best exemplified by simulated defense systems. Indeed *real* air defense systems are of this sort to the extent that the situation is assessed by men (who respond to, say, visual signals on radar screens) and the information is processed by computers.[49] The simplest example is the servomechanically operated antiaircraft gun and its crew. The crew recognizes an object as a hostile aircraft. The gun makes all the "decisions" about when and in which direction to fire.

The system with automated decisions is the big bugaboo of the cybernetic age, celebrated in satires and cartoons. To what extent the actual decision processes are in fact coming under automatic control is not the issue in this book, and so these matters will not be discussed here. Simulated defense systems as examples of gaming are used almost exclusively in tactical military training.[50] I have not been able to find diplo-military games of this sort.

SCENARIOS

Several examples of scenarios are given by Kahn. In one of them (59, p. 150), Kahn imagines that the Russians have three hundred ICBM's and that each has a 50 per cent chance of destroying its target. At the time this occurs (during the much publicized "missile gap") the United States, it is assumed, has fifty Strategic Air Command bases. In allocating six ICBM's to each base, the Russians could count on 63 chances out of 64 that each base in turn would be destroyed, which means that with two chances out of three all of them would be destroyed and that with a very great likelihood no more than one base would be missed.

The problem now is to imagine whether the Soviet Union would launch a nuclear attack under these conditions. The pros and cons are presented in an imaginary conversation between a cautious Khrushchev and the General, his strategist-in-chief, who is trying to convince Khrushchev that the attack should be launched because Russia can get away with it. Kahn has reproduced this conversation in both *On Thermonuclear War* (58, pp. 198–199) and in *Thinking About the Unthinkable* (59, pp. 151–152). It must be read verbatim to be believed; so with apologies to the reader's sensitivities we reproduce it here.

G: So you can see that if you press these three hundred buttons there is a good chance of our getting away scot-free, a small chance of our suffering moderate damage, and no chance at all of our suffering as much damage as we suffered in World War II.

K: The Americans are on a fifteen minute alert. If they have any spies or even if we have a defector, we will be destroyed.

G: Don't worry. I have arranged to have a training count-down operation at noon every Saturday. All you have to do is pick up the telephone and give the order. You will be the only one who knows when the attack is going to take place.

K: I don't believe it. What if some Ukranian who is still mad at me presses one of the buttons ahead of time just to get me in trouble? Or else some don't fire and leave five or six American bases untouched.

G: Don't worry. I know that some Ukranians are still harboring unjustified grievances against you. There are no Ukranians in this force. In addition to being specially selected for reliability, every officer is married and has children and we have told these officers that if they fire early not only will they be shot but their families will be severely punished. We can take this extraordinary measure without hurting morale because every officer realizes that this issue is of overriding importance.

K: I still don't like it. I can imagine what will happen. I will pick up the phone and say, "Fire!" The officer will reply, "What did you say?" I will repeat, "Fire!" He will say, "There seems to be a bad connection. I keep hearing the word 'Fire'." I will say, "If you don't fire, I will have you boiled in oil." He will say, "I *heard you* that time. Don't fire! Thank you very much!"

It seems, then, that Khrushchev is *not* likely to think that he can get away with it, and so we are reasonably safe on that score.

"However, this conclusion does not finish the problem," Kahn warns and goes on to describe what is more likely to happen. He describes an escalated crisis over Berlin. When things get to the point where a showdown is inevitable, Kahn imagines a "sophisticated" attack which the Russians may launch (59, p. 153). It is a much smaller attack, avoiding local fallout by using smaller war heads and air-bursting the bombs instead of ground-bursting them. In this way they kill fewer than five million Americans—just a warning shot in the air, so to say. The real punch is not in the attack but in the ultimatum delivered simultaneously with it. The ultimatum contains first a warning that for every Soviet city which we destroy in retaliation, five American cities of comparable magnitude will be destroyed (the exchange list is specified: Moscow = New York + Washington + Los Angeles + Philadelphia + Chicago; Leningrad = Detroit +

Pittsburgh + etc.). Next the ultimatum offers a peace treaty in an "enclosed brochure to be studied."

Situations which Kahn calls games are also scenarios according to our definition. One of them deals with a nuclear explosion at an SAC base near Mobile, Alabama. The source of the explosion is not clear. "We" naturally believe, or at least would like to believe, that the explosion was an act of sabotage by Soviet agents. But we cannot prove it. The imagined sequence of events refers to our attempts to pin it on the Russians and to their well-known evasive actions, including protestations of innocence.

In one version of the scenario our President orders the manufacture of false evidence indicating that the Soviets caused the explosion. However, this well-meaning but imprudent ploy backfires to the detriment of United States prestige. In another happier version, the President is more clever. He orders a *single missile* fired against a Soviet atomic bomb plant.

"The world is horrified and frightened by the news. However, the United States' claim that the Mobile explosion was caused by Russian sabotage is believed. *It is the only psychologically adequate rationalization for the two smoking ruins.* . . . It is at this point in the game that world attitudes toward each side begin to benefit the United States" (59, p. 163, emphasis added).

Kahn goes on to argue that it is not to the Russians' advantage to retaliate *our* blow.

"This is true," he writes, "even if the Mobile explosion was in fact an accident rather than Soviet sabotage, *so long as the Soviets think the President actually believed it was Soviet sabotage.* They cannot believe that the United States staged the Mobile explosion. They know their denials will not be believed because they have cried 'wolf' too often. It is impossible for them to prove that the explosion was not caused by a Soviet agent . . . The true facts about the cause of the explosion are irrelevant" (59, p. 164, emphasis Kahn's).

WHY SIMULATE?

The designers of simulations, gaming, and scenarios agree that the principal value of these procedures is in furthering the development of theory and as teaching aids. It is in the nature of theory to be concerned with "If so . . . then so" statements. Thus, the conclusions of a genuine theory are always conditional. In computer simulations, one always gets answers of the following sort: If the situations resulting from decisions were determined in such and such a manner (assessment) and if the decisions were guided by such and such rules (formulated policy), then such and such results would obtain. To argue that neither "if" approximates reality is to argue against believing that the simulated results *will* indeed obtain. But this argument is not relevant against the theoretical value of simulations, since the *conditional* conclusions are valid and it is one of the tasks of theory to draw as many and as valid conditional conclusions as possible.

The same remarks apply to gaming. About the results obtained in gaming one could say, "If the assessments were made by such and such rules and if people who made decisions on the basis of assessments behaved like the participants in the game, then such and such would be the results; or else if people assessed the situation as our participants and the decisions were made by such and such rules, such would be the results."

On the matter of theoretical value, therefore, I agree entirely with the proponents of simulated procedures, even of the scenarios. (It is interesting to see of what depravity the human intellect is capable.) I would only add that the theoretical value of simulated procedures would be greatly enhanced if the range of the simulated situations were enlarged to include not only power game maneuvers, nuclear exchanges, and blackmail but also radically different procedures. For it is certainly desirable to deduce or even to imagine, as it is done in the scenarios, the results of accommodation, compromise, tension reduction (unilateral and bilateral), and cooperation. From the point of view of developing a comprehensive theory, the range of alternatives and the repertoire of conceptualizations is a pure good.[51]

My reservation concerns the pedagogic value of the simulations, gaming, and scenarios, as they are predominantly used. To quote Charles McClelland (79), his game, called World Politics, is "intended to build interest in the geography of world affairs, to increase sensitivity to the disparities in the distribution among countries and regions of resources and capabilities and to provide simulated experience with some of the strategies of statecraft. Perhaps the most important function is to encourage imaginative and manipulative constructions of possible international systems."

It is difficult to argue against this intent. Certainly we need more imagination, more flexibility, more awareness of the conditions which make states and their relations with each other what they are. However, if we examine the actual games which are used pedagogically, we see how strongly they are involved with the strategic modes of thought. If any decisive evidence were lacking of the strategists' interpretation of global conflict as a game, their preoccupation with gaming provides it.

Here we observe the operation of all the pressures for simplification which we have discussed in Chapters 10 and 11. For example, even with the operation of chance factors, simulation games have much more determinism in them than the situations warrant. Typically Nature is assumed to act on the results of actions but not on the implementation of decisions. It is assumed that what is decided on can be carried out to the letter. When chance does act, it usually acts in accordance with simple known odds. This is especially evidenced in McClelland's world politics game, in which each "confrontation" is treated as a game of chance, not as a genuine two-person game.[52] The misconception that a "calculated risk" applies in such situations is firmly built in. Further, although non-zero-sum features are present in some of the games (100), the emphasis is overwhelmingly on zero-sum features. The games are for *stakes* (like any parlor games).

We may well raise the question about what these games actually teach and whom they are intended to teach. The most likely targets of such teaching are students of international affairs, people who in the future may be influential in the conduct of these affairs. Presumably, the implied absence of conscience considerations, characteristic of most of these simulation games, reflects political reality. Knowledge, it is almost universally accepted, means knowledge of "existing" reality. Illusion is the assignment of non-existing features to reality. But is this indeed the case in all areas, including international relations? Do not people who make international relations make the reality which underlies it? And having made it, do they not perpetuate it by declaring it to be *the* reality. How do games teach "flexibility" if the admissible "reality" is stiffly circumscribed by the rules of the game?

This objection is admittedly removed in the scenario. There "flexibility" and imagination are given free play. But in what direction?

Kahn defends his scenarios from charges that they are products of a paranoid or a schizophrenic mind by pointing out that this criticism may be pertinent to the content of the scenarios, not to the methodology, and in this he is on solid ground. We have already absolved the methodology. But why avoid the discussion of content, especially if the scenarios are used to stimulate the imagination?[53] Is it of indifference what people are led to imagine?

The stock rationale offered for "thinking the unthinkable" simulates a defense of the open mind. By implication, those who deplore the unfettered fantasies of blackmail, genocide, and betrayal are accused of having closed minds. They are compared to the prudes of yesterday, who stood in the way of combating prostitution by denouncing the subject as indecent (59, p. 17). But the essential issue is not what we shall be permitted to think about; the essential issue is what *shall* we think about? Images of the world compete for selection. And it is by no means true that having selected an image, we remain free to discard it "if we don't like it."

I do not believe that I am restricting my child's intellectual freedom when I induce him to read *Winnie the Pooh* instead of *Gory Comics*. On the contrary, I believe I am enhancing his future intellectual freedom by directing his choices. Nor am I advocating the censorship of Dr. Kahn's scenarios. I am merely deploring them, not because they are unpleasant, but because they are stupid and malign like *Little Orphan Annie* and *Smiling Jack,* from which the conversation between Khrushchev and his strategist appears to have been cribbed.

The paranoid's logic rests on the incontrovertible assertion that what he imagines is possible. I will not only admit that the scenarios proposed by Kahn and other strategists are possible but also that they are not too implausible. I readily absolve the strategists of charges of paranoia. A more appropriate term for this type of thinking is psychopathic, that is, thinking utterly devoid of moral sense. In our days, it is easy to sell such thinking as "objective," and the bulk of Kahn's persuasive efforts are directed to that end. To me, however, it seems that Raymond Aron's apology in his Introduction to *Thinking about the Unthinkable* is more pertinent:

> The analyst who calculates in millions or tens of millions of deaths resulting in a matter of a few minutes from thermonuclear exchanges does indeed forget the human significance of these figures, just as a reader of detective stories calmly accepts recitals of choice murders.

This *is* to the point. The strategists do live in a world similar to that of the detective story, where murder is a game of reversed blind man's buff and every one can be It. I know many people addicted to detective stories, but confess I have never met anyone who thinks he is living in one. If he did, he would have to be locked up. The strategists cannot be locked up, because they do what they do with our blessings. The world of their imaginings is believed to be the real world and, in fact, can be shown to be real, at least in part. But the crucial fact is forgotten: The nightmare world of diplo-military strategy owes much of its "reality" to the efforts of the strategists themselves.

OPPORTUNITIES

Although there is little likelihood that the "answers" one gets in simulations, in gaming, and in scenarios will be taken as bases of diplo-military policy, the question is always pertinent of the extent to which simulated situations approach reality. The question is pertinent with regard to the research and teaching aims of these methods.

The real world is complex; the simulated world is necessarily drastically simplified. The closer to reality one wishes to bring the simulated world, the more complications have to be introduced. For this there is a price to pay: The "answers" one gets to the questions one puts become increasingly specific to the situation depicted. The aim of theory, however, and also of pedagogy (on a certain level) is to derive or to display general conclusions (or hypotheses) which would apply to a variety of specific situations. In order to generate such general ideas, situations must be made sufficiently simple to be theoretically tractable. If one is extraordinarily lucky, one may get ideas that are both general and pertinent to real life. This happens if in simplifying the situation one removes the incidental and inessential factors and retains the most essential ones. The reason physical science has been so phenomenally successful, both in the generality of its theory and in its relevance to the real world, is that the physical scientists hit upon just the right concepts: Mass, energy, force field, time are all of them elements from which physical reality, as we know it, is constructed.

The behavioral sciences are still far from having such an inventory of fundamental concepts. A principal aim of theory in these sciences is to construct such an inventory. Traditionally this was done by reflective speculation. But with the development of experimental methods suitable for behavioral science, experimentation became an important *theoretical* tool. That is to say, the results of many behavioral experiments are to be viewed not primarily as answers to specific questions (what will happen under such and such conditions) but as the raw material from which general hypotheses can be generated. Reviewing his results, the experimental behavioral scientist can say something of this sort: "Now I have deduced certain regular relations between the conditions I have imposed and the behavior I have observed. How general is this relation? To what range of conditions or situations does it apply?" The important end-product of such research, then, is not an answer but a question. One hopes in this way to have an inventory of important questions. Important concepts arise from these.

CHAPTER 14

SIMULATION OF INTERACTIONS
MOTIVATED BY TRUST AND SUSPICION

We have seen how the analysis of prisoner's dilemma suggests this simple game as a genuine paradigm of characteristically human ambivalence. Since the normative theory of games provides no satisfactory recommendations for a choice of strategy in PD, only an empirical investigation of actual behavior can serve as a point of departure for the construction of a theory of this game.

Systematic experiments with prisoner's dilemma were started in the United States about 1958 or 1959, mostly by psychologists. For the most part these were separate studies by different investigators, conducted according to traditional methods of experimental psychology.

THE METHOD OF EXPERIMENTAL PSYCHOLOGY

Where the man in the street (and the metaphysician) speak of causes and effects, the experimental psychologist is wary of assigning these roles to events. He speaks instead of independent and dependent variables. The independent variables are those which he himself manipulates or those which are not affected by the experiment, e.g., time; the dependent variables are those which are "read" as the results of the experiment. In this way, one relates values of observed quantities (dependent variables) to values of manipulated quantities (independent variables). If these relations can be expressed mathematically, one has a compact statement—a "result."

Frequently the manipulated variable is not a quantity but a condition under which the experiment is performed or else a characteristic of the population of subjects. For example, if one wishes to establish whether men or women are better in discriminating tones, one compares tested samples of men and of women, being careful to establish by a statistical argument the degree of confidence one has in the result.

Such, then, is the usual context of published research in experimental psychology. The method has brought scientific rigor into psychology. To the extent that the results are reproducible and the findings are stated in terms of observables, one is within the realm of science. To the extent that the results indicate regularities in the relationships among the variables, one has reason to suppose that "laws" are operating in the realm of the investigation. To the extent that there is evidence for such laws in observed patterns of behavior, experimental psychologists can claim to be following the paths blazed by the natural scientists.

On the other hand, the limitations of this method are serious. A "law" is supposed to link a great number of "facts" and so to bring order into accumulated knowledge which would otherwise be like an untidy heap of disconnected records of observations. But even "laws" are not much help if they proliferate, for a heap of disconnected "laws" soon comes to resemble a heap of disconnected facts. If the establishments of "laws" at the rate of one law per experiment were all there was to scientific psychology, one would be at a loss how to apply what one has learned. Complaints are sometimes heard that the situation in psychology is nearly of this sort. We expect psychology, like any other science, to provide knowledge about its field of investigation, which includes the entire gamut of human behavior and its underpinnings. However, as we look through the literature of scientific psychology (that is, reports of experiments) we see little that sheds light on how people behave in real life and why. One finds formalized hypotheses and decisions, determined by conventional statistical criteria, of whether to accept or reject the hypotheses.

Early experiments on prisoner's dilemma were conducted in the accepted framework of experimental psychology. The game situation provided an opportunity for studying cooperative and non-cooperative behavior. The extent of such behavior could be easily quantified, for example, as a fraction of C choices in a given experimental run or the percentage of a population choosing C in a single play of the game. One could then ask questions about relations between this "measure of cooperation," the dependent variable, and some independent variable chosen for the occasion. These questions could be answered within the framework of the situation which comprised the experiment.

In particular, it was established in various experiments that by and large people tend to play the non-cooperative strategy more frequently than the cooperative (80, 105); that the instructions given to them influence their playing (34); that the tendency to cooperate shows a weak but discernible correlation with some independently assessed personality traits in the expected direction (76), etc.

Most of these conclusions could be clearly anticipated on common sense grounds. Thus not much is learned from the experiments except that our expectations are justified. It is hard to see what relevance findings of this sort have to the intriguing questions suggested by prisoner's dilemma as a paradigm of the present impasse in the relations between the hostile blocs.

However, the early purely empirical investigations can be seen as stepping stones to a more penetrating analysis which brings the experiments considerably closer to real life. For the analysis points to a theory which may have a much broader field of application than the laboratory situation in which it was conceived. In this approach, instead of posing specific hypotheses to be answered by specific experiments, one concentrates on the over-all properties of the *system* suggested by the dynamics of the prisoner's dilemma game. The meaning of this statement will, I hope, become clear from the discussion to follow.

In experiments conducted in this writer's laboratory at the University of Michigan, pairs of college students were asked to play games of the prisoner's dilemma type several hundred times in succession without communication. The payoffs were in money.[54] In the preliminary analysis of the data, we proceeded in the usual way, relating various statistics of the data to each other and to experimentally controlled variables. We have found out how the frequency of cooperative responses, averaged over several pairs of subjects playing the same game, depends on the payoff matrix of the game, on the number of plays already made, and on other factors. There is, of course, a great deal of variance among the pairs. Some play predominantly cooperatively; others, predominantly non-cooperatively. Some pairs show equal propensities to cooperate on the part of both subjects; others are strongly "skewed," with one subject a persistent cooperator exploited by the other subject, who keeps defecting and winning money.

A list of such results is hardly more than a contribution to the "untidy heap" mentioned earlier. It is possible, however, to construct a mathematical model of the process in which these results are unified, in the sense that they become logical consequences of rather simple assumptions. Moreover, these assumptions are related to similar assumptions underlying other psychological experiments. We have thus an opportunity for the systematic construction of a general psychological theory.

THE STOCHASTIC MODEL

Our model is of the stochastic type. It is based on assumptions that the events comprising the process occur with certain constant or variable probabilities. The "laws" governing the process, then, appear as the relations of the probabilities to each other. The model has two kinds of implications, namely "forward" and "backward." The former are the predictions one derives from the model. Such predictions can be compared with the observed data, and the degree of agreement constitutes the test of the model. The latter are the *interpretations* which can be made of the parameters of the model. These interpretations constitute the psychological theory suggested by the model.

A stochastic process is best described in the language of mathematics. Since not everyone reads this language, we will attempt to describe it in words. We must caution the reader, however, that such attempts can be at most partially successful.

Consider the pair, playing prisoner's dilemma sequentially. The pair constitute a system. The term system has a great variety of meanings, but here it means only the following. A system is something that can be in one of any (finite or infinite) number of *states*. At any given time the "something" is in a certain one of these states. The states are distinguishable by an observer, so that at any given time the observer can tell, by inspecting the system, in what state it is. Moreover, the transition of the system from state to state is governed by certain laws. The goal of a theory purporting to describe such a system is to discover (1) all the states in which the system can be and (2) the laws which govern the transition from one state to another. The laws may be deterministic or probabilistic.[55]

Consider now the system defined by our two players. As far as our theory is concerned, the system at any given time will be in one of four clearly distinguishable states, namely, CC, CD, DC, and DD, according to the pair of choices just made by the two players.

Suppose now the system passes from state CC to CC (i.e., remains in the double-cooperative state for two consecutive plays.) How does this happen? This happens if each of the players, having cooperated and having been rewarded for cooperating (since the double-cooperative state is rewarding to both) cooperates also on the next play. Or suppose the system passes from state CD to DD. This happens if one of the players, having cooperated, and having been punished (for the single cooperator is punished) does not cooperate the next time, while the other player, having defected and been rewarded (for the single defector is rewarded) defects also on the next play. All the sixteen transitions from state to state (from each of the four states to each of the four states) can be similarly described in terms of what each individual does after what he did last and after what has happened to him.

People playing PD sometimes choose C and sometimes D. What they choose depends on a great many circumstances. A task of a theory is to classify the circumstances into relevant classes. The theory would be complete if our classification allowed us to predict with certainty how people would choose in each of the circumstances. But no theory of human behavior yet exists which makes such predictions possible. At most we can determine the probabilities with which people will make the choices. Let us define such probabilities.

We shall denote by x the probability of cooperating on the next play, after having cooperated and been rewarded. This probability has a suggestive psychological interpretation. Let us designate it by "trustworthiness." One could, of course, dismiss this interpretation as unjustifiably sentimental. After all the theory of conditioning can explain such a tendency without making use of moralistic overtones: Reinforced responses tend to become fixated; hence x can be considered simply as a measure of the extent to which the rewarded response C has been fixated by conditioning. This is so. But we must keep constantly in mind that we are dealing with a potentially "rational" player, who, according to *strategic* analysis should be constantly driven to defect, which temptation is constantly reinforced by the knowledge that the other is also being tempted to defect and therefore that one *certainly* ought to defect. It is against this whirlpool trap of strategic thinking that "trustworthiness" is a defense. The complement of x, that is $1 - x$, can be called, accordingly, a measure of "perfidy".

Next, let us define y: the probability of cooperating on the next play after having cooperated and having been punished (for being the only cooperator.) The closest moralistic term for this measure is "forgiveness." The complement of y, $1 - y$ can be called "vengefulness."

Next we define z: the probability of cooperating on the next play after having defected and having been rewarded (for being the only defector.) This quantity could be conceived as a measure of "repentance." Its complement, $1 - z$ suggests "greed" (continuing to defect and to reap the rewards at the cooperator's expense.)

Finally we define w: the probability of cooperating on the next play after having defected and having been punished. The propensity for doing so speaks for "trust", since escape from the punished DD state is possible only if the other also goes along instead of sticking with D and reaping the single defector's payoff. The complement of w, $1 - w$, is a measure of "distrust."

We can now propose a mathematical model of the entire process, which comprises several hundred successive plays of PD by many pairs of subjects. The mathematical model is a set of assumptions. We know that every one of these assumptions is false. Nevertheless we make them, for our purpose at this point is not to make true assertions about human behavior but to investigate consequences of assumptions, as in any simulation or experimental game. These consequences must be rigorously derived, i.e., derived by mathematical techniques; and this can be done only if the assumptions are translatable into mathematical statements and if the resulting problem of derivation is tractable. Moreover, we shall want to interpret the derived consequences, so these too should be sufficiently straightforward to yield to interpretation.

Thus the exigencies of the hypothetico-deductive method dictate the kinds of assumptions that can be used in constructing a model. We note that this is exactly the same sort of restriction which is imposed on the strategists' formulations of global military-diplomatic problems.

The assumptions which constitute our model are the following:

1. Every one of the individuals playing a particular PD game is characterized by the same values of the psychological parameters x, y, z, and w.

2. The parameters x, y, z, and w depend on the payoffs of the particular game played and on the conditions under which the game is played but not on the pattern of outcomes preceding a particular play.

As we have said, these assumptions are almost certainly false, nor are they tenable on common sense grounds. For the first assumption implies that all people have the same propensities for trustworthiness or for its opposite, for forgiveness or for its opposite, etc. The second assumption says that the propensities remain the same, that is, that people do not *learn* to trust or to distrust one another, to repay betrayal by betrayal, or to refrain from doing so, etc. Neither assumption, we feel, is in accord with what we know about human nature.

However, from the mathematical model we can see what *would* happen if the assumptions were true. We can then compare these results with what *does* happen and see to what extent our model must be modified to approach a reasonable facsimile of what actually underlies people's behavior in this situation.

By the use of mathematical techniques, we deduce the following conclusion from our assumptions. Regardless of what the initial probability distributions have been of the four states of the system, after a while these frequencies will be given by the following formulas. The P's represent the probabilities (or the relative frequencies) of the states. The subscripts refer to the states; $\tilde{x}$ stands for $1-x$, $\tilde{y}$ for $1-y$, etc.

$$P_{CC} = \frac{w^2(1-\tilde{y}z-y\tilde{z}+2w\tilde{w})-2w\tilde{w}(w^2-yz)}{(1-\tilde{y}z-y\tilde{z}+2w\tilde{w})(1-x^2+w^2)-2(w^2-yz)(w\tilde{w}-x\tilde{x})}$$

$$P_{CD} = \frac{w\tilde{w}(1-x^2+w^2)-w^2(w\tilde{w}-x\tilde{x})}{(1-\tilde{y}z-y\tilde{z}+2w\tilde{w})(1-x^2+w^2)-2(w^2-yz)(w\tilde{w}-x\tilde{x})}$$

$$P_{DC} = \frac{w\tilde{w}(1-x^2+w^2)-w^2(w\tilde{w}-x\tilde{x})}{(1-\tilde{y}z-y\tilde{z}+2w\tilde{w})(1-x^2+w^2)-2(w^2-yz)(w\tilde{w}-x\tilde{x})}$$

$$P_{DD} = \frac{(1-\tilde{y}z-y\tilde{z}+2w\tilde{w})(1-x^2)-2w\tilde{w}[(1-x^2)-yz]}{(1-\tilde{y}z-y\tilde{z}+2w\tilde{w})(1-x^2+w^2)-2(w^2-yz)(w\tilde{w}-x\tilde{x})}$$

These equations tell us that if we know the values of x, y, z, and w, we can substitute them in the right side of each equation and calculate (i.e., predict) the frequencies of the four states "after a while," when the system has settled down to its steady state.

Our conclusion contains the far from precise phrase "after a while." We shall return to it and define it more exactly. For the present we note the following features of our equations:

1. $P_{CD} = P_{DC}$. This is, of course, a direct consequence of our first assumption. If all the people are alike, then the frequencies with which the two unilateral states will occur must be equal. This should be true even if people are not alike, if our population is big enough. For in a large population the average behavior of subjects named A should not be different from the average behavior of subjects named B.

2. $P_{CC} + P_{CD} + P_{DC} + P_{DD} = 1$. This is a tautology, since the P's represent the mutually exclusive and exhaustive probabilities of the possible states of the system.

3. From the foregoing it follows that only two of the four states are independent, say P_{CC} and P_{CD}. The other two are determined when the first two are known.

4. Our equations have four variables (x, y, z, and w) on the right side, and only two on the left side. Therefore, although knowledge of x, y, z, and w completely determines the four P's, knowledge of the P's is not sufficient to determine x, y, z, and w.

Now there is a way in which the parameters x, y, z, and w can be inferred. Recall that the P's will become stabilized only "after a while." In the beginning of the process, the P's will change even though x, y, z, and w remain constant. Accordingly, if we take several successive readings of the P's (the relative frequencies of the states) in the beginning of the process, we could (in principle) estimate x, y, z, and w, if these are indeed constant.[56]

However, there is also another, more direct, way of estimating x, y, z, and w (again supposing they are constant.) One can count all the instances where following a CC state, subject A cooperated (and similarly for B). The average of these two numbers divided by the total number of occurrences of CC gives us x. The other propensities can be similarly computed. Knowing x, y, z, and w, we are in a position to deduce *theoretically* the expected time course of the P's, i.e., the path along which the system approaches its steady state. We can now put our theory to a test. Does the observed time course of the P's coincide with the predicted time course? If it does, we have a satisfactory model from which we can draw further conclusions. It will remain satisfactory until we draw a conclusion contradicted by evidence. If there is a disparity between the predicted and the observed time courses, we must dig deeper.

Figure 5 shows the comparison.

A discrepancy is apparent. The predicted time course of P_{CC} reaches its steady state value around the thirtieth play of the game, while the observed value gets there on about the two-hundredth play. Evidently at least some of our assumptions were false.

The most vulnerable of our assumptions was that relating to the constancy of x, y, z, and w during the course of the experiment.[57] The assumption amounted to saying that the average individual's propensity to play cooperatively depended only on what he did and on what happened on the immediately preceding play of the game. It is reasonable to suppose, however, that these propensities *themselves* change with experience (i.e., during the course of the game). Fortunately, we have a ready-made theory to provide a model of this process, the recently developed stochastic theory of learning.[58] It is this theory which we now plug into our stochastic model. In its simplest version, the model deduced from stochastic learning theory superimposed on our original stochastic process requires twelve parameters. These are:

1. The rate of increase of trustworthiness (x) when trustworthiness is rewarded.

2. The rate of decrease of trustworthiness when it is betrayed.

3. The rate of increase of forgiveness (y) when forgiveness is successful (i.e., when the defector is converted).

4. The rate of increase of vengefulness ($1-y$) when forgiveness is in vain.

5. The rate of decrease of forgiveness when greed ($1-z$) is rewarded.

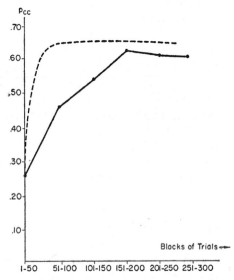

FIGURE 5. *Solid line:* Actual time course of average Pcc. *Dotted line:* What the time course should be if x, y, z, and w were constant.

6. The rate of increase of forgiveness when greed backfires (is reciprocated).

7. The rate of increase of repentance (z), when repentance is rewarded.

8. The rate of decrease of repentance when repentance is betrayed.

9. The rate of increase of greed when greed is rewarded.

10. The rate of decrease of greed when greed is punished.

11. The rate of increase of trust (w) when trust is justified.

12. The rate of decrease of trust when trust is betrayed.

By properly selecting values of these twelve parameters, we can fit the time courses of x, y, z, and w, and, since the time courses of the P's depend on those of the propensities, the time courses of these too will be fitted.

Now it is by no means surprising that four curves can be fitted by twelve parameters. The more parameters one has at one's disposal, the easier it is to fit theoretical equations to a curve. If the curve is not too erratic, two parameters often suffice. The observed time courses of x and w are quite well behaved (x keeps increasing, and w keeps decreasing). We have two parameters for each of these curves. The observed time courses of y and z are somewhat more erratic, but we have four parameters to fit each of these curves with our equations. Thus, we must admit that the predictive power of our model cannot be considered as a dramatic triumph of our theory. The test to which the theory was put was not severe enough because of the large number of free parameters available.

But our result need not be the end of the investigation. We can proceed from this point in two directions: (1) Restrict the freedom of the parameters, for example, by obtaining independent estimates of their values. (2) Use the psychological interpretation of the parameters in experiments designed to inquire how these psychological traits are affected by changing the conditions of the experiment. The former course of action (the "forward" implication) aims at putting the model to more severe tests and so at strengthening our confidence in its "reality." The latter course of action (the "backward" implication) proceeds on the assumption that the model does represent a real psychological process and aims at determining the range of generality of the process and so the range of application of the theory.

RESULTS AND INTERPRETATIONS

In our work we have been inclined to follow the second course. We assume (tentatively, of course,) that we have isolated certain important variables characterizing the behavior of human subjects (college students) in the prisoner's dilemma game. These variables have psychological interpretations. Hence we are in a position to ask how these psychological features vary under various conditions.

Note that our variables or parameters are on four levels:

1. The over-all frequency of cooperative response, denoted by C. This single variable represents the grossest level of analysis.[59]

2. The frequencies of the four states, CC, CD, DC, and DD. Of these only two are independent if the two subjects are assumed to be identical; otherwise three are independent. The independent frequencies constitute the data on the next level of analysis.

3. The propensities, $x, y, z,$ and w. All four are independent. They are taken into account on the third level of analysis.

4. The twelve learning parameters, all independent, represent the deepest level of analysis that we have attempted.[60]

About each of these sets of variables or parameters, we can ask questions pertinent to the level of analysis where it is found. The questions relate to the way the values of the variables or parameters vary with some chosen independent variable. Of the latter there are many. But here we shall consider only a few.

1. *The payoff matrix.* We have used seven different games in the experiments. The games are shown in Matrices 19 to 25.

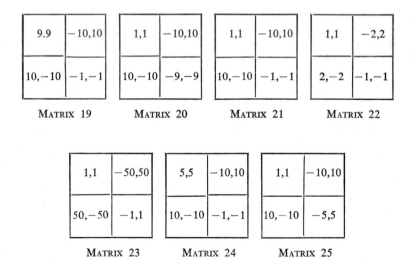

9.9	−10,10	1,1	−10,10	1,1	−10,10	1,1	−2,2
10,−10	−1,−1	10,−10	−9,−9	10,−10	−1,−1	2,−2	−1,−1

MATRIX 19   MATRIX 20   MATRIX 21   MATRIX 22

1,1	−50,50	5,5	−10,10	1,1	−10,10
50,−50	−1,1	10,−10	−1,−1	10,−10	−5,5

MATRIX 23   MATRIX 24   MATRIX 25

2. *Time*. Time is measured by the number of plays elapsed.

3. *Knowledge of the game matrix*. In some experiments subjects kept the matrix of the game or games which they played in front of them. In other experiments, the matrix was not shown to the subjects. In both cases, however, the subjects were told of their own and of the other's payoffs. In principle, they could easily infer the game matrix from this information. (There is no memory load to speak of, because the game has only four possible outcomes and only two strategies to choose from.)

Here is a list of questions and answers derived from the data.

Level 1 (over-all frequency of cooperation).

Q_1: How does the over-all frequency of cooperation depend on the payoff matrix?

A_1: If we compare Matrices 21, 24, and 19, in which reward for cooperation changes while the other entries remain the same, we find that C increases with reward. If we compare Matrices 22, 21, and 23 in which the defector's payoff and the "sucker's" loss change, while the other entries remain the same, we find that C decreases as defector's payoff and sucker's loss increase.

If we compare the games represented by Matrices 21, 25, and 20, in which punishment for double defection changes as other entries remain the same, we find that cooperation increases as the punishment increases.

These results are shown in Figure 6 on page 155.

These results are, of course, expected on common sense grounds. The experiment does little more than corroborate the expectations.

Q_2: Does the amount of cooperation depend on whether the players see the matrix?

A_2: Yes. Cooperation is about twice as frequent when they see it as when they do not.

The comparison is shown in Figure 7 on page 156.

Here we have a result which is not obvious on a priori grounds. In fact, we had conjectured the opposite. We thought the matrix would be a constant reminder to the subjects of the fact that D dominates

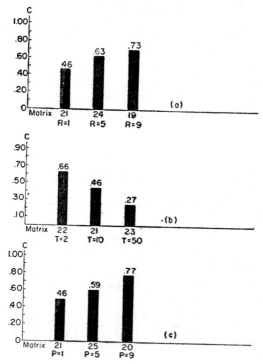

FIGURE 6. Frequency of cooperative choice depends on

      (a) R, reward for cooperation

      (b) T, temptation to defect

      (c) P, punishment for double defection

C (cf. p. 49). Instead, the matrix seemed to remind them that the mutually beneficial CC solution was available (if they would only trust each other).

Q_3: Does the frequency of cooperation change in the course of the game?

A_3: When the matrix is seen, cooperation generally increases as the plays are repeated. However, the increase is preceded by an initial decrease, which lasts about twenty-five plays. The low point is passed about then. Thereafter an upswing starts until the top level of about 65 per cent is reached on about the two-hundredth or two-hundred-and-fiftieth play and persists thereafter.[61]

It should be stressed, however, that this figure represents the population average (seventy pairs). Actually, most of the pairs either "lock in" on CC or on DD. It is just because more pairs (about 50 per cent) lock in on CC than on DD (about 15 per cent) that the average goes up.

When the matrix is not displayed, the initial decrease is much longer. It is quite gradual, and the low point (about 25 per cent to 30 per cent

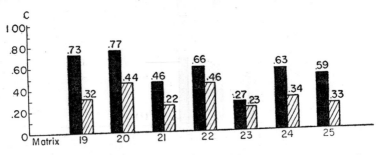

FIGURE 7. Comparison of frequencies of cooperative choices when game matrix is displayed (*black columns*) with when it is not (*hatched columns*).

C) is reached after about 150 plays. Thereafter there is a recovery, but also quite slow. At the end approximately the initial frequency of cooperation is reached, which is about 35 per cent.

We see, then, that the apparently simple question, "Do people playing prisoner's dilemma learn to cooperate?" has no simple answer. Initially the frequency of cooperative choices decreases. Later, more people learn to cooperate than to defect, but both kinds of behavior are observed. Thus the "dilemma" is reflected in the results of the experiment.

Level 2 (the frequencies of the four states).

Q_4: Are the responses of the two players correlated?

A_4: We have examined the correlation coefficients of the responses in the various runs.[62] A positive value of this coefficient would indicate that cooperative responses of one subject tend to elicit cooperative responses of the other. A negative value would indicate that opposite responses tend to be elicited. A value of the correlation coefficient near zero would indicate that the responses are essentially independent of each other. A priori, one could argue for any one of these possibilities. It is commonly observed that people respond in kind. On the other hand, in prisoner's dilemma it pays to defect when the other cooperates. It is also reasonable to expect independence of responses for lack of communication opportunity. It turns out that the values of the correlation coefficient are strongly biased toward the positive end. (The average correlation is about $+0.5$) Moreover, the coefficient increases with time, starting about 0.2 and reaching values of 0.7 to 0.8. The players not only play like each other; they tend to play more and more like each other as plays are repeated.

Q_5: What about the unilateral states, CD and DC?

A_5: These tend to disappear in the course of a session. However, an occasional long unilateral run is observed. We call such runs "martyr runs." They look like attempts of one player to induce the other to cooperate by example, even though he loses money doing this.

Q_6: How do martyr runs end?

A_6: A martyr run can end in a "success," i.e., conversion of the defector, or in a "failure," when the martyr gives up and himself becomes a defector. Switches are also observed, when the martyr gives up just as the other starts to cooperate. Failures outnumber successes about 2½ to 1.

Level 3 (propensities).

Q_7: What are the average values of the four propensities in the subject population?

A_7: Our subject population (University of Michigan students) is characterized by the following average propensities:

Trustworthiness—About 0.95
Forgiveness   —About 0.4 or 0.5
Repentance   —About 0.3
Trust   —About 0.1 or 0.2

Operationally, these figures mean the following. Once a pair has "locked in" on cooperation (CC), it is highly unlikely (one chance in twenty) that one of them will defect on a particular play. Next, the "betrayed" cooperator is somewhat unlikely (slightly less than odds-on) to continue cooperating on the next play. The defector who got away with it is rather unlikely to repent on the next play (about three chances out of ten). When a pair has locked in on DD, one of them is quite unlikely (one or two chances out of ten) to try to break the deadlock.

Here, then, is the clearest demonstration of the characteristic instability of prisoner's dilemma. Both of the "double" states, CC and DD, exert a "pull" on the system in opposite directions. Once a system gets to one or the other of these states, it tends to stay there.[63]
Level 4 (rates of change of the propensities).

Q_8: How do the propensities change in the course of a session?

A_8: The average x starts high and climbs still higher to practically 1.00. The average y increases slightly. The average z is erratic but the fluctuations are not large. The average w starts low and becomes still lower. According to our interpretations, the average subject learns to be more trustworthy and more forgiving but also more distrustful when betrayed. (The contradiction is only apparent. "Forgiveness," in our context means a tendency to persist in the unilateral cooperative state; "trust" means a tendency to break out of the double-defecting state.)

This is as far as our analysis has gone at this writing. The learning parameters, i.e., the constants presumably underlying the entire process have not yet been examined.

The question most frequently asked about this work is:

Q_9: What can be learned from these experiments?

A_9: What can be learned depends on what one sets out to learn. Should one look to results of the experiments just described for information about human nature or the nature of international relations, one will be disappointed or else deluded, if one tries to interpret the results by direct analogies. Knowledge about human behavior does not come in the form of straight answers to straight questions because the art of selecting and formulating questions is an integral part of such knowledge. Natural science, as we know it, took centuries to build. Its foundations were laid by people who did not ask at each step, "What will I learn of practical value from this experiment or from the solution of this equation?" The building of knowledge places its own demands on the builder. The next step in the process usually suggests itself naturally and forcefully.

In my opinion, the chief value of the experiments just described is in the fact that they suggest intriguing questions, which, in turn, suggest new experiments and alternative theoretical approaches. Thus experimental and deductive techniques are linked and reinforce each other. Next, in performing these experiments, one learns the method itself—how to design experiments in which (1) conflict of motives is a prominent feature and (2) the data are objective, quantifiable, and suggest fruitful theoretical schemes. The context of the experiments is admittedly thin, but this is the price one has paid for the high degree of theoretical tractability. A theory of prisoner's dilemma promises to be rich and complex. It seems sensible, therefore to develop such a theory from the ground up to be used as a tool in future experiments and observations in the hope that they can be brought closer to real life.

CHAPTER 15

ANSWERS AND INSIGHTS

~~~~~~

> *With mere instruction in command*
> *So that people understand*
> *Less than they know, woe is the land;*
> *But happy the land that is ordered so*
> *That they understand more than they know.*
> —LAO-TZU

THE USES OF KNOWLEDGE

Research, it is universally understood, is an activity designed to increase our store of knowledge. To the question "Why should the store of knowledge be increased?" different answers have been given. One view holds that knowledge is an end in itself, and that there is something uncouth about asking why we should pursue it. Euclid is said to have ordered a slave to give a penny to a student, when the latter asked of what use knowledge of geometry would be to him. To me it seems that if the question was asked in good faith, it should have been answered in good faith. Euclid might have told the student that there is a deep satisfaction in seeing the fragments of knowledge combine into a coherent picture. Had the youth been patient and diligent, he would have seen such a picture unfold as he came to understand geometry. The acquisition of insights, Euclid might have gone on, is a rich source of satisfaction because it awakens a vigorous appetite for more of such experience. Unlike other appetites, which are dulled by indulgence or else become addictions, destructive of health or values, the appetite for insight is both wholesome and insatiable.

A contemporary American high school teacher usually gives a different answer to the question why geometry should be studied. He stresses the instrumental aspect of knowledge, either in terms of its technological applications or in terms of the opportunities for advancement it confers. Here the emphasis is not on the insights one derives from knowledge but on power.

Knowledge and power were not always so closely related. In prescientific societies, knowledge was imparted to the young in order to acquaint them with what is expected of them as members of the community. Another important aim of instruction in prescientific societies was to inculcate wisdom, that is, an awareness of "how things are." Both of these aims were directed at the acquisition of attitudes rather than of techniques or "advantages." The object lesson was a favorite vehicle for such instruction. A proverb, for example, is a generalization in reverse, as it were. Instead of drawing a general conclusion from a number of specific observations, the proverb disguises the general principle as a concrete event. "Birds of a feather flock together" refers not to animal behavior but to the fact that people of like habits, interests, and values tend to form bonds. A parable or a fable is a story constructed on the same principle as the proverb.

We tend to dismiss this method of teaching as primitive and the knowledge so imparted as unreliable. Let us, however, venture to look at a real scientific experiment from the "object lesson" point of view. Certain caterpillars progress in "follow the leader" fashion. One caterpillar assumes the role of the leader and is presumably guided by his receptors to where the caterpillars are supposed to go. The others form a chain so that several of them become in fact a very long caterpillar with the head of the leader serving as the head of the synthesized beast. If now the chain is closed, the resulting ring has no leader. Rings of this sort have been observed to march around the rim of a bowl filled with leaves on which these caterpillars feed. The caterpillars may keep marching for days without breaking the chain to descend into the bowl, until they die of exhaustion.

Now this piece of information constitutes a portion of knowledge. To what use can we put it? Would it be feasible to harness the power generated by the moving caterpillars? Can we use this method to exterminate caterpillars? Joking aside, is nothing to be derived from this demonstration but a feeling that nature is at times bizarre? Or does the phenomenon evoke in us an uneasy recognition? Is the experiment not a parable? Do we not often observe the blind leading the blind? Do we not often assume that the leaders are guided by reality-testing while the rank and file are guided by leaders? And do not situations occur where the rank and file erroneously believe that a leadership exists, since everyone believes that someone else knows what he is doing?

Object lessons are supposed to guide the formation of attitudes. We clearly recognize that the formation of attitudes is an important goal of education. Aside from some extremely vague attempts at "character building" and religious instruction, backed by myths, we have hardly anything in our formal educational system aimed consciously and squarely at inculcation of attitudes. Science in particular is taught for the most part as a collection of "objectively verifiable facts" and at best as a method of relating facts and theories. Deriving object lessons from science is deemed old fashioned.

But are there indeed no object lessons to be derived from scientific discovery? Did the heliocentric theory, then, tell us nothing about how awfully mistaken we were in supposing that the clod of dirt we live on was the center of the universe? Did not the theory of evolution throw a shadow of doubt on our presumed exalted position in the living world? And do not the current findings of the biophysicists suggest that the cockroach with his magnificent toleration of high radiation doses may be a "higher" level of life than we with our hypertrophied brain?

The constantly heard complaint is that science, having endowed man with awesome power to mold and control nature, did not endow him with power to control himself. This platitude has been uttered in a pretense of humility so many times that we overlook its shallowness and its anthropomorphism. Science is not a fairy godmother and has not "endowed" man with anything; nor has science withheld anything from man. Science is a certain type of social activity in which a portion of mankind engages and which organized societies encourage within certain limits. Depending on how this activity is motivated, men with different interests will engage in it and will guide its direction.

There was a time when scientific activity was devoid of utilitarian motives. Whatever practical needs may have given the impetus to a systematic study of geometry (as is evidenced by its name), there is little reason to believe that the Greeks, in constructing the stately deductive system which *they* called "geometry," were guided by any practical aims. Neither Pythagoras nor Plato, nor Euclid, nor Appolonius were land surveyors; nor were they employed by surveyors, nor, as far as we know, did they teach any.

The purely intellectual content given to science by the Greeks worked both ways: It stimulated creative intellectual power in the "scientists" and also limited severely the scope of science for want of application, i.e., interaction of thought with concrete experience.

All this was changed in the Renaissance, when the link between thought and active impact on the environment was established. Leonardo Da Vinci may well serve as the patron saint of science as we have come to know it. Still, the impact of science on Western man's way of thinking in those first exciting centuries was at least as great as its power-endowing potential. The Renaissance is justly associated with humanism, and Michelangelo symbolizes that age as well as Da Vinci. Much of Renaissance technology was still largely on paper. Da Vinci, the prophet of modern technology, did not make flying machines. He just drew them and asserted that they were possible. In other words, Da Vinci did not have an "answer"; he had only an insight, namely, that man could set about doing things for himself instead of waiting for Judgment Day. In a way, this insight was not so different from Michelangelo's, whose message must be seen to be received. For example, you must see how Michelangelo depicted the human figure (e.g., Adam coming to life) in order to realize what the artist thought of man and of his mission on earth.

By and by the dreams of technology became realities, and more and more answers were required. The insight of the Renaissance, the idea of man for himself, became the prevalent attitude and no longer needed to be reiterated in inspired forms. The *implementation* of the idea became the order of the day. Science branched off from art and philosophy and went its own way, developing its own epistemology en route. In this epistemology little room was left for insights, because only what was publicly demonstrable (not internally revealed) was admitted as "true." To be sure, the criteria of demonstration departed radically from simple-minded seeing-is-believing tests. Intricate deductive reasoning became incorporated into scientific demonstrations; so the chains leading from that which was presented directly to the senses as evidence to that which was inferred as an underlying model of reality became long and involved. But it came to be demanded of every scientific demonstration that the chain, however, long, should be unbroken. Every link in the chain had to be justified by a legitimate step of induction or deduction. In short, a subjective feeling that something was true ceased to count for anything whatsoever as a criterion of what was accepted as scientific truth.

There were good reasons for excluding subjective components from the pursuit of truth by scientific method. For science as a way of pursuing truth emerged as an antithesis to the primitive view of the world which was thoroughly profused with desires, hopes, fears, and anthropomorphic interpretations of natural phenomena. In fact, science as we know it began as a separation in men's minds of what is from what ought to be, of the objective from the subjective world views.

The ideal of objectivity pervades science to the present day. The criterion of objectivity is most effective as a defense against the wishful thinker, the charlatan, the bigot, the dogmatist, and the deluded sentimentalist. The defense has served scientists well in their struggle against traditional views. As men became more aware and more interested in the material world about them, appeals to the evidence of the senses could challenge entrenched authority. As the world became more understandable, it became less frightening. Curiosity overcame fear in one area after the other.

It is this view that permitted science to be geared to technology. Having discovered the laws of electromagnetic dynamics, men were able to harness various sources of energy to do useful work. Having discovered sources of disease, men could make hygienic arrangements to diminish its incidence. Also having discovered how to harness power, men could inflict damage on each other.

Military research is, of course, largely directed toward these latter ends. Most of it is concerned with designing physical apparatus of ever greater destructive power (hardware research). An increasingly important sector, however, is concerned also with the design of effective *strategies* of destruction and of threat. To the extent that these strategies serve to coordinate the use of weapons systems, they are merely supplementary to hardware research. There is, however, a gradation ranging from purely military strategy to diplo-military strategy which is concerned with maneuvers and "postures." A proper sequence of timing of these postures is supposed to confer an advantage on the poseur. At times it is maintained that the purpose of diplo-military strategy is to achieve certain objectives without war, or to postpone war as long as possible; or else to improve one's position at the outbreak of war. At times it is even declared that the objective of diplo-military strategy is to make war altogether impossible.

In fact, strategic thinkers have proposed the idea that peace research ought to be an extension of their own activities. Since their own methods are "hardheaded" (or are depicted as such), the strategists claim that they could make peace research also hardheaded.

WHAT CAN WE EXPECT FROM PEACE RESEARCH?

Now what could the products of "strategic" peace research be? Conceivably they might be hardware, for example, weapons so much more terrible than those already stacked that war would *really* become unthinkable. Research directed toward the discovery of such devices would, of course, be identical with military research. Because of its avowed purpose, however, it could be labeled "peace research." Although the switch of labels could serve to allay somewhat any pangs of conscience which may be troubling some of the people presently involved in weapons research, it hardly serves the purpose of delineating an area which could justifiably be called peace research in contradistinction to war research. The same applies to the design of diplo-military strategies "calculated" to prevent an outbreak of hostilities but aimed primarily at enhancing the intimidating potential of either of the power blocs. "Deterrence" sounds better than intimidation and, in fact, *assuming rationality of both sides*, a weapons system and a diplo-military strategy can be made to appear to be designed for deterrence only. Therefore, research aimed at the creation of stable and effective deterrence can, with somewhat greater justification than pure weapons development, be called "peace research."

There are, however, two reservations with regard to the relevance of deterrence to peace. First, the reliability of a particular deterrent system can be established only in terms of determining the *tested range* of its reliability. For example, when we step into an elevator, we are reassured by a sign on the wall which asserts that the elevator has a capacity of twenty-eight persons or six thousand pounds. Backing up this statement are the tests to which the cables have been put. All loads smaller than the experimentally determined critical load, are "safe." The maximum allowed load, being only a fraction of the critical load, can, in view of the reliability of physical laws, be considered safe beyond all reasonable doubt.

If deterrence is to be realistically considered as a war-preventative, and if hardheaded criteria of the sort demanded of peace research are to be applied, then something like a measure of the "load" or "stress" has to be developed in the context of international tensions in order to determine the "safe" limits of a deterrence system. But even if such measures are proposed, who would care to put a deterrence system to a test? On second thought, some people might; but then it would take quite a stretch of imagination to subsume such an experiment under "peace research."

Second, the assumption of rationality is an exceedingly strong one. The examination of this assumption brings up all the questions we have raised in Part I. We have seen that there is no satisfactory unambiguous definition of rationality in conflict situations outside the context of the two-person zero-sum game, unless norms are invoked which are beyond the conceptual scope of strategic thinking. And even in the context of decisions within the scope of strategic analysis, normative theory is powerless, as we have seen, unless the utilities of the decision-makers are precisely known.

It follows inexorably that any research which can seriously claim to be directed toward the prevention of war or especially toward the establishment of peace must be *essentially* concerned with psychological matters, with man, his motivations, and his social behavior.

Now the "actors" in the situations which fall within the strategists' field of scrutiny are not men. They are by definition "players," motivated by payoffs. The content of these payoffs is either not mentioned at all or is assumed as self-evident. For example, in the context of "international relations" the players are usually taken to be nations or nation blocs, and their "interests" are assumed as given. Next to no attention is paid to the *non-political* or *non-military* genesis of these interests. When the possible importance of such non-political or non-military determinants (for example, psychological or cultural-historical ones) is pointed out, the strategists may actually concede that certain types of psychological, historical, or sociological knowledge are relevant to the problems with which they are concerned. But the sort of knowledge they seek is the sort that can be plugged into their own systems. It is not difficult to "sell" psychology in the context of military research, as an adjunct to the development of man-machine systems, since the reaction characteristics of a man who serves as a component in such a system must be known. At times anthropologists are called upon to provide information about attitudes of non-Western people who live in strategic areas, in order that Cold War intrigues may be more effectively pursued. "Kremlinologists" profess to have knowledge about evaluative habits, predilections, and compulsions of Soviet leaders. Research directed toward obtaining knowledge of this sort is called "software" research. It is becoming a modest but respectable sector of the strategic research effort.

As has just been said, respectability is conferred on research of this sort by its potential applicability to strategy, that is, to a design of maneuvers calculated to modify or control the "political environment" of a state. Largely excluded from the range of respectability is the sort of knowledge which results in *altered perceptions* rather than increased power of those who gain it. This is the sort of knowledge that leads to insights rather than answers. Because insight knowledge has no legitimate place within contemporary scientific epistemology, it can easily be dismissed as vague, unsupported by evidence, etc.

In a recent meeting sponsored by the American Orthopsychiatric Association, there was an encounter between Arthur I. Waskow and Adam Yarmolinsky.[64] The subject under discussion was the problem of civil defense, but the real issue quickly became the role of the social scientist in the formulation of policy.

Taking exception to certain passages in Waskow's book (127), Yarmolinsky said, among other things:

I can't imagine, and the report does not tell us on what basis "available social science knowledge" teaches us that to "almost all the people" civil defense and disarmament are "dissonant." Do "almost all the people" drive recklessly because they are insured? Or if they have seat belts? Do "almost all the people" oppose American support for the UN or the Peace Corps because we are also at the same time putting emphasis on military defense? The report does not tell us the "available social science knowledge" on which this peculiar view is based. Quite the contrary, it goes on to assert that "even the small group of disarmament enthusiasts might wane and weaken under the impact of the physical existence of shelters." In other words, this "dissonance" is so compelling that even those sophisticated enough to be actively concerned about the arms race might be swept up by it. Can such assertions, lacking even detailed argument, never mind any pretense of evidence, be seriously called "scientific." Yet that is the kind of thing we are presented with in the name of "available social science knowledge and research data."

What I am complaining about is a basic abandonment of a rational attitude toward a world that is not terribly rational. . . . Social scientists particularly have to deal in situations in which any sensible person would throw up his hands and go home. We can't afford to throw up our hands and go home—because there isn't any place to go. We have to face up to the problem of civil defense, we have to face up to the problems of arms control and disarmament. We have to build weapons which are fearful even to think about while we negotiate with people whom we really do not understand about issues which involve the continuation of the world as we know it.

This is a terribly difficult business and it is getting more difficult all the time, and it makes the behavioral scientists more important all the time. The only plea I'm going to make to you is that if you are going to perform the function to which you dedicate yourselves, you've got to be rigorous in your thinking.

"We want answers, not insights," Yarmolinsky seems to be saying. Contrast this with Jerome Wiesner's[65] remark:

"Some problems are just too complicated for rational logical solutions. They admit of insights, not answers" (68).

INSIGHT KNOWLEDGE

Insight knowledge does not immediately and appreciably add to the knower's ability to change the environment. Rather, it produces changes within the knower. These changes may be very profound, as, for example, in perceptions and attitudes concomitant to maturation or in the growing identification with others or in the process of socialization. There is no doubt that changes of this sort do occur in individuals and even in entire nations. In view of the absence of universally acceptable "objective measures" of such changes, they are not demonstrable to any one who does not care to see them. Yet we all know that they occur and we know we are deceiving ourselves when we declare discussions of such matters "meaningless," simply because they do not satisfy the criteria of scientific rigor.

Moreover, it seems fairly evident that just such elusive factors are among the decisive determinants of war and peace at the present time. The truth of the matter is that we do not know how and why nations become or cease to be "aggressive." We do not know how the actions and wills of millions of people are welded into a war machine. Our understanding of this phenomenon is dulled by its very familiarity. Historians, strategists, and experts on international relations contribute to this sorry state of affairs by presenting the international power game as "reality."

"But this *is* the reality of international relations," might be the rejoinder. To some extent it is, but it is, of course, not the whole reality. The relations between the United States and Canada, between Denmark and Norway, between Switzerland and Italy are of a different sort than those between the United States and the Soviet Union. There is very little likelihood that a Danish espionage ring operates in Norway or that the Italian general staff has worked out several alternative plans of defense againt a possible Swiss invasion.

If mutual suspicion and continual squeeze play are assumed to be normal relations between states, then the absence of these symptoms has to be somehow explained away. This is usually done with great ease, for example, by attributing the existing cordial relations between states to the absence of vital incompatible "conflicts of interests" between them. But this explanation begs the question, for among the listed "interests" of a nation is quite frequently security from attack by another nation or a strategic advantage over it, and these are "interests" only if the other nation is perceived as an enemy.

We know next to nothing about the really important aspects of human behavior, individually, institutionally, and en masse. So much will be admitted by the strategists. However, their responses to this recognition of ignorance are grossly inadequate. To most of them, this ignorance makes no difference since there is no place in their scheme where knowledge about human behavior would help. As we have said, their actors are players, not people. These strategists simply cannot be bothered.

There is, to be sure, another (minority) class of strategists who would appreciate the closing of the "behavioral science gap." These people would like the psychologists and social scientists to get busy and dig out the answers so that the strategists can make their calculations with more confidence. They realize that a nuclear attack on the United States may have other effects than a reduction of population and of productive capacity and a disruption of communications. These more enlightened strategists are understandably uneasy about calculations which show on the basis of known rates of industrial development that with the remaining population and the remaining productive capacity the *status quo* can be restored in so many man-years (58 pp. 84–95). Possibly, through their contacts with the military, who have seen combat, they have a nodding acquaintance with "morale." Consequently, they would welcome an assist from psychologists and social scientists on how to "figure morale in."

What the strategists of both classes have generally no use for at all are analyses and prognoses that are not supported by the kind of data or the kind of arguments with which they are familiar. Specifically, they are likely to dismiss summarily the arguments of thinkers such as Erich Fromm, Erik Erikson, Bruno Bettelheim, Paul Tillich, George Santayana, C. Wright Mills, Jean-Paul Sartre. These men, in their estimation, neither marshal evidence in support of their views nor provide any usable "answers." Instead of reasoning, they preach.

It goes without saying that works of fiction seem to the strategists even less relevant to the problems of global conflict. We are not likely to find either Swift's *Gulliver's Travels* or Golding's *Lord of the Flies* on the strategists' reading lists as contributions to the understanding of the present global conflict. Perhaps it is too much to expect those specialists to concern themselves with questions about man's nature and fate. But perhaps it is not too much to demand that those who design strategies to protect our freedoms understand *what it means* to subvert freedom; that is, to understand both the nature of freedom and the nature of totalitarianism.

Totalitarianism, for example, is not to be understood in terms of the changes in the formalities of the social decision process, e.g., the replacement of parliamentary procedures by a dictatorship. The professional life of a symphony orchestra is also run by an absolute dictator, but this does not make it a totalitarian system. Nor were all autocracies, e.g., czarist Russia, necessarily examples of totalitarianism. To understand totalitarianism (distinctly a twentieth century phenomenon) one does not examine the number of political parties, nor the mechanism of elections, not even the restrictions of expression and the brutalities of the police. All these features were present at one time or another in practically all regimes. How then does one come to understand the nature of totalitarianism? One might gain such an understanding from the proceedings of the trial of Adolph Eichman or from the books of Hannah Arendt (1, 2), or from the discussion of her views by Bruno Bettelheim (8).

It is impossible to spell out just what this understanding consists of. When one has understood, one knows that one has understood. This may sound like a reference to religious experience; but it is a mistake to dismiss all such references as belonging to strictly non-discursive or mystical modes of speech and therefore irrelevant to rational discussion. Some of our most common experiences cannot be communicated without an appeal to *inner* experience. For instance, it is impossible to describe verbally an olfactory experience in an effective way. The only way to get someone to know what a skunk smells like is to tell him "That's it" when he is smelling it. From then on, he will know what skunks smell like, and you will know that he knows, and both of you will "know" that each has "the same sensation" when he smells a skunk, even though there is no way to prove it except by inferences from principles which already assume what is to be proved.

The understanding of art and of ethical imperatives is of this sort. This is not to say that there is no "objective" basis for art appreciation, any more than it is to deny the objective basis of olfactory experience. The "smell of a skunk" is the impact of certain, in principle, exactly specifiable molecules on chemo-receptors and the resulting chain of also, in principle, specifiable neural events. And so it is with the "voice of conscience." But we need not pretend that we do not know what a skunk smells like or what feelings are evoked by a statue of Michelangelo or what compassion or remorse feel like just because we cannot describe the associated "objective" events. We can communicate about these matters *directly*; and this ability to communicate about them without knowing their minute structure is as much a distinguishing mark of humanity as the power of analysis.

The acquisition of insight is an expansion of one's ability to encompass situations directly, bypassing analysis. Concomitant to an insight is an increase in receptivity to certain stimuli, external and internal. To gain insight into the nature of a problem is not necessarily to solve the problem (the solution is the "answer"). With insight one is led to ask the right *questions* about the problem. These questions may lead to an answer, but they may also lead to a new insight, for example, that the problem is unsolvable as posed and must be reformulated.

Now if the insight-inducing potential of peace research is discounted, if "answers" are demanded, it is difficult to say how such research could be of practical value. The greatest obstacle to "objective" peace research is the absence of opportunities for experimental verification of proposed theories. Some such opportunities could, to be sure, be created, one would think, if only governments were willing to make experimental moves. But even if this were feasible, the results of such "experiments" would be anything but conclusive from the "scientific" point of view. In the pervading atmosphere of strategic thinking, the probings of one side would be likely to be interpreted by the other side as "moves," i.e., as the same old plays in the Game. Under these conditions the probings would not constitute "changes of political environment" whose results could be objectively ascertained, but rather events in the *same* environment and so worthless for comparing environments. On the other hand, some probings might conceivably change the environment for the better. But the results, though possibly highly desirable from the point of view of outlooks for peace, would be no more conclusive than negative results. To pin down the results, one would have to "replicate the experiment," that is, go back to the old conditions and try again. However, it may not be possible to go back to the old conditions. Physical conditions are frequently restorable; political and psychological conditions are typically non-restorable (the processes are irreversible, as the physicist says). *Status quo* is a fiction invented by eighteenth century diplomats.

In some quarters, hopes are pinned on the historical method as a substitute for the experimental method in international relations. One could make a thorough study of *cases* and attempt to derive from their analysis important factors conducive to war or to peace. Examples of such studies are found in the work of Quincy Wright (131) and of Lewis F. Richardson (97). Richardson's work, dormant for many years, has recently received considerable attention and is being continued by several investigators (28, 29, 56, 111, 112, 128).

The direct value of this work in providing "answers" on how to cope with the danger of war is also an unknown quantity for want of experimental procedures. For all we can get from historical research is hypotheses based on analogies. We do not know whether the "laws" so discovered (if they should be discovered) are valid in our environment, so radically different sociologically, psychologically, economically, and technologically from the environment in which war was a normal instrument for pursuing "national interests." And even if the knowledge so gained were valid, the problem of applying it still looms, especially if promising preventive measures turn out to be at odds with existing diplo-military policies.

Finally, the laboratory approach (psychological experiments, simulations, etc.) should be least expected to yield "answers." Here the analogy between the simulated situation and real life is even more far fetched than historical analogies. On the other hand, if the results are taken simply as hypotheses to be tested, the problem of verification again presents itself.

The situation is seen in an entirely different light if peace research is evaluated for its insight-inducing potential. Experimental probings on the level of actual international relations are viewed from this standpoint not as trial balloons "to see what happens" but as actions which *in themselves* can induce a reorientation in thinking about international relations, that is, actions which bring about changes in the political climate. The same potential resides in thorough historical research and in laboratory experiments.

Note that the sacrosanct objectivity of the scientific mode of thought must be modified in this context. Attitudes are a vital ingredient in this sort of research. Research conducted with one set of attitudes may yield nothing but inconclusive hypotheses. Undertaken with another set of attitudes and expectations, research with the same content may induce fundamental changes in the way of thinking of the researcher. Here the magnitude of the research effort becomes important, not in the sense of getting a lot of "answers" from a "crash program" but rather in the sense of the impact that research *as a social activity* can have on the society which supports it.

If we start asking different questions, we may become different people. This in itself might induce profound and salutary results.

CHAPTER 16

IS A DIALOGUE POSSIBLE?

By a dialogue I mean a verbal interchange in which positive as well as negative responses of the participating parties occur. This definition would exclude the exchanges of diatribes and invectives which characterize so much of political discourse (national and international). The definition also excludes many instances of formal debate, such as take place in courtrooms, legislative chambers, and forums. Although these encounters are aften kept within bounds of politeness by certain rules of decorum, they nevertheless seldom amount to more than exchanges of verbal blows. At best, they consist of statements of opposing points of view "in parallel" as it were. The participants actually address their remarks not to each other, not even at each other (although at times they seem to do so) but rather past each other to third parties—the audience, the electorate, the jury, etc. In other words, the participants do not seriously try to change the views of their *opponents*. They merely compete for attention and for the sympathy of the bystanders.

In a dialogue the efforts of the participants are actually directed toward changing or at least modifying the opponent's point of view. Accordingly, if a participant in a dialogue is seriously concerned with this aim, he will be concerned with appropriately effective techniques. It may turn out that the usual forensic techniques, while effective in scoring points, influencing juries, "public," etc., are useless for the purpose of the dialogue itself, namely, for effecting a shift in the thinking of the opponent.

In an earlier book (92) I listed what I believe to be the essential features of a dialogue (ethical debate), namely:

1. The ability and willingness of each participant to state the position of the opponent to the opponent's satisfaction (exchange of roles)

2. The ability and willingness of each participant to state the conditions under which the opponent's position is valid or has merit (recognition that any position whatever has *some* region of validity)

3. The ability and willingness of each opponent to assume that in many respects the opponent is like himself; that is to say, that a common ground exists where the opponents share common values, and each is aware of this common ground and, perhaps, of the circumstances which have led the opponent to the position he holds (empathy)

The question I am now raising is whether a dialogue is possible in the United States on the basic issues related to international relations. The question is important to us Americans because we have always taken pride in living in an "open society," i.e., one characterized by earnest exchanges of views between unintimidated people.

It should be noted that I am not asking whether the critics of the present mode of foreign policy have a voice. They have. A voluminous "peace literature" freely produced and distributed attests to it. Nor am I asking to what extent this voice is heard or is listened to. I am asking whether a fruitful exchange is possible between groups committed to practically incompatible approaches to problems of war and eace.

WHO ARE THE STRATEGISTS?

The ills plaguing the world have frequently been blamed on identifiable groups of people, nations, minority groups, adherents of assorted creeds, professions, etc. In my references to "the strategists," I may have given the impression that I have singled out a group of people who are exerting a pernicious influence on United States foreign policy. My intent, however, was to examine a way of thinking, not a group of people.

When I say "strategist," I mean someone who at the moment conceives international problems in strategic terms. At other times, he may think about the same problems in other terms, and so the same person may at times be a "strategist" and at other times may not. Therefore, the fact that strategists are "like everybody else," i.e., share their psychological make-up with a broad spectrum of the population, are motivated or constrained by the same impulses and norms —this fact is irrelevant in the matter of identifying "the strategists." The strategists constitute not a sector of the population but a sector of social roles. They are strategists when they are playing out their roles, i.e., when they are thinking strategically.

Another misunderstanding which should be forestalled lurks in the temptation to link the strategists with certain political views. There are people in the United States who nurture deep hatreds against the Enemy. Such hatreds lead those people to advocate courses of action which can hardly be supported by "rational" considerations, however rationality is defined. These people call for immediate cessation of negotiations with the Enemy, a declaration that a state of war already exists, and similar histrionics. There are few, if any, strategists, among the "total victory" enthusiasts or among compulsive flag wavers. Indeed, many strategists express considerable contempt for these gentry.

THE ABSTRACTIONISTS

I believe there are two types of strategists in the United States. One type I shall call the abstractionists. The abstractionists have at times been called the "cool young men." Their habitat is the research factories which service the armed forces. Their mode of thought is largely apolitical. That is to say, in formulating strategic problems, the abstractionist would feel quite comfortable if the players were relabeled. In fact, he is used to labeling them "A" and "B" in the first place. It is among the abstractionists that the impact of game-theoretical formulations is most strongly felt, and it is to them that the motto is addressed which is said to adorn an office at the Rand Corporation: "Don't think—compute!"

The abstractionists' contribution to the present conduct of international conflict is largely in the fields of operations research and logistics. Military problems, given certain norms, have "optimal" answers. For example, on the basis of known effects of nuclear blasts and thermal effects, calculations can be made concerning the number of bombers which are able to wreak a given level of destruction. On the basis of attrition rates which can be reasonably expected, assuming a certain effectiveness of the enemy's defenses, one can calculate the number of bombers which should be sent in order for the required number to get through. In replacing bombers by missiles, one calculates what one is exchanging for what: to what extent the heavier development effort is compensated by cheaper production, to what extent the "capabilities" derived from missiles will be matched by the opponent's efforts, etc., etc. (122).

On the defense side, one must know what to expect from ground-to-air defenses and air-to-air defenses against bombers; what one can hope for in the way of antimissile missiles and, if one really wants to think ahead, in the way of anti-antimissile missiles. One must know how much concrete can withstand how must blast pressure and how much heat, and one must translate this knowledge into designs of "hardened" missile sites, or "shelters" for civilians. These are clearly the same old problems of war "economics." Only the content has changed. Where one hundred years ago it was necessary to think about how much hay a calvary regiment would require, fifty years ago about how many railroad cars (40 *hommes*—8 *chevaux*) were optimal for an echelon, twenty-five years ago about the fire power of a Sherman tank, one has now graduated to the mathematics of missile guidance and overkill factors. The technical knowledge required for the really advanced problems of this sort is enormous. Specialization is, of course, mandatory, and the joints between the specialities must also be welded, which requires still another class of "integrating specialities."

Into this picture, the game-theoretical orientation fits most naturally. For the logistic efforts of one side are, of course, opposed at all times by corresponding efforts of the enemy. No doubt this feature has always been present in strategic formulation. But game theory seems to have given the formulations of logistic problems a new, exciting luster and a rigor comparable to that conferred by advanced methods of mathematics upon the physical sciences.

Game-theoretical models are not confined to military tactics and strategy. As an example consider the following situation. Assume that an agreement has been concluded between Country A and Country B on some method of arms control or a disarmament procedure or, perhaps, on a ban against testing nuclear weapons. Suppose the agreement provides for a maximum number of inspections per year by either party on the territory of the other. The timing and the places of inspections are to be at the discretion of the inspecting party. Here is an opportunity to formulate a genuine two-person game involving mixed strategies. For clearly, secrecy about when and where an inpection is to be made is of central importance if (1) the inspected party is to be discouraged from attempting evasions and (2) if the chances for discovering evasions are to be maximized. Accordingly, a game can be formulated between two parties, one called Inspectors, the other Evaders. The payoffs accruing to the Inspectors are of two kinds, namely: (1) negative payoffs associated with the extent of undiscovered violations perpetrated by the Evaders and (2) positive payoffs associated with the number of violations discovered. For the Evaders, naturally, these payoffs have the opposite sign: It is in their interest to get away with as many violations as possible.

The game calls for mixed strategies. For example, if a violation is the possession of mobile missile-firing installations, the idea is to keep moving them around to minimize the chances of their being discovered. (If the missile launchers stay in one place, then the Inspectors, having failed to find a launcher at one site, can safely choose a different site on their next inspection and eventually close in on their prize.) The Inspectors, on the other hand, must also randomize their inspections geographically and possibly in time so as to minimize the number of launchers which the Evaders can hope to get away with and/or to maximize their chances of discovering one.

The theory of the two-person zero-sum game states that there exists an optimum strategy for the Evaders, namely, a maximum number of illegal missile launchers (or nuclear test explosions or whatever) and a certain randomization pattern in space and, perhaps, in time. Also for the Inspectors there is an "optimal" mixed strategy of randomized inspections.[66]

The challenge offered by problems of this sort is formidable and understandably intriguing to the specialist. There is practically no limit to the complexities that can be introduced. For instance, in the case of mobile missile launchers, not all locations may be equally valuable as launching sites. Therefore, the payoffs necessary to the Evaders involve the number of undetected launchers weighted by the frequencies with which they can be placed in the tactically preferable locations. If the relative "values" of the locations are also known to the Inspectors, they must weight their inspections accordingly with frequencies.

One cannot hope to solve the problem in all of its complexity at once, but as in the case of any mathematicized science, one can begin with some drastically simplified models and work one's way up to more and more realistic ones. In doing so, one follows the tested methods of applied mathematics: One brings to bear the greatest intellectual prowess on man's most excellent mode of thought—problem solving. In this mode, it is irrelevant to ask who are the Evaders and who the Inspectors and why the ones are so anxious to cheat and the others to catch them at cheating. In fact, the "solution" of the game reveals an optimal strategy *both* to the ones and to the others. The services of the same mathematician are available to both sides (as once were the services of the Prussian military specialists). There is even no point to keeping research of this sort classified; for the same solution can be obtained independently by the other side.

In short, the abstractionist works in a context devoid of content. It is in this sense that the abstractionist is characteristically apolitical.

THE NEO-TRADITIONALISTS

Strategists of another type, whom I shall call the neo-traditionalists, think in somewhat more political terms. Unlike the abstractionists, who are likely to have received their training in mathematics or in the physical sciences, the neo-traditionalists are more likely to have a background in political science, occasionally in history or economics. To them the participants in the present conflict are not interchangeable players A and B, but specific nations, the great powers, their allies, and their satellites. The powers also play a game, but theirs is the real game of indentifiable "interests" instead of hypothetical parries, thrusts, and "nuclear exchanges." I call these writers neo-traditionalists because the most conspicuous feature of their mode

of thought is the revival of traditional views of international politics.
This trend is most clearly discernible in the writings of Henry A.
Kissinger. It is epitomized in a tribute to Clausewitz.

War, argued Clausewitz, can never be an act of pure violence because
it grows out of the existing relations of states, their level of civilization,
the nature of their alliances, and the objectives in dispute. War would
reach its ultimate form only if it became an end in itself, a condition
which is realized only among savages and probably not even among them.
For war to rage with absolute violence and without interruption until the
enemy is completely defenseless is to reduce an idea to absurdity (65,
p. 65).

This paraphrase of Clausewitz occurs in the context of attributing
Clausewitzian ideals to the Communists. In fact, the immediately
succeeding paragraph Kissinger quotes a Soviet military authority: "If
war is a continuation of politics, only by other means, so also peace
is a continuation of struggle, only by other means" (107). I came
across this statement after I started to write this book and was startled
with its striking similarity to my own opening sentence. However, as
the reader must have gathered by now, this book is a polemic *against*
the view that politics ought to be equated to a struggle for power,
while the views of Kissinger, as those of Shaposhnikov (the Soviet
strategist, whom he quotes) and of Clausewitz amount to an acceptance of the power-struggle definitions of both war and peace.

At this point some of the neo-traditionalists may well point out the
distinction between what ought to be and what is. There may be some
among them who will readily admit that the perpetual struggle among
the powers is not a desirable state of affairs. But they will insist that it
is an actual one, and that therefore a theory of international relations
ought to be predicated on this actuality. This is the traditional position of *realpolitik*. Later we shall inquire into the nature of the difference between the two senses of the word "accept," the sense of recognition and that of approval. For the present we shall confine ourselves
to the non-controversial meaning of "acceptance," with which the
strategists will readily agree. They accept (in the sense of recognizing
as real, perhaps as inevitable) the power struggle as a normal relation among sovereign states and see international political "reality"
rooted essentially in the issues of that struggle.

Why, then, one might ask, if the reality of the power struggle is axiomatic, and if the "rational" use of force is an obvious desideratum, is it necessary to reiterate this with so much emphasis, as is done in the writings of the neo-traditionalists?

The answer to this question is quite clear in the writings of Kissinger. Since World War I, we have been witnessing a *perversion* of the rational power principle, he says. War has ceased to be a tool by means of which rational participants in the power game pursue their "interests." A particularly vicious symptom of this degeneration of war as a rational pursuit, according to Kissinger, is found in American thought about war. There is a reason for this in our recent experience with war. He writes:

> The literalness of our notion of power made it impossible to conceive of an effective relationship between force and diplomacy. A war which started as a surprise attack on us had of necessity to be conducted in a fit of righteous indignation, and the proper strategy for waging it was one of maximum destructiveness. By the same token now that the risks of war had grown so fearsome, the task of diplomacy was to attempt to settle disputes by the process of negotiation, and this, in turn, was conceived as a legal process in which force played a small role, if any. The objective of war was conceived to be victory, that of diplomacy peace. Neither could reinforce the other, and each began where the other left off" (65. p. 29).

Observe what is being said. Diplomacy and war have become separated. They ought to be reintegrated. This is exactly what Clausewitz was saying in his famous dictum. His magnum opus *On War* was written shortly after the Napoleonic Wars. These wars had departed from the accustomed patterns of the eighteenth century. The objectives of pre-Napoleonic wars were not "total." No state sought to deprive another state of its sovereignty. A war was simply one way of conducting disputes. For example, if the crowned heads had an argument as to who should succeed to the throne of Spain, they sent their armies on marches. After some maneuvers and perhaps a pitched battle or two, the monarchs would have a family reunion (most of them were cousins) and settle the business. This was *not* Napoleon's way. He was not anybody's cousin, and he played for keeps. An upstart corporal wearing an emperor's crown had no use for the niceties of the European "system."

The system was restored (or was thought to have been restored) in 1815, and for a century Europe reverted to the old game called the balance of power. It is of this game that the neo-traditionalists write with sometimes undisguised nostalgia. The rules of the balance-of-power game are spelled out by Morton Kaplan (60, p. 23).

1. Act to increase capabilities but negotiate rather than fight.

2. Fight rather than pass up an opportunity to increase capabilities.

3. Stop fighting rather than eliminate an essential national actor.[67]

4. Act to oppose any coalitions or single actor which tends to assume a position of predominance with respect to the rest of the system.

5. Act to constrain actors who subscribe to supranational organizing principles.

6. Permit defeated or constrained essential national actors to re-enter the system as acceptable role partners or act to bring some previously inessential actor within the essential actor classification. Treat all essential actors as acceptable role partners.

The over-all objective of the balance-of-power game, then (the objective of all the players as distinguished from their individual objectives) was not the preservation of peace but the preservation of the system. The victor must make sure that the defeated participant is re-integrated into the system, so that he can fight another time; for, who knows, next time he may be an ally.

The strategists are seldom so naive as to believe that the European system can be restored in its entirety, and they note the features of our era which make this impossible.

First and foremost of these is the destructiveness of modern weapons. Nowadays, the decision to "fight" rather than allow this or that is a decision to stake "national survival" on the outcome. Indeed as even many of the strategists admit, a decision to employ all the existing technical capacity in a war may be tantamount to a decision to commit national suicide *regardless* of the outcome.

Second, specifically with regard to the United States, the all-or-none conception of war and peace is incompatible with the rules of the balance-of-power game. The United States has never been a member of the system. Consequently, the Clausewitzian conception of war as a rational pursuit of national interest has never been internalized in our way of thinking. We still harbor the illusion (or so it appears to the strategists) that war is a dirty business and that the goal of diplomacy is peace.

Finally, there have appeared on the scene other powers to be reckoned with who have no use for the "system," namely, the U.S.S.R. and China. Kissinger calls them revolutionary powers (analogous to France of 1794). Kaufmann calls them aggressive powers: "It has long been a basic assumption of American foreign policy that both the Soviet Union and Red China are aggressive powers, that they assign a very high priority to expansion in the hierarchy of their goals, and are likely to use any and all means, including violence to attain their ends" (61, p. 1).

In view of the acceptance of the power struggle principle by the neo-traditionalists, it seems strange that any power would be singled out as an "aggressive" power simply because it is likely to "use violence to attain its ends." What is meant here (it should be understood, in fairness to the author) is that there are no apparent limits to *how much* power the U.S.S.R. and China will try to attain. In other words, they will not, according to this view, play the game according to the rules set up by the old established members of the club.

What, then, is to be done? Time was when the United States Secretary of State could announce that any encroachment by the revolutionary powers on the status quo would be likely to be countered with a nuclear attack on their homelands. But this did not work. For one thing, "public opinion" is to be reckoned with in a democracy. Kaufmann writes:

> . . . a policy of deterrence will seem credible only to the extent that important segments of public opinion in domestic [sic] and allied countries support it. . . . This consideration suggests a rather crucial and specific requirement that a policy of deterrence must fulfill. Its potential costs must seem worth incurring. In other words, there must be some relationship between the value of the objective sought and the costs involved in its attainment. A policy of deterrence which does not fulfill this requirement is likely to result only in deterring the deterrer (62, p. 20).

The central idea in the writings of the neo-traditionalists is the Gilbertian notion that the punishment ought to fit the crime. The trouble with the doctine of massive retaliation is that the magnitude of the threat mitigates against our willingness to use it. A threat of massive retaliation which is not believed by the threatened party can have disastrous consequences for the would-be retaliator. For if the threat is not believed, the bluff can be called. And if the bluff is called, the fist-shaking party faces a choice between nasty alternatives—to unleash a nuclear war or to back down and so reduce the credibility of future threats. The massive retaliator appears, then, to be talking loudly and carrying a stick so big that he may not be able to lift it.

The prudent thing, according to the neo-traditionalist, is to have a range of both decibels and sticks at one's disposal and *to use* either or both as the situation warrants: small transgressions—small punishments; big transgressions—big punishments. And the important thing is to keep the *capability* of the biggest punishment which technology allows and also the determination to use it "if necessary."

This is the gist of the limited war theory, the neo-traditionalists' answer to the threat of mutual annihilation. To their credit, it must be stressed that both the "need" for the theory and its aim are spelled out in the clearest terms. The "need" arose from the bankruptcy of the massive retaliation doctrine. It was impractical to bomb Moscow every time a riot occurred in Caracas. The Communists, knowing this, could proceed to "nibble away at the edges of the Free World." The aim of the theory was to restore war to its rightful and honorable place in international affairs.

". . . the problem is this: How can the United States utilize its military power as a rational and effective instrument of national policy?" (87, p. ix).

If limited war was to become a rational and respectable substitute for total war, its strategic theory ought to occupy more of the strategists' attention; consequently, all-out war became a topic to be avoided, and so it is, in most of the writings of the neo-traditionalists.

Herman Kahn played the part of the *enfant terrible* when he broke through the tacit taboos and plunged into the "extended" theory, into the oh, so evermore exciting challenges and potentialities of thermo-nuclear war.

The neo-traditionalists had stopped at the edge, because it seemed to them that "the pursuit of national policy by thermo-nuclear war" was a contradiction in terms. Kahn's greatest achievement was to show, at least to his own satisfaction, that this was not necessarily the case, first, because there were untapped potentialities in the art of blackmail against the background of thermonuclear annihilation; second, because if nuclear war were to be fought after all, the strategist should not shirk his duty—he should work out (well in advance) the best way of fighting such a war if only to "prevail" (since "victory" in the accepted sense was difficult to define); third, because there was a public relations job to be done: What sort of impression do we make if we keep sniveling about the horrors of war?

Kahn became the loudest and clearest spokesman of the "cool young men."

WHO ARE THE OTHERS?

I have now identified the strategists and have presented their framework of thought. As the reader may have gathered from the title of this book, I juxtapose to the mode of thinking in which strategy is central another mode in which conscience is central. My task is now to describe this other mode and the camp to which people who think in it belong.

I do not know what to call those people, and I will not bother. The designing of strategies is a profession; an appeal to conscience is not. At least the professionalization of this activity tends to degrade it, as the history of organized religions has shown. Therefore, one cannot always recognize members of the conscience camp by what they do publicly. To be sure, many of them engage in agitation and in organization of community and political action, just as the strategists are frequently found among consultants to military agencies. But just as the way of thinking of the strategist is spread far beyond the circle of professionals, so the other way of thinking is not confined to the "professional" peace worker. It will be useful, therefore, to mention some other divisions of views which are correlated with the division between the strategic thinkers and the others, but do not quite coincide with it.

In the press, the dichotomy "warhawks vs. peace doves" was coined. This dichotomy implies commitments to war and to peace respectively and is not useful, since the coldest blooded of the cold warriors can protest his devotion to peace. One cannot challenge this protestation without questioning its sincerity, and this will not be done in this book.

Another dichotomy, proposed by Singer (110), is between the "armers" and the "disarmers." On this scale, positions are clearly discernible, and the distinction coincides more closely with the one we are concerned with. Also, the individuals who line up along the armers-disarmers axis line up pretty much the same way on the strategy-conscience axis. Yet the armers-disarmers division makes for a confrontation on matters of *policy,* not modes of thought. It is possible to arrive at a position favoring disarmament without leaving the strategic mode of reasoning. There are disarmers who write effectively on this issue entirely in the strategic mode.[68]

A dialogue on the level of a policy debate is certainly possible. Such a dialogue between, say, the armers and the disarmers might be fruitful if in its course the underlying assumptions made by both parties were brought out, provided some agreement could be reached at the outset about desirable goals. One such agreement appears plausible. Many of the armers are firmly convinced that their program is most likely to prevent the outbreak of a nuclear war (if not of "small" limited wars). Whatever the disarmers may feel about the feasibility or the morality of limited wars, most of them would agree that the prevention of nuclear war is a desirable goal under any circumstances. The two camps can thus agree on at least one goal. Since the disarmers are equally convinced that only disarmament can ultimately prevent nuclear war, the disagreement is seen to be about means. This sort of disagreement can be fruitfully discussed. It is, in fact, easy to take the next step, that is, to state the fundamental assumptions of both sides with regard to some proposed policy, say the policy of deterrence. The armers, it seems, believe:

1. That the capacity to destroy the opponent is *necessary* to prevent him from destroying you. (In other words, if it were not for our retaliatory capacity, we would have been destroyed by now);

2. That the capacity to destroy the opponent is *sufficient* to prevent him from destroying you. (In other words, deterrence is a workable safeguard).

Most disarmers deny both of these assumptions. The debate, therefore, is joined at the very base of the two positions.

If a debate crystallized around the choice of a policy (e.g., a "hard" versus a "soft" policy on a specific issue), the armers and the disarmers could also formulate their respective positions in terms of pos-sible outcomes, their estimated probabilities, and utilities assigned to them. They would then find that the disarmers assign greater proba-bilities and larger negative utilities to escalation and war; the armers, on the contrary, assign higher probabilities and greater utilities to the other side's backing down. In this sense both positions are seen to be based on "rational" considerations. Their differences are traceable to different subjective estimates and values which are unavoidable in decision problems.

It will thus be found that up *to a point* disagreements arising in the pursuit of strategic analysis can, in principle, be resolved, not in the sense of effecting agreements but in the "optical" sense of being re-solved into components, so that the analysis can proceed to the next stage. Ultimately, no further resolution will be possible, because the basic values will have been reached. Polite dialogue must stop at this point: One can only agree to disagree on subjective estimates of unique future events and on preferences. Beyond this point, attempts to continue the discussion in the same mode will either get nowhere or will explode into hostile exchanges.

But the dialogue could continue if the mode of discourse were changed. It could continue if one allowed introspection, insight, and conscience to guide the discussion. Therefore, whether a dialogue is possible beyond the point of the "irreducible" clash of values de-pends on whether the strategist is able and willing to talk in another language and to think in another mode.

What, then, is the way of thinking of those who are concerned primarily with conscience, and how does it differ from the strategic mode?

First, whereas the strategic thinker conceives of each choice of action primarily (perhaps exclusively) in terms of its effects on the environment, the conscience-driven thinker conceives actions pri-marily with regard to their effects on the actor.

Second, whereas the strategist can begin his work only when values (utilities) are given or assumed, the conscience-driven thinker con-siders the determination of these values to be the principal problem. He rejects the relativist notion that all values are matters of pref-erence like brands of cigarettes. To be sure, one cannot "prove" the superiority of one set of values over another if one confines one's self to methods of proof appropriate to other inquires. Nor can one prove by rational analysis that *King Lear* is a more profound work than *Tarzan of the Apes*. The conscience-driven thinker will not relinquish the problem of discerning human values simply because the problem does not yield to rational analysis; nor will he divorce any important sphere of human activity from this problem.

Third, while the strategist frequently recognizes the importance of self-fulfilling assumptions, their role is hardly ever actually taken into account in strategic analysis. The strategist assumes not only that the values are given but also that the "state of the world" at a given moment (including the values and the thinking processes of the enemy) is an objective fact to be ascertained. The critic of strategic thinking, on the contrary, while admitting that the state of the non-human environment may be considered as an "objective fact" at a given time, denies that values and predispositions are "objective facts." What they "are," in his way of thinking, is to a significant degree determined by what we think of them. Therefore in this area the aphorism of Henry Margenau is especially appropriate: "All of man's facts have become acts."

It is extremely difficult for one who subscribes to this orientation to join in a dialogue with a strategist, even with the best intentions. The basic question in the strategist's mind is this: "In a conflict how can I gain an advantage over him?" The critic cannot disregard the question, "If I gain an advantage over him, what sort of person will I become?" For example, he might ask what kind of a nation the United States might become if we succeeded in crushing all revolutions as easily as in Guatemala. With regard to deterrence, the critic might ask not "What if deterrence fails?" (everyone worries about *that*) but, on the contrary, "What if deterrence works?" Erich Fromm asks just this question: He inquires into the kind of *reality* behind the strategist's prescriptions of security:

. . . the biggest and most pervasive reality in any man's life if deterrence should 'work' is the poised missile, the humming data processor connected to it, the waiting radiation counters and seismographs, the overall technocratic perfection (overlying the nagging but impotent fear of its imperfection) of the mechanism of holocaust (46).

The critic is convinced of the corrupting effect of power, especially of unimpeded power. And this, for him, is not simply "something to think about" in off moments, but a fundamental insight. Moreover, he is convinced that this insight is not a symptom of softheadedness. It stems from looking at the facts of history, not ignoring them. If Stalin's Russia is to be used as an example of pure despotism (as the rationalizers of the Cold War frequently insist), it ought to be an object lesson on the results of power unimpeded by conscience. Moreover, conscience is silent when the wielders of power are convinced that it is being used to achieve good ends.

The neo-traditionalists' acceptance of international relations as a power game seems self-defeating to one who questions the value of power. Here the strategist will, of course, argue that his "acceptance" of the power game is not predicated on approval, that he merely takes the world "as it is." But the strategists' conclusions are not mere descriptions. They are frankly recommendations, predominantly recommendations to try to get more power in the power struggle, and so are predicated on the tacit assumption that power is a "pure good." The conscience-driven thinker challenges this assumption.

In my grandmother's time, body weight was considered a "pure good." I remember a passage from one of her letters written long ago from the Old Country. "Your aunt Rose, glory be, has added to her health (knock on wood). She has gained 16 kilograms since the birth of her baby and now tips the scales at 102." Similarly, financial standing is considered a "pure good" in our society, certainly as it applies to firms and often to individuals. Yet it seems as reasonable to question this assumption and even to deny it, as it is to question the assumption that health is reflected in obesity. With regard to power, we also have weighty reasons to question its value and to inquire into the mentality that considers the power game among nations as a normal, civilized state of affairs. For that is what Clausewitz implied when he said that only savages fight wars for the sake of fighting. We may forgive Clausewitz, writing before Victoria's accession, this cavalier distinction between civilization and savagery. But after what the descendants of Clausewitz brought about in Europe, it seems odd that this distinction is still made by the new traditionalists, who seek to restore respectability to war by making it "an instrument of policy."

In spite of occasional protestations on the part of strategists that their job is rational analysis, not value judgments, value judgments are unavoidably included in their analyses, because the end results of these analyses are policy recommendations. For example, some strategists pride themselves on having broken through the inhibitions which delayed a strategic analysis of thermonuclear war. In assuming the posture of staring this eventuality in the face, they liken themselves to the surgeon who does not permit himself to be swayed either by the horror of what he sees or even by empathy with the patient (for he needs detachment to cut human flesh.) This comparison may be valid if thermonuclear war is viewed as a disaster to be guarded against and coped with, if, in spite of precautions, it does occur. However, thermonuclear war is not a natural disaster. It is being carefully planned and prepared by the strategists themselves. It could not occur if the strategists of both sides did not put forward convincing arguments about the necessity of possessing "nuclear capabilities" and the "will to use them." In this context, the "detachment" of the strategist resembles not so much that of the surgeon as that of a butcher or still more that of all the other organizers of mass exterminations. Those technicians too were for the most part "detached" in the sense that their work was not charged with affect. German chemists were detached when they prepared the poison gas; German engineers were detached when they built the gas chambers; German transportation experts were detached and efficient as they kept the trains moving, carrying people to the slaughter sites; German bookkeepers were detached while keeping tallies of the despatched, etc. Doubtless many of those responsible for this activity took a certain pride in having overcome any inhibitions they might have had in this matter. They might have been sincerely convinced that the "Jewish question" was a problem to be solved in a detached and definitive manner, possibly for the good of humanity. In other words, the charge of depravity, sadism, etc., can be made convincingly only against certain isolated individuals. It cannot be made against the entire corps of specialists who planned, designed, and carried out the exterminations of the 1940's. These people did not go berserk. They were carrying out their duties methodically and systematically. They were "normally functioning" human beings.

Our strategists are also exactly like other people of their social class, education, and background. They enjoy the same sort of personal relations as the rest of us, appreciate the same gifts that life bestows, suffer from the same griefs and misfortunes. The monstrosity of their work carries little or no emotional meaning for them, not because they are mentally ill, but because they share with the rest of us or perhaps are more richly endowed than the rest of us with the most creative of human faculties, which becomes also the most dangerous one when coupled with a lack of extensional imagination—the faculty of abstraction.

To the mathematicians among them equations on the blackboard are just equations. Mathematics is a great leveler. When a problem is mathematically formulated, its *content* has disappeared and only the form has remained. To the strategists "targets" are indeed only circles on maps; overkill is a coefficient; nuclear capacity a concept akin to heat capacity or electric potential or the credit standing of a concern. The logic of abstract reasoning applies in the same way to all problems which are logically isomorphic.

The logician, the mathematician, the statistician, and the strategist all derive their competence (and so their social status) from an ability to handle abstract chains of reasoning detached from content. This, rather than freedom from preconceived notions and from the bias of vested interest, is the true meaning of their detachment.

If a dialogue is to take place between strategy and conscience, these are the things that must be said.

Given the etiquette of civilized discussion, especially in the English-speaking world, it is difficult to bring such matters up without eliciting accusations of foul play. The strategists accuse the moralists of prudery, of refusing to face certain facts of life. But the moralists can claim with equal, I would say with much greater, conviction that it is the strategists and their supporting hosts of bureaucrats who refuse to look facts in the face.

At a recent trial of a group of British pacifists (who engaged in a sit-down protest at Wethersfield Air Base on December 1, 1961), one of the defendants, acting as his own counsel, was cross-examining a government witness, an air force officer. The following is an excerpt from the cross-examination.

Q: So actually there is no order which you would not accept?

A: It is my duty to carry out any order that is given to me.

Q: Would you press the button that you know is going to annihilate millions of people?

A: If the circumstances demanded it, I would.

Q: Would you slit the throats of all the two-year-old children in this country, Air Commodore?

Mr. Justice Havers: I think you must stop all that (47).

This line of questioning was forbidden by the judge as irrelevant. But from the point of view of the defendants, the picture evoked by the questions was far more relevant to the issue tried (whether the war resisters acted against the interests of the United Kingdom) than are the concepts in which the military thinks. The military concepts of defense have only a "logical" relevance to the country's national interests. That is, they are connected to the conventional ideas of "national interest" by the force of our thinking habits, but by hardly anything else. On the other hand, the horrible deaths of a nation's two-year-olds has a *direct* relevance to the country's "national interest." These deaths are expected as *actual,* not merely logical, consequences of nuclear war. Nevertheless, the demand for "rational argument" is a demand that the moral aspect of genocide be dismissed as "irrelevant."

I heard this attitude stated quite frankly by an official of our Department of Defense, a man not only of superlative intelligence but also easy to talk to, in the sense that he listened carefully, got the central point of what was said, and replied directly to it.

"You keep worrying what is going to happen to the two-year-olds," he said, when I kept harping on the subject, following the example of the British defendant, "but what I want to know is who is going to get West Berlin, if we do what you propose."

And again, "No, I don't see them [the Communists] as fiends or criminals. To me the whole thing looks more like a basketball game between Pekin, Illinois, and Peoria, Illinois."

The moral issues are beyond the scope of military and political decisions. Moral convictions are private and so should not be injected into the formulation of public policy. But more effective than any explicit arguments against bringing in the moral issue is the functional deafness developed by the strategists to any discourse in other than strategic mode. Consequently, if someone wants to *reach* the strategists, to induce them to listen seriously, he must either gloss over the moral issues or lay them aside altogether. Someone with a facile knowledge of weaponry and logistics has an excellent chance of catching the strategist's ear. Someone moved by a passionate concern for human values but with no understanding of the intricate strategic issues and their highly proliferated ramifications may as well be speaking a dead language.

The emphasis by the critic of strategic thinking on the vital importance of the self-predictive assumption is, perhaps, the crucial stumbling block to the dialogue.[69] For the strategist's deeply internalized conviction is that he takes the world "as it is." To the critic, however, the world looks somewhat as it does to the wisest of the three umpires. The first umpire, who was a "realist" remarked, "Some is strikes and some is balls, and I calls them as they is." Another, with less faith in the infallibility of the profession, countered with, "Some is strikes and some is balls, and I calls them as I sees them." But the wisest umpire said, "Some is strikes and some is balls, but they ain't nothing till I calls them."

A value is not a fact. The act of choosing a value and the act of guessing the other's values are facts. It is, therefore, by no means a matter of indifference what values one puts into one's own matrix and what values one will assign to the payoffs of the other. The game one will play depends vitally (sometimes irrevocably) on the values one has put in. But in real life it is the way the game is played that reveals the values. How "objective," then, are the strategists' estimates if there is good reason to suppose that the strategists themselves have made the game what it is? In no laboratory would the results of observations be taken seriously if there was reason to suspect that the methods of observation had influenced the results. Nevertheless it is precisely in their claims to "scientific objectivity" that the defenders of strategic analysis are most vociferous when confronted with questions of value. On the basis of their "objectivity" they accuse of muddleheadedness and naiveté anyone who asks embarrassing questions about whether their games are worth playing, or whether one ought to identify with actors whose moral code resembles that of Louis XIV, Frederick the Great, and Catherine II at its best and that of Attila, Genghis Khan, and Hitler at its worst.

If dialogue becomes impossible on these matters, it is because neither side can really listen to the other. In most cases, such blocks to communication are unfortunate. The improvement of communication is one of the crucial problems of our time, and brave efforts go into this enterprise. Books are written and courses taught on this subject; innumerable techniques are proposed, ranging from forensics to semantics. I often wonder whether it is worthwhile to try to bridge the chasm between strategic and conscience-inspired thinking. It may be feasible and advisable to broaden the views of both management and labor: The industrial process must keep functioning, and both sides may stand to gain from increased mutual understanding. It is imperative to establish avenues of communication between Blacks and Whites and between East and West, because they all must either learn to live with each other or perish. In the case of strategy and conscience, I am not sure. Here, I believe, is essential incompatibility, not merely a result of misunderstanding. I do not believe one can bring both into focus. One cannot play chess if one becomes aware of the pieces as living souls and of the fact that the Whites and the Blacks have more in common with each other than with the players. Suddenly one loses all interest in who will be champion.

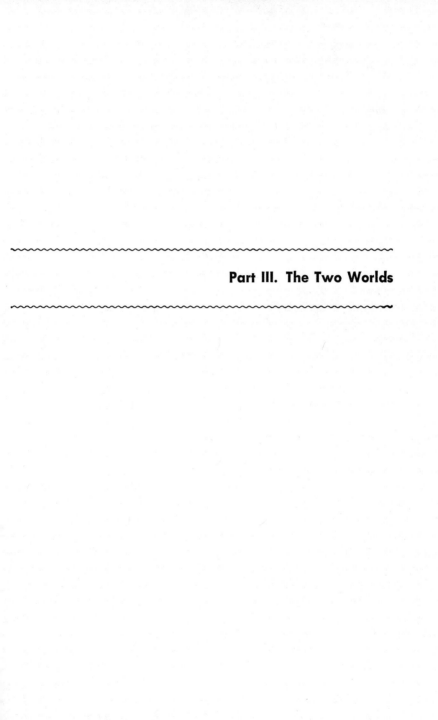

Part III. The Two Worlds

CHAPTER 17

INTRODUCTION

~~~~~~

We have attempted to show that the strategist's thinking is hemmed in by a compulsion to approach all stituations in the "problem-solving mood." There is nothing wrong in this approach per se. As a matter of fact, it characterizes the rational man and distinguishes him from the mental patient, the child, the neurotic, and the primitive. But when the compulsion to formulate "tractable" problems shuts out other modalities of thinking, the particular professional handicap of the strategist makes itself felt.

We have listed ways in which the pressure for simplification induces inadequate formulations of decision problems, the way in which preoccupation with the zero-sum-game paradigm masks the fundamental feature of the impasse between hostile armed blocs. Most of all, we suspect, it is the professional involvement of the strategists that blinds them to the enormity of the evil associated with being positively and "creatively" involved in a "game" in which the suffering and death of untold millions of innocent human beings are the payoffs. The evil is further aggravated by the exclusion of moral considerations from the stakes for which the Game is played. Our strategists, as a rule, do not preach about the "evils of communism." The extensional meaning of losing (or, for that matter, of winning) the Game concerns them hardly more than such matters concern the chess player. Just as the latter plays the Game and plays it well (i.e., ruthlessly) because he is a chess player, just as a businessman competes not necessarily because he is greedy but because he is a good businessman, so the strategists play out their gruesome scenarios because they are strategists.

But how about the rest of us who are professionally not so committed? I suggest that three factors are involved in our tacit acceptance
of the strategist as a member of a legitimate profession. One is tradition. The military have always been around; so they are still around,
in spite of the fact that their role today has little or no relation to
their historic role in the affairs of the nation. Strategy is a necessary
adjunct to military planning, and so the strategist's job is assumed to
be a part of "national defense" in spite of the fact that the term "defense" has lost all of its original meaning (to defend—to protect).
Another factor is ignorance or apathy. The vast majority of us simply
do not know or do not care about what is going on and what is being
prepared. (We can say it in words, but we do not envisage the extensional meaning of those words). Finally, many of those who do know
or care are seduced by the Devil image. Our strategists, as we have
already pointed out, do not need to see the adversary as the Devil.
Being specialists concerned with the intricacies of the Game, they
play it for its own sake. But the ordinary person, who is not an addict
of the Game, would be horrified by it if "to lose the game" did not
mean for him the worst possible outcome, worse than all the obscene
horrors of the nuclear holocaust. It appears, then, that the military
with its technical and intellectual cohorts retains its grip on the popular mind in somewhat the same way that the medieval church did,
namely, as a protector against the Devil.

Why do people cling to the Devil image?[70] Explanations have
been offered by drawing parallels with paranoid perceptions and reactions. But it is hard to believe that a vast majority of the populations of the two superstates are "paranoid." To claim that they are
because they cling to the Devil image is to beg the question. Ordinary
people give no evidence of paranoia in the business of everyday living.
Why should their attitudes about the large scale world be any more
accurate indications of their psychic states than their attitudes about
the small scale world? After all it is in the latter that the people actually live. It seems the "paranoid obsession" explanation must be
rejected as oversimplified.

We suspect that the people of both worlds cling to the conventional
Good versus Evil view of the conflict, because an attack on this view
is instinctively interpreted as an attack on the central core of one's

ethos. Such an attack must be repelled. Therefore whatever supports the conventional view (with which fundamental positive values are linked) is eagerly embraced.

We have, then, the following links in the chain which leads to the present impasse. The central core of one's ethos must be defended. It is most easily defended if it is seen as an absolute Good threatened by an absolute Evil. The Good-Evil dichotomy nourishes the Devil image. The Devil image justifies the model of current history as an apocalyptic struggle. This being the age of science, not only technology but also scientific modes of thought must be mobilized in the conduct of the struggle. Hence the hegemony of strategic thinking in international affairs and the impasse which results from exclusive reliance on it.

Where can this chain be broken? I believe the weakest link is that which connects the defense of the central core of one's ethos to the idea of the struggle between Good and Evil. In the last generation or two, the parochial bases of such conceptions have become apparent to ever more people, and in the age of vanishing distances and increasing contacts (despite restrictions) the trend is likely to continue. It is not necessary to assume a posture of complete ethical relativism in order to attack provincial views of good and evil. The problem is to broaden people's ethical outlooks without threatening (as ethical relativism usually does) the central cores of their ethos.

This problem I consider central to the task of breaking the spell which the exclusively strategic conception of national goals has cast upon us. If one feels secure in keeping the central core of one's own ethos, one can eventually gain the freedom to examine another central core. That other core may be profoundly different, but it need not on that account be incompatible with one's own. The Western world has already achieved such insights with respect to religion. Among deeply religious but enlightened people, the conviction that one's own religion is right need not be coupled with a conviction that someone else's religion is "wrong." Heresy may still be used as a technical term in some systems of theology, but certainly the word has lost all practical significance in enlightened religious life.

I believe that given a period of relative peace, the present passionate convictions about the rightness or wrongness of capitalism, communism, etc., will retain at most a ritualistic significance. People may still be living under arrangements which will still be called by these traditional names (as monarchies and republics are still distinguished in spite of the fact that the distinction has become an anachronism in many instances); but they will not for that reason entertain the idea of wiping each other off the earth.

This resolution may come "of its own accord," as it were, if there is a period of relative peace. But there is no guarantee of this. Therefore, we cannot rely on the gradual "dissolution" of the Devil image. If we see in it a source of mortal danger, we must attack it at once. At the same time we must be careful, as has already been pointed out, of preserving the central cores; for it is the defense of the central cores against threat which nourishes the Devil image.

Our first task in the remaining chapters, therefore, will be to examine the central cores of "Americanism" and "communism," the two world views which in the United States are popularly thought to be locked in a struggle for survival. We shall then be led to questions which have been excluded from the strategic framework, partly because they do not fit into it and partly because they threaten to disrupt it. Such questions are "Is the enemy an enemy?" "Need he be an enemy?" "If not, what must be done in order that he become an enemy no longer?" These questions I believe to be far more relevant to our security and to our dignity that those with which the strategists are overwhemingly preoccupied.

CHAPTER 18

THE CENTRAL CORES

The central core of Americanism comes from the roots of American history. The best features of American civilization, as well as the sources which nurture American genius, in turn derive from it. This idea may sound like an apology or a mystique, especially to hostile ears, but there is really nothing apologetic or mystical about it. On the contrary, the sources of Americanism, being of recent origin, are quite easy to trace and their modern manifestations are easy to identify.

The dominant sources of Americanism are two: the conquest of the frontier and the break with European society. The two are related, because the drive for the frontier, like emigration from Europe, also involved a pulling up of stakes. The break with Europe, epitomized in Washington's Farewell Address also meant establishing the American identity. The early American cry was "Leave me alone!" (cf. "Don't tread on me," an early motto of the Republic). The theme finds rich expression in classical American literature (22).

One's identity is discovered (Americans largely believe) in the process of being freed from domination by others and through experience with molding the environment in the pursuit of one's personal needs. The escape into the wilderness and the conquest of the frontier were the primitive phases of this experience. Later came the euphoric era of invention.

"I am an American. My father was a blacksmith, my uncle was a horse doctor . . . I could make anything a body wanted—anything in the world, it didn't make any difference what; and if there wasn't any quick new-fangled way to make a thing, I could invent one" (21).

In so introducing himself, the Connecticut Yankee glorifies self-reliance and ingenuity as the supreme American virtues. The worship of personal success is still the most significant theme in American culture. Features which are obvious are nonetheless significant on that account.

It would be a mistake, however, to suppose that this most essential source of American motives is the only one. In addition to the principal theme we distinguish a subordinate one—the theme of social virtue. This theme is "tacked on," as it were, to the other. *First* the individual establishes himself as a free agent, self-reliant, ingenious, and the focus of his own energies. *Then* he fulfills his obligations to other, perhaps less fortunate, individuals or to society at large. Philanthrophy fits well into this scheme. So does a career of public service, in which the individual is pictured as *giving his already well-formed self* to the service of his society, not as being *made* by his society. Thus even in the context of social responsibility the individual is still seen as the primary object of attention. His fulfillment of social responsibility is a mark of generosity, possibly even a sacrifice, but not an integral part of self-fulfillment.[71]

The genuinely social or communal aspects of the fundamental American ethos are ordinarily confined to the local level. The barn-raising tradition, the town meeting, the school board, the church—these are felt to be the foundations of American democracy.

The emergence of the "good society," then, is seen through American eyes as proceeding from the individual *out*. Free individuals (it is taken as axiomatic) make a good community. By some tacit extrapolation, it is assumed that good communities add up to a good society. This is the element of the scheme which Americans only dimly perceive. At any rate, the good society is viewed as a matrix in which the individual has maximum opportunity to make something of *himself*, to pursue happiness. This is the American Dream. Its philosophical expression is Benjamin Franklin's autobiography; its manifesto is the Declaration of Independence; its nourishment came from an environment ideally suited to its realization—a vast, rich, practically empty continent. Its continual reiteration, ranging from the artless through the pious, to the blatant and the vulgar, is found on every page of the *Reader's Digest*.

The sources of the Communist ethos are more difficult to trace.

This may be because in contrast to a golden age of individual initiative, which actually existed in the America of the nineteenth century, no such golden age of fulfillment ever existed to nourish Communist ideals. Some see the sources of the Communist ethos in the primitive communism of early Chrisitianity; others in the Roman ideal of the justice-dispensing state. St. Augustine's *Civitas Dei* appears to be an amalgamation of these two sources.[72] The long history of proto-Communist fantasies can be traced in the utopian literature, of which Plato's *Republic* and Thomas More's *Utopia* are the best-known examples.[73]

THE COMMUNIST ETHOS

What is the Communist ethos? It is as explicit as the American and quite as emphatic in terms of universal human values. (Note that we are not speaking here of Communist social reality any more than we were speaking of American social reality when we were describing the American creed). The starting point of the Communist ethos is different from that of the American ethos. In the Communist version, the individual with his "natural" inclinations and ideas of happiness is not taken as a given. Characteristically, Marx, in criticizing the foundations of classical economics laid down by Smith and Ricardo, dismissed as fictitious the hypothetical primary economic units, the lone hunter and the lone farmer who come together to barter. He argued that even before man became man, he was already a member of a community, family, herd, or tribe, and so on. These social factors are the givens. They shape the individual's consciousness and therefore his ambitions and notions of happiness. A particular manifestation of the "pursuit of happiness," such as the amassing of wealth, is not indicative of basic human nature. It is a reflection of the social values of the society in which the wealth-amassing individual finds himself. According to Marxist theory, values are neither naturally given (a denial of the "natural rights" doctrine) nor freely chosen (a denial of some Christian doctrines). They are imposed upon the individual by his social milieu, for example, by his class interests. As long as there are social classes in conflict, values will clash, and man will know no peace. His energies will be expended in the social struggle, and he will not be really free. To speak of free-

dom under these conditions is misleading. The way to peace and freedom lies through an organization of the classless society. For Marx
this meant primarily the abolition of the private ownership of the
means of production.

So much for the Communist prerevolutionary ethos.

Let us now look at the postrevolutionary Communist ethos, particularly the Soviet variant. The Social Revolution has occurred. Has the
Classless Society come into being? No. "Why no?" we ask. "No one
expected it to come like the sunrise," the Russian Communist typically
replies. "But now that we have taken our fate into our own hands,
instead of being driven by the blind forces of history, we can build a
classless society. In fact, by herculean effort we *are* building it."

This standarized declaration contains the key to the present Soviet
ethos. Just as we Americans assume that the individual can be free
to pursue his ambitions, provided only that his social milieu is sufficiently permissive, so the Russians assume that a society (e.g., a portion of humanity, ideally all humanity) can embark upon the true
road to progress, provided only that it has freed itself from fratricidal
strife. Moreover, just as the American believes that the individual
ought to be free to pursue his ambitions, and therefore society *ought*
to be permissive of these ends, so the Russian believes that society
ought to move in a certain direction, and therefore its members *ought*
to be socialized in such a way that they see their future happiness as
the goal which society as a whole pursues.

We have depicted the American and the Soviet rationalizations
of their respective social creeds. This is the way *idealized* American
and Soviet societies appear to the *average* American and to the *average*
Soviet citizen, neither of whom tends to be critical of the official
(or the conventional) view of the sort of society he lives in. At least
each thinks that his society *would* be as it is described, officially (in
the U.S.S.R.) or conventionally (in the United States), if only it were
not for certain imperfections.

BACKWARD AND FORWARD VIEWS

Now we must compare the prevailing American and Soviet ideas of
what is responsible for the dissonant elements in their respective

systems. There are two main views on these matters in the United States, the conservative and the liberal.[74] The conservative view faces backward. It places the American Golden Age somewhere in the end of the last century, when the ideal of liberty (as the conservatives understand it) came closest to being realized. In the conservatives' estimation, American ideals have become *corrupted* by the infusion of alien elements, perhaps imported by immigrants from abroad, perhaps generated by a weakening of the moral fiber due to the "soft life," perhaps introduced by a hypertrophy of government institutions. The conservatives' cure for social ills is the re-establishment of un-fettered individualism, which they believe can be accomplished by removing all governmental regulation of economic activities.

The liberals reject this view. They see the classical or primitive American ideals as inadequate to cope with the problems of the fully industrialized frontierless society. The liberals accept the necessity of modifying the private enterprise system by introducing social legisla-tion and some controls of economic activities. Typically they view such regulations as *ad hoc* measures. They are empirically oriented and shun the vision of a Golden Age either in the past or in the future.

In the Soviet Union, the vision of the Golden Age is dominant, and it is placed always in the future, never in the past. The short-comings of the present are attributed simply to the fact that the Golden Age of communism has not yet arrived. It is to be established, the people are told (and believe), when an adequate material base for it has been prepared and when new generations have grown up under new conditions. The official view is that although Soviet society is far from perfect, it is progressing toward perfection.

Because of the comparative meagerness of open criticism of public policy in the Soviet Union, we can only surmise that the role analogous to that of our conservatives is played in the U.S.S.R. by the Stalinists. To be sure the Stalinists have no Golden Age in the past to extoll, and it is doubtful whether there are men in the Soviet Union who are nostalgic about the tyranny of the Stalinist era. Even the hack bureaucrats, among whom Stalinist sentiments are said to be smolder-ing, cannot very well long to return to the system of secret police terror in which everyone's life (including the life of the most loyal henchmen of the system) was in constant jeopardy. But they have a "heroic" age to point to and can rationalize the shortcomings of the present system in terms of the corruptive influence of "liberal" ideas. Like our own extreme right, the Stalinists can easily identify these ideas as "alien." In short, both future-oriented views, the American and the Soviet, assume the perfectability or at least the workability of the respective systems. Both conservative (acually reactionary) views are obsessed with the corruption of primitive virtues brought about by "modernistic" innovations.

The common idea underlying both of the future-oriented views, namely, the positive acceptance of change, derives from a confidence in man's ability to direct change toward desirable goals. The common idea underlying the two past-oriented views, American ultra-conservatism and Stalinism, is orthodoxy.

SIMILARITIES AND DIFFERENCES

Let us now look at the pragmatically oriented, future-oriented factions of both worlds. The fundamental concern of both is the age-old problem of man-in-society. Both contend that the goal of human existence is fulfillment. Each individual, both insist, has certain potentialities. Under certain conditions these potentialities will come to fruition; under certain other conditions they will be stifled.

Americans contend that these potentialities grow out of the individual's own urges and that ideally the individual should be free to attempt to satisfy these urges; that only the demonstrably necessary restrictions should be placed on the freedom of the individual, necessary in the sense of preventing some individuals from frustrating others in the pursuit of fulfillment.

The Russians maintain that the individual's motivations stem from his social environment and that therefore the primary emphasis of social action should be on the construction of a social milieu conducive to eliciting socially constructive motivations.

Even here there is still not much room for quarrel, because the principle of *mens sana in societatis sana is* acceptable to many non-Communists, even to anti-Communist liberals. The sharp disagreement with the Communist view on the part of the liberals comes when the Communists claim to know just which urges should be encouraged and which discouraged. This *total* manipulation of the psyche and the frank espousal of such manipulation by the Communists appears despotic to liberals. Not the cruelties themselves, not the repressions, the horrors of forced labor camps, the blood purges are the real foci of conflict between the Communists and the non-Communists. For is is easy for the Communist (at least today) to disavow the excesses as deplorable aberrations. The incompatibility is rather between the liberal's conviction that a deliberate molding of the psyche *must* lead to excesses and oppression and the Communist's conviction that excesses and oppression are only unfortunate by-products of strenuous social effort and must disappear as success is reaped. *Mutatis mutandis*, the liberals usually maintain that social irresponsibility is only an unfortunate by-product of the ideal of freedom, while the Communists maintain that the neglect of social welfare in the name of profit is an inevitable consequence of tolerating the individual's commitment to pursue his private advantage.

Who is right? Excesses and oppression have occurred under Communist regimes. Were they inevitable or only avoidable "unfortunate by-products?" Are they inherent or are they redeemable? No answer to this question can be verified. History is not a record that can be played over. On the other hand, deterioration of social responsibility has occurred in capitalist societies and is especially rempant in the United States.[75] Same question. Same answer. Since either answer to either question must remain no more than an affirmation of faith (at least within our lifetime), the questions are not really questions but simply invitations to affirm faith or else invitations to disavow a faith, depending on who addresses such questions to whom. Affirmation of faith may be emotionally satisfying but its most pronounced effect is an equally emphatic affirmation of faith by the other side. Invitation to a believer to disavow his faith is even more futile and serves no other purpose than to make further communication difficult or impossible.

CHAPTER 19

PREREQUISITES OF UNDERSTANDING

To understand something means to see it as a special instance of a general principle, one already known. This criterion applies both in science and in everyday affairs, to understanding of events as well as to understanding communications. Contrariwise, to fail to understand something means not to be able to find anything in one's experience with which to identify or compare it.

To take an example, we are baffled by a magician's tricks until the tricks are explained for us. They are explained by pointing out circumstances of which we had not been aware—the existence of strings, mirrors, etc. When these are taken into account the trick is revealed as a *normal,* i.e., expected, occurrence. Similarly when we are baffled by the way people act, our bewilderment is sometimes relieved when circumstances are pointed out to us of which we had not been aware. The question that led to the discovery of the law of gravity was not (as legend has it) "Why does an apple fall?" but rather "Why does not the moon fall?" The equations of motion show that the moon does in fact "fall," if the more general idea of "falling" (i.e., accelerated motion) is understood in mathematical terms.

Thus understanding a baffling event can come from two sources: (1) discovery of hitherto hidden circumstances which, when revealed, make the event appear expected instead of unexpected and (2) enlargement of one's range of experiences, that is, the range of what is expected.

Once events have been explained, they fit into a *framework* of explanation. Everyone has such internalized frameworks, the man-in-the-street with his common sense notions, the natural scientist with his "natural laws," the mathematician with his axiomatic bases, the professional with his accepted operational codes. These frameworks are remarkably stable. Once established it is difficult to change them. Our experience, or rather the ways of thought which have developed in us on the basis of our experiences, contribute the totality of our self-awareness. We cling to the existing pattern of self-awareness as tenaciously as we cling to our lives, sometimes more so. Attempts to change these patterns, especially when made in certain contexts (which will be described in a moment) are consciously or unconsciously interpreted as threats.

Let us look at the conventional explanations of the Communists' action in the light of what has just been said. In primitive explanations of behavior, people are said to behave as they do because they are what they are: policemen, barbers, teachers, parents, bankers, thieves, Communists, Africans, good people, bad people.[76] This is the level of explanation offered by our own primitives of Soviet behavior. The Soviet leaders behave as they do because they are what they are, namely, Communists.[77]

It is frequently argued that explanations of this sort are worthless, because they are circular. However, ultimately all explanations must reduce to an argument of the same sort, namely, to an appeal to see the particular as part of a general pattern. Thus the explanation of a particular cat's behavior may refer to the generally observed behavior of cats. This cat chases the mouse because cats chase mice. This "explanation" is trivial but becomes less so when we can go a step further in generalization. Not only cats chase mice, but many animals chase smaller animals. Cats are a subclass of a larger class of *predatory* animals. In a way, we can say that cats chase mice "because" pike chase perch, foxes chase hares, etc. The "because" here is of a very primitive sort. It does nothing but point to analogies. Analogies are very weak explanations but explanations nevertheless, both logically and psychologically quite related to the sophisticated explanations of advanced science, for these are also given in terms of general situations which include the given situation as a special instance.

ANALOGICAL EXPLANATIONS OF SOVIET BEHAVIOR

Let us now look at the analogies frequently offered in the United States as explanations of Soviet behavior. The most common analogies are those which link Soviet foreign policy with policies of would-be world conquerors and those which picture the Soviet system as a fountainhead of a vast conspiracy or as a crime syndicate. These analogies are acceptable to the American man-in-the-street because they suggest familiar interpretations of recent history. In the case of Nazi Germany, aims of world conquest were frankly spelled out and pursued by Hitler. Hence a precedent exists for attributing ambitions of world conquest to possessors of military might, driven by a sense of historical destiny. The primary requirement of an explanation is satisfied.

The alternative explanation—a world-wide conspiracy—is also based on the existence of familiar analogies in American experience. As a nation we have the dubious distinction of being chronically plagued by rackets, legal and illegal. That is not to say that concentration of political and economic power is confined to the American scene. There have been and continue to be despotisms far more extensive and ruthless than the House of Morgan and the Mafia. But our own despots (the magnates, the political bosses, the racketeers) have acquired in the estimation of our public an extra dimension of evil, because they arose in what is stubbornly believed to be a "free society." The power of the combines derives directly from conspiratorial and subversive coups, whose crassness is undiluted by centuries of "legitimate" privilege and aristocratic tradition. To us Americans, therefore, subversion has an especially frightening and evil connotation. Moreover our sense of justice, derived from egalitarian ideals, is easily aroused when power is exercised brazenly. Unoffensive and hard-working people among us have been time and again browbeaten by assorted bullies, hoodlums, strike breakers, and desperadoes. This picture is frequently invoked as an analogy to a Communist "take-over." The image of the commissar thus coupled with that of the gangster and the straw boss as well as with the SS gunman becomes terribly real.

THE CAPITALIST BOGEY

A frightening image of capitalism is just as real to the Russians and for the same reasons. The propaganda clichés have successfully linked the Capitalist to the Russians' historical experience. Who were the "capitalists" with which Russians had had direct contact? They were first and foremost the landlords. To be sure, the landlord was rarely a capitalist, but the social roles of the two were hardly differentiated. A capitalist to the Russian masses is a person who *owns* and by reason of his ownership *does not work*. Others work *for* him. He consumes without producing.

We must also appreciate the connotations of the Russian words denoting "work." There are two words, *trud* and *rabota*. (cf. *work* and *labor*). *Trud* carries the connotations of dilligence. *Rabota,* on the other hand, stems from the same root as slave (*rab*), and so does the word *rabochi* (worker), which is the word used to denote a member of the working class.[78] Our word *robot,* which is of Czech origin, is similarly derived. Thus the division between people who lived by toil and those who enjoyed the privilege of ownership was sharp and is reflected in the language. The Russian peasant or worker could be distinguished as easily from a *barin* (landowner, merchant, professional) as a Negro field hand from a plantation owner.

The smooth-skinned arrogant masters lived in a world entirely apart from the world in which the toilers lived. Nor could the toilers nurture any realistic hope of passing from their world of back-breaking labor into the world of entertainment, elegance, and luxury. Although few remain in the Soviet Union today who have personal recollections of those times, the image is kept in sharp focus all through school, in the movies about old times, and, of course, with the help of Russian classical literature, about which we shall have more to say below.

All through the Stalinist era the world "outside" was pictured as rather similar to prerevolutionary Russia. Here is an excerpt from a story written apparently for the young, dealing with a sojourn of a Soviet family (the husband is in diplomatic service) abroad. The time is before World War II.

The journey across Europe was interesting and weird. In Poland Tonia [the young wife] saw a landowner for the first time in her life. He was riding in a buggy—a fat bewhiskered man in a canvas raincoat. He was inspecting his scanty oat crop with a strict mien. Kostia [the husband] had never seen a landlord either. Both of them watched this strange figure for a long time. It seemed to have stepped out of a textbook of political education (57).

To the vast majority of Russians, then, "capitalism" means first of all a cleavage of a society into two classes, of which one is condemned to do all the work and to live in poverty, while the other is privileged to do no work and to live in luxury. It is a primitive image and false in many respects, but it is based on historical reality, first and foremost Russian historical reality. The fact that the social system of prerevolutionary Russia was feudal rather than capitalistic is irrelevant in this context. Although Communist textbooks of political education distinguish between feudalism and capitalism and even point out the progressive feature of the latter compared to the former, in the historical memory of the Russians the two systems appear fused into one. This was, in fact, the case. Although Russia began industrializing toward the end of the last century and although the emancipated serfs did trickle into the cities, becoming industrial workers or even small traders, the vital feature of full-fledged capitalism, as we have known it in the United States, complete with class mobility, simply did not exist.

THE REVOLUTIONARY VISION

Against this background image of "capitalism," socialism appears to the Russians as a result of a heroic cataclysmic event, called (*The*) Social Revolution. The image of the social revolution is also rooted in historical reality and is kept in focus by the same means. The preparation of the Russian revolution is credited to a generation of fearless men and women. These people were constantly hunted by the cruel police and led difficult but romantic, utterly dedicated lives. Their task was first to explain to the oppressed the causes of their misery and so to point out to them their friends and their enemies; second, to build a feeling of solidarity among the oppressed and a hope in an ultimate victory; third, to build a network of organized revolutionary activity under their own leadership.

In this planning for the revolution, specific postrevolutionary problems were not included. It would not be accurate to say, however, that the revolutionists never gave these problems a thought. There were in fact protracted theoretical disputes about what sort of post-revolutionary society was best suited for Russia. Primarily the post-revolutionary vision split into two, on the one hand a democratic agrarian society (as the Social Revolutionaries pictured it), on the other a socialist-industrialized one, envisaged by the Social Democrats. The exponents of the former view held that the Russian peasant was a carrier of values specific to Russia, and that these values should be preserved uncontaminated by Western materialism. The Social Democrats were oriented toward the West and Marxism, with its glorification of the industrial worker as the dominant actor in the new society. However, this difference in social philosophies was not very relevant to the overwhelming task facing the revolutionaries—the overthrow of the czarist regime and of the social structure that supported it—the social structure built on the privilege of ownership, which in Russia was primarily the privilege of land ownership.

We have mentioned the connotations of the word "work" in the mind of the Russian. The connotations of "ownership" are no less important. To appreciate them properly we must compare them with their counterparts in our own culture.

OUR CALVINIST ORIGINS

As has been already pointed out, the historical basis of our social experience was the conquest of the frontier. In our folk conception, the conquest was accomplished by individual pioneers.

Coupled with the rugged mores of frontier conquest were the Puritan mores which the typical pioneer brought with him. In the Puritan conception, work was not only a necessity but also a virtue. A virtue, in turn, in its Calvinist-Puritan interpretation brought earthly rewards. There is a curious paradox in this fusion of initiative-worship with the Calvinist doctrine of predestination. According to that doctrine, who shall be saved and who shall be damned has already been decided, and the individual can do nothing to alter that decision. It would appear, then, that the efforts of the individual to lead a virtuous life are pointless, and it is hard to explain the constant stress the Calvinists lay on the importance of a virtuous life. A way out is offered in a curious argument. It is assumed that although those to be saved or damned are *already* marked for their fate, nevertheless because God is just, the saved ones will be also for the most part the virtuous ones. A man does not know whether he is among the saved. His efforts to practice virtue are not directed toward insuring his actual status (already determined) but are rather efforts to convince himself and others that he *is* among the saved. If he is not, his efforts will avail him nothing, but if he is to be saved, he will have a good reason to expect that he is, if he is virtuous.

It turns out, then, that the pursuit of virtue (which in the Calvinist tradition is tightly bound up with self-reliance and industry) need not be motivated exclusively or even primarily by material rewards. Pursuit of virtue in this light is an effort to *prove* to oneself (and to others) that one is indeed among the saved.

Now it goes without saying that modern American society is not composed primarily of Calvinists. Nor is our ethos any longer derived from theological formulations. It is, however, quite likely that the erstwhile hegemony of Calvinist thought has given a direction to American social philosophy. A direction, once established, favors the development of certain institutions. Institutions mold social attitudes. Social attitudes are self-perpetuating and put a stamp on a society which persists long after the original impulses have been spent.

Consider an analogy. A living organism develops from a zygote— a single cell. Within this cell are certain vastly complicated structures, chromosomes, upon which a "message," a definite sequence of units selected from a four-letter "alphabet"[79] is "written." The particular sequence determines whether the future organism will be a human being, a cobra, or a tomato. Let us now look at our finished organism. It is hopeless to find "the" cell which made it what it is. No material trace of it remains. All the molecules in it have long been replaced by other molecules. The cell has lost its own identity, but the identity it has stamped on the organism remains, as big as life, because each step in the development of the organism was determined, not perfectly, perhaps, but to a large degree by the preceding steps. The fact remains that the differences between tomatoes and cobras are incomparably vaster than between different tomatoes. Yet all these differences stem from the difference in the original arrangement of "letters" (certain atom complexes) *in a single cell,* which has long since dissolved as an entity.

In view of the way biological organisms are determined, it is not fantastic to suppose that something of the sort may be happening in the development of social organisms. The main point here is not that different historical conditions give rise to different social organisms (this should be obvious), but that it is possible for the character of the organisms to persist long after its determining factors have disappeared. Thus the difficulty of demonstrating an all-pervasiveness of Calvinist mores in modern American life (though they certainly persist here and there) does not invalidate the argument that they may well have been the determining "code" in somewhat the same way as the genetic code determines the nature of the developing organism.[80]

And so let us assume that our idea of American virtue is strongly colored by Calvinist ideas. That is, virtue and work are related. Work is seen as a way of demonstrating one's virtue and, by implication, a way of proving that one has been chosen to be among the saved. The fruits of work in the American conception are wealth. Hence the accumulation of wealth is a virtue. The right of property is a social institution which guarantees to the virtuous the fruits of their virtue, not only in the sense of material rewards but also (perhaps primarily) in the sense of enabling them to proclaim to the world that they have been virtuous and so are probably among the chosen.

SAINTLINESS AND RUTHLESSNESS

This chain of connection has no counterpart in the old Russian ethos. There industriousness was never an important component of virtue. Indeed virtue as such had no direct counterpart in the old Russian ethos. Instead, one finds saintliness—a denial of self. Characteristically the saint in the flesh was frequently the village idiot, who was usually treated with a mixture of kindness and awe. Again we have occasion to refer to semantic evidence. The simpleton is often called *blazheny* (cf. *blago*—blessing). The *blazheny* could say anything to anybody.[81]

THE OLD AND THE NEW

Now it may be argued that the present culture hero of the Soviet Union has come a long way from the saintly idiot. Let us therefore look at the Soviet product. But before we do so, we must look at their prototypes in the classical literature. The most famous of these is Turgeniev's Bazarov in *Fathers and Sons* (120), the science-worshipping "nihilist." Bazarov calls himself a nihilist because he professes contempt for the traditional values (more properly, the sentimental rationalizations of these values). Bazarov had, of course, enormous faith in new values, those of enlightenment, activism, and science. But, as is typically the case, to the older generation he seemed to negate all values because he belittled *their* sentiments.

A somewhat more realistic portrait is that of Chekhov's Lopakhin in *The Cherry Orchard* (19). Lopakhin was born a serf on the estate of the family who own the cherry orchard. On the stage we see him as an enterprising businessman and a friend of family. He offers them a way out of their financial straits: the cherry orchard, commercially worthless, is to be converted into subdivisions for *dachas* (summer homes). His advice falls on deaf ears, and eventually the orchard has to be sold at auction. The climax of the tragedy (which Chekhov calls a "comedy") is Lopakhin's announcement that he himself has bought the property. The little urchin, whom the gracious manor lady once consoled when he was hurt, becomes the destroyer of everything the family had held dear, their ties with the past, their homestead, their very way of life.

Now the theme of dispossession is familiar to us as the stereotyped theme of the American folk melodrama. It occurs also in our serious literature (116). But observe how in the American version the good and evil are sharply separated. The holder of the mortgage is the standardized villain of the melodrama or a faceless bank. The other theme of *The Cherry Orchard,* the rape of nostalgia, is treated by Tennessee Williams in *A Streetcar Named Desire* (130). Here too, the rapist is the outsider, a second-generation Pole totally impervious to the suffering of his genteel wife and her sister.

But in Russia, the struggle between the Old and the New was much more complex than a confrontation between opposed interests or between total strangers. In *The Cherry Orchard* it is not clear who is hurt more, the living anachronisms or Lopakhin, the unwilling source of their impotent grief. The revolutionists were equally ambivalent about the world they were destroying.

This may seem paradoxical in view of the vast gulf between the owners and the workers and in view of the seething hatred which the revolutionists professed for the old regime. But one must bear in mind that the revolutionary leadership was recruited to a large extent from the gentry and from the intelligentsia. These were people well aware of the fact that in preparing to destroy the regime, they were also digging the grave of the world from which they themselves sprang, the world of intense and intricate personal affect-ridden relationships. To the uncompromising Russian this meant that an irrevocable decision had to be made. It also meant that in making the decision a man had to cleanse himself from all vestiges of commitment to the other side.

In Dostoyevsky and in Lenin, two gigantic world figures nurtured by Russian ideology, we have the prototypes of the two opposite choices. Dostoyevsky, after initial allegiance to the Revolution, turned his back on its ideals and became a bitter enemy of the new Western ideas (atheism, liberalism, socialism). Lenin, whose origin was in the gentry, committed himself to the Revolution and in doing so deliberately purged himself and insisted that his colleagues purge themselves of all sentiments which he felt would stand in the way of accomplishing the impending transformation of social and personal relations.[82] Stalinism, a monstrous perversion of Leninism, was the gruesome harvest that sprang from the seeds recognized already by Dostoyevsky (38).

Now one might argue that it is a far cry from the revolutionists of the turn of the century to Stalin's secret police and the entrenched Soviet bureaus; but so it is from the Puritan Pilgrims to the modern operator, chiseler, and racketeer. Nor is the full-grown organism recognizable in the zygote. Still there is a continuous chain of development that leads from embryo to beast. Only mechanically deterministic systems can be understood without regard to their history. When it comes to systems too complex to be understood as mechanisms, knowing how they got that way is a prerequisite for understanding.

CHAPTER 20

WHAT THEY LACK

To us Americans it seems that the Russian lacks two kinds of blessings: those that come from mail order houses and those subsumed under "freedom." With regard to the first class of blessings, the Russian will readily agree that he has a shortage. He may be somewhat defensive in response to our tendency to boast of our affluence and will cite current projected production figures and estimates about the expected time when Russia will "overtake America." But on the whole, the Russian will cheerfully admit our lead. Our lead is a challenge to him, and he knows exactly what is to be done about it.

With regard to the second class of blessings, those having to do with freedom, it will be a different matter. Here the talk will be more diffuse, defensive counterthrusts will be more persistent, and certain aspects of freedom, dear to us, will be compulsively belittled. The Russian's defense against the charge that he "has no freedom" may proceed along several lines, but there will be an amazing uniformity in his counterarguments. When we point out to him that a single political party and a single slate of candidates in elections offers no choice of policy nor of candidates for a given office, he will reply that our two-party system does not offer any meaningful choice either. And even if there were discernible differences between the programs of our two parties, the Russian will insist that the "choice" between them has little to do with freedom. Such a choice would simply reflect a conflict of class interests. In the U.S.S.R., he would say, while there still exist "classes" (workers, collective farmers, and intellectuals), their interests do not clash and hence they have no need for separate political parties to represent them. Moreover, he will point out (and this can be verified) that there are representatives of all three classes in all elected bodies in Russia.

With regard to the "classical" civil liberties, e.g., freedom of speech and assembly, he will argue that Soviet citizens enjoy these freedoms to the fullest extent; that only those who are hostile to "the aspirations of the people" are curbed. He will also accuse our press and other mass media of presenting points of view overwhelmingly favorable to the interests of only a small sector of our society.

The Russian will maintain that Soviet citizens enjoy freedom of worship and will mention the open, unimpeded functioning of several churches. In response to our questions about freedom of artistic expression, we may get an answer similar to that given by the Soviet delegate to the United Nations at a recent press conference, to the effect that the Soviet government has a perfect right to express its opinion (sic) on abstract art.

We have guessed the probable replies of a conventionally thinking or, at any rate, a conventionally speaking Russian. We guess that on these matters he would speak in very much the same terms in 1963 as he spoke in 1953 in the darkest days of the *Stalinshchina*. Yet reality has undergone tremendous changes from that time. Millions of people have been freed from slave labor camps. Literary works have been published which at one time might have endangered the life of the reader, let alone that of the writer. In science and scholarship, the taboo has been lifted from a whole host of fields, such as cybernetics, symbolic logic, genetics, mathematical statistics. Work has appeared in behavioral sciences outside the narrow confines of reflex physiology and educational psychology which had been the only "safe" areas during the days of Stalinist orthodoxy. All these events were, of course, by-products of de-Stalinization.

De-Stalinization is one of the most significant developments of our times. I am using "significant" in its literal meaning. The event signifies the currents in Soviet popular moods and beliefs, a phase of development of the Soviet Communist party, and the changing relations between the population and the party. These are historical, psychological, and sociological matters vitally important for understanding the real issues of the East-West conflict. The fact that these matters have little or no bearing on the strategic analysis of the conflicts is evidence that strategic analysis is not concerned with issues.

STALINISM

The brutalities of Stalin's regime as revealed by Khrushchev (64) fit into the conventional pattern of political despotism. But Stalin's power was expressed also in another way which has had no precedent, at least among secular potentates. He could force people who were passionately devoted to truth (practicing scientists) and to esthetic ideals (practicing writers and artists) to utter blasphemies against their ideals. Now I am not a religious man, conventionally speaking; so the term blasphemy in its literal sense has little terror for me. But I think I know through analogous experience the more general meaning of the word and so its frightening connotations, Blasphemy is a symbolic act which defiles what is held holy. For those who hold nothing holy, blasphemy has no meaning at all. For example, George Bernard Shaw's Roman emperor (108) cannot understand why the Christians will not go through a simple ceremony (burning a pinch of incense) and so avoid being devoured by lions. Thoroughly brainwashed pragmatists are immune to the meaning of blasphemy. Thus the prevailing explanations of the actions of the accused in the Moscow trials is that the confessions were motivated either by practical considerations (responses to threats or promises) or by morbid exhibitionism. The deeper meaning of the confessions escapes the pragmatist, namely, that the confessions were genuine acts of blasphemy. So were the innumerable hand-kissing recantations of the scientists, artists, and writers accused of heresy during the purification rites following the contaminating contacts with the West in World War II (132).

THE EITHER-OR DISEASE

The idolatrous worship of Stalin was the crassest symptom of the disease which struck Russia almost immediately after the Revolution. I say Russian, not Soviet, society, because there was no Soviet society at the time of the Revolution. Indeed there was at that time no society of any kind in Russia, if by society we mean a matrix of social obligations in the discharge of which the necessary coordinated work of a nation (or of a comparable unit) is accomplished. Soviet society was being built while the disease ravaged Russia, and perhaps this is why severely pathological features were built into that society.

The disease was what sematicists call the two-valued orientation. Its victims recognize two and only two "positions" on every issue— the correct one and the wrong one. This dichotomy *defines* every issue. To a victim of the either-or disease it seems that one has understood an issue only when one has singled out the two positions and has committed oneself to one or the other of them.

A strong case can be made for tracing the either-or obsession to Lenin's influence. Lenin survived the Revolution by only six years. But even during these years he did not operate at full capacity. A would-be assasin's bullet struck him only a few months after his regime was established. After that Lenin's strength steadily declined. It is idle to speculate how Lenin would have met the formidable problems of constructing a society from scratch on the ruins of the old order. When he died in 1924, hardly anything had been started. Lenin's active life, therefore, was almost entirely dedicated to a destructive goal, namely, the total destruction of Russia's social system.

It is hard for us Americans to understand a mentality so dedicated. Few of us experience directly an oppressive power which is so totally alien to us and so destructive to our values that its existence appears only as unmitigated evil. The closest analogy can be found, perhaps, in the power of some criminal syndicates, which exact a tribute from small people and so play purely parasitic roles. But the analogy is not a very good one. The small businessman can make a stoic adjustment to paying the tribute, and as long as he pays it, he can lead a comparatively normal life. A better parallel is found in a military occupation by foreign forces; but we have never experienced this plight. The plight of the Negro under white supremacist rule is also somewhat similar, but only a relatively small minority of us are in that position. Actually none of these forms of oppression comes really close to a tyranny which is both total and institutionalized. The racketeer's victim can still hope to escape. At any rate, the extent of his injury is largely limited to a financial tribute. The victims of racism have for generations nurtured a hope that the system will eventually atrophy. But this expected demise of racism is not, as a rule, associated in the minds of the victims with a complete collapse of the social, political, and economic institutions of our society.

Not so in the case of the Russian revolutionary in the last decades of the Romanoff dynasty. The complete collapse of the *entire* social system was what he normally envisaged as the way out of hell. That is to say, he pictured the hunters (the police, the gendarmery) becoming the hunted; the oppressors (the landowners, the nobility) stripped of their power and of their glitter, which meant, of course, of their possessions; for their power was wielded by their ownership of what *rightfully* (in the eyes of the revolutionaries and of the people themselves) belonged to the people. In short, the revolutionary did not seek to rectify the abuses of privilege; he sought to abolish the social roles associated with those privileges. He was convinced that the *pristav* (Czarist police chief), for example, should not exist at all rather than that he should exercise his power with more discretion.

IDEOLOGICAL STRUGGLES

There were several schools of revolutionary thought in Russia. All of them were more or less in agreement on the impending demise of the czarist feudal system. But they were in vociferous disagreement on ideology. Again it is hard for us Americans, with our pragmatic outlook on politics, to understand what is meant by an ideological struggle. We see plenty of political strife. The speeches in legislatures, editorials in newspapers, the activities of lobbies, election campaigns, all attest to such strife. But overwhelmingly these clashes are over whether or not to do something; and if so, how to do it. There is hardly any ongoing public debate on the nature of man in society and on the course of future history, the ideological debate which makes enemies of opponents.

The gist of the polemic that claimed large portions of energy of the Russian revolutionary leaders was just this sort of thing. There was, to be sure, a goodly measure of pragmatically oriented debate. Questions were discussed like "Is assassination of government officials an effective revolutionary tactic?" or "Should revolutionaries be candidates for elective offices?" or "Where and when should strikes be called?" all questions about explicit actions, hence "practical" questions. Yet the polemic always gravitated toward the ideological. The revolutionary found his motivating force not in immediate achievements resulting from his successful acts (as the empirically oriented pragmatist does) but from a "world picture," from a feeling that he has understood the nature of man, of society, and of history.

We have the clearest evidence of the world picture which inspired Lenin. This was the picture emerging from the sociological views subsumed under historical materialism and from the philosophical views subsumed under dialectical materialism developed by Marx and Engels. These views have been amply described elsewhere, and we will forgo recapitulating them. We will only stress the connection between the Marxist views, as Lenin interpreted them, and the either-or orientation which eventually came to underlie the "ideological disease" which has plagued Russia since the Revolution, has inhibited in many ways the normal process of her social development and maturation, and continues to this day to be a great obstacle to the realization of the positive aspects *of the Communists' own program.*

THE INCONTROVERTIBLE DOCTRINE

To Lenin, Marxist socialism was distinguished from all other kinds because it was based, he was convinced, on a scientific theory. The difference, in Lenin's view, between pre-Marxian and Marxian socialism was somewhat like the difference between a system of healing practices based on hand-me-down beliefs and a medical art based on scientifically established facts. As long as socialist ideas were centered upon notions of social justice or humanitarian ideals or even on rationally argued utilitarian principles, socialism remained a pipe dream like the wish fantasies in fairy tales (flying carpets, horns of plenty). What Marx and Engels did, in Lenin's estimation, was to discover the "laws of transformation of society," somewhat in the way Newton discovered the law of universal gravitation. Just as the discovery of this law transformed a vague metaphysical cosmology into a physical science, which subsequently drove God out of celestial mechanics and also instigated the industrial revolution, so the "laws of transformation of society," supposedly discovered by Marx and Engels, were destined to transform social myth into social science, drive utopian ideas out of revolutionary movements, and give the ascendant class (the proletariat) not merely a just cause to fight for but a weapon with which to fight for it.

If we take the parallel with physical science seriously, this is by no means an absurd idea. Science began when man began analyzing instead of wishing and discovered what was *necessary* in nature (laws). Having discovered what was necessary, he began to see how to accomplish the possible. Moreover in the development of physical science, knowledge and action were tightly interwoven. Not idle speculation, nor even accurate but passive observation, but only an active *impact* on the environment via the controlled experiment, via the trial and error of invention and via exploration provided the necessary experience and the necessary state of mind to pursue scientific knowledge and to utilize the power conferred by it.

Lenin argued essentially that Marxist social science was following the same road and offered similar opportunities, and his argument seems plausible. Marx did not preach. He *analyzed* the relations which obtain among men. This analysis led him to the conclusion that these social relations (dominance, submission, cooperation, competition, oppression, exploitation, etc.) derived from the way production and distribution of commodities was organized in the society in question. Note especially the direction of the implied cause-effect relationship. The relations determined by the productive process are primary; they are the cause. The other relations (e.g., ethical, legal, affective) are derivative or secondary. This way of putting it is critical for the argument that follows.

The supposed discovery of these laws (analogous to the discovery of the physical laws) established what was necessary in the course of history. But the necessity remained a necessity only so long as it was hidden from man. Once discovered, it gave man the freedom to use the laws of historical development to further his ends. To Lenin, "man" in this context meant creative man, and this, in turn, meant the workingman, the member of the ascendant class.

It is not hard to see how a brilliant and bitter young man, living at the turn of the last century, could become completely possessed by the idea that a marvelous and all-illuminating truth was discovered. Of Lenin's exceptional brilliance there can be no doubt. His bitterness has been frequently traced to the execution of his idolized elder brother, who had been involved in an attempted assassination of Czar Alexander III in 1887, when Lenin was seventeen years old. It seems psychologically plausible that the mixture of intellectual power, a passionate commitment to science, and a burning thirst for vengeance made Lenin what he became—an intellectual giant among fanatics.

TECHNIQUE OF REVOLUTION

Let us now follow Marx's theory of revolution, as it was transformed by Lenin, into a *technique* of revolution. According to Marx, the regime immediately following the social revolution was to be a "dictatorship of the proletariat." Marx did not spell out how that dictatorship was to be wielded. Dictatorship means the imposition of a single will. But does "the proletariat" have a single will? In view of recent history, we may not think so, but the question apparently did not occur to Marx. The proletariat, in his analysis, had a single *class interest,* and since he held class interest to be the ultimate source of motivation, he may well have taken it for granted that for this reason the proletariat possessed a single will. The purpose of the dictatorship was to create new institutions appropriate to a socialist society. The power of the state, residing in the working class, was to be used coercively to channel social life into the framework of the new institutions. (For Marx a non-coercive state was a contradiction in terms). Once the new social relations had been established and the bases for economic exploitation abolished, the need for coercion would disappear, and the state, having lost its (only) function would automatically "wither away."

Now most of Lenin's life was spent before the Revolution. His concern, therefore, was not with what to do when proletarian dictatorship would be established but how to overthrow the old order and how to establish the dictatorship. All Marx said was that the social revolution *would* occur when the time is ripe. On how to *make* it occur (even when the time is ripe) he said next to nothing. Moreover, Russia was the last country in which Marx would have expected his social revolution to occur. *England,* industrially the most advanced country, was to be the scene of the first revolution. Lenin, however, cared little about England. His concern was how to overthrow the old order in Russia. On this question he could naturally find no guidance from Marx. Accordingly he developed a theory and a revolutionary tactic of his own, and the entire subsequent history of Soviet Russia bears the stamp of it.

Lenin's conception of a revolutionary party was a curious amalgam of democracy and military discipline. In retrospect, especially with a view to what the Communist parties became in the Stalin era, the military discipline aspect of the organization is entirely obvious, and it is difficult to see how this feature can be made compatible with democratic principles. For Lenin, however, the principle of "democratic centralism" (as it later became known) was not a contradiction in terms. This is understandable if we remember that Lenin imagined a Marxist revolutionary party to be guided by scientific analysis.

Democratic centralism works as follows. Suppose that the revolutionary party is faced with the problem of charting a course of action at a particular historical moment. Equipped with the tools of Marxist analysis (in the same way the engineer is equipped with his knowledge of physics and of mathematical techniques) the membership of a revolutionary party is supposed to arrive at the best (strategic) decision which circumstances permit. Thus it is not a leader's whim that dictates the decision but the "objective situation" itself. It is therefore *the* correct decision. Subsequent events may dictate changes, may even indicate that the decision was mistaken. But at the time the decision is made, it is presumably made on the basis of objective fact and of the best available prognoses. *For this reason,* it is an absolute obligation of every member to carry out the decision. In doing so, he is not submitting to the whim of human authority. He is exercising revolutionary discipline, that is, placing the rationality of science over his personal predilections. An individual guided by subjective biases, sentiments, prejudices, and fears is certainly fallible. But a scientific analysis uncovers "objective reality." Hence revolutionary discipline is equated, in Lenin's theory of the revolutionary party, with rationality and with the scientific outlook. Lenin's faith in science and rational analysis was unbounded, and he believed that "scientific method" is directly applicable to the conduct of the revolutionary struggle. Lenin was a strategic thinker par excellence.

THE SELFLESS EGOTIST

For all his egotism (unshakable conviction of being right), Lenin was not unaware of human frailty nor unsympathetic toward it. He knew that sentiment and personal bias could exert an influence on anyone, including a revolutionary, who was, after all, only a human being. Nor was he blind to the dangers of corruption and abuse of power. On the latter score, however, he was utterly sure of himself and justly so. Seldom, if ever, has the world seen a man bestowed with so much power who was more modest and unassuming as a person. Nevertheless, I do not know of a single instance when Lenin conceded that he was wrong and someone else was right on some theoretical or tactical issue. On the contrary, the others always knuckled under whenever it came to a showdown in his own party. On at least one occasion he threatened to resign if he did not have his own way, and this convinced the others that he was right. When he won victories over his colleagues, they were always total victories, and he could not see how it could be otherwise. Indeed Lenin had no positive concept of compromise. He knew the value of a tactical retreat and of a political deal. But these maneuvers had nothing to do with compromise as it is understood in practical politics. They only served the function of allowing him to jockey for positions from which to launch the next assault on his opponents. Both politics and polemics were to him struggles of annihilation. He was thus as completely authoritarian as any despot except for two vitally important differences. First, as we have already said, Lenin was free of vanity; second, he was free of malice.

To reconcile these statements with his total inability to admit error or to compromise even with his own colleagues, imagine a mathematician teaching willing but immature students. For such a teacher the concept of "difference of opinion" about what is true does not exist. A mathematical conclusion is either right or wrong; a proof is either valid or invalid. Lenin, like a mathematics teacher, saw no relevance of "opinions" to the pursuit of truth. His convictions seemed to him to have been derived from an unimpeachable analysis of "objective facts." His impregnable self-assurance, therefore, could be very well combined with genuine personal modesty. It was not *Lenin* whom Lenin claimed to be always right. It was Marxist analysis, for which Lenin saw himself serving as a human channel.

Lenin's freedom from malice is well attested to by his ability to forgive and forget the "errors" of his colleagues and by his trusting attitude toward them. Again his attitude is comparable to that of a sincere teacher. Such a teacher will attribute the aberrations of a student's conclusions to one thing only, namely, error. When faced with error, there is only one thing a teacher must do, namely, correct it. There is no occasion for punishment, revenge, or bearing a grudge. The student *must* see his error; else he would not be a student. When he sees his error (Lenin's disciples always did) he is congratulated for having seen it, not punished for having erred.

As far as the world outside his own party was concerned, in particular the doomed world of bourgeois society, Lenin's aim was simply to destroy this world. It is not likely that he envisaged this annihilation as a physical extermination of human beings. Rather he conceived it as rendering completely void the network of social obligations which made that world, for example, class privileges, property rights, the legal system, etc. It is, of course, true that resistance to this sweeping nullification started at once and was immediately met with terror. One must not, however, confuse these excesses with the terror which raged later in Stalin's day. The latter was systematically planned and implemented through a highly organized network of spies, professional inquisitors, and executioners. The terror of the early years was still largely spontaneous, and much of it can be traced to popular outbursts, drumhead courts, lynch mobs, etc. Lenin's dictatorial government tolerated or even condoned this violence but did not design far-flung plans for a systematic physical eradication of all *persons* against whom the very shadow of suspicion fell. An individual's working class or peasant origin and his appearance attesting to it were usually fairly good insurance against arbitrary liquidation. And persons in this category were, after all, the vast majority.

Thus Lenin's attitude toward the doomed world which he went about destroying could be described as "total estrangement free of personal malice." I have frequently tried to understand this attitude by invoking an analogy. I suppose Martin Luther King feels toward the world of white supremacy something of the sort that Lenin felt toward the bourgeois world. I am not, of course, comparing the totally different methods used by the two revolutionaries, Lenin's coercion and terror and King's non-violence. I am drawing a parallel between their attitudes toward the *impersonal* worlds which they committed themselves to destroy. King's actions, like Lenin's, are guided by a singleness of purpose. There will be no compromise (except temporary arrangements for calculated reasons); no retreats except tactical retreats. The world of white supremacy, that is, the entire network of dominant and submissive relationships, the white man's conception of the Negro's social role, the system of custom and law reinforcing these conceptions—all this, in King's estimation, will be destroyed. What white supremacists think about this prospect simply does not matter. They need not be asked. There will be no voting about it. The racists have neither equity nor bargaining power on their side. Their world is irrevocably doomed. And all this has nothing whatsoever to do with malice toward any particular white persons, even rabid ones, or even toward the segregationists as a group. This freedom from malice is much clearer in the case of King than in the case of Lenin, because the actual conduct of King's non-violent campaign bespeaks the attitude, which, in Lenin's case, can only be inferred from a retrospective analysis of Lenin's character. Nevertheless, there are reasons to believe that Lenin came from the same cut of human material that produced leaders like King and Gandhi. Only historical and geographical circumstances made Lenin pursue his aims by violent means where King and Gandhi could forgo them.

This singleness of purpose, coupled with purity of heart, seen through the mist of intervening terrible years, makes Lenin a saint in the eyes of most Russians, all the more so because the avowal of his sainthood is now coupled with an officially sanctioned condemnation of Stalin's corruption.

LENIN'S HERITAGE

Now I reject the Carlylean idea that single individuals can will-fully put the stamp of their personality on the course of history. When this appears to be the case, as with Lenin, I believe that the seemingly responsible individuals come to the forefront in a selective process. I think it stands with human society somewhat as with the biological world. Organisms adapt themselves to their environment not be-cause adaptive changes are the responses of the organisms to their environment but rather because the genes which eventually manifest themselves in the adaptive features are *already* in the population when the opportunities for manifestation present themselves. There were, perhaps, several "Lenins" at various times and places who left no mark. The Russians' aspirations evolved in consequence of their own dynamic. Lenin gave these aspirations the clearest expression, and so they crystallized around his person. I do believe, however, that there is also a "back action." Because these aspirations were crystallized around Lenin and his mode of thought, the present mode of thought of the Russians has been much more firmly established than it might have been.

It is the Leninist mode of thought which underlies the Russians' lack of freedom. Stalin's terror was made possible, I believe, because the people accepted it, and this acceptance is traceable to the convic-tion (which stems from Lenin) that in politics, as in mathematics, there is a "correct" view, associated with every situation, and there is a method of analysis which enables properly trained and properly *emancipated* individuals to come by the correct view. Dissenting opinions are due either to error or to a commitment to the enemy camp. There can be no compromise with error nor with the "class enemy."

The all-or-none disease or the two-valued orientation, so clearly evident in Lenin's writings, pervades the whole thinking process of the Communists on matters of doctrine. However, their thinking on matters of policy (i.e., strategic thinking) is not at all as rigid as we would expect it to be. On the contrary, Communist leaders have shown great flexibility in formulating and pursuing strategies. There is no contradiction here: The Communists combine singleness of goals with a variety of means. This was shown dramatically in the very first months after the November Revolution.

Lenin sent Trotzky to negotiate a peace treaty with the Germans with instructions to agree to practically anything, just to put an end to the fighting. Lenin justified this policy on two grounds. First, a breathing spell was essential in order to consolidate Soviet power. Second, the territorial concessions to the Germans would not mean much anyway, since proletarian revolutions would soon break out (Lenin was convinced) in the countries of the belligerents or in Germany, at any rate, and so national boundaries would become obsolete.

Trotzsky did not follow Lenin's instructions and instead announced to the Germans that Russia would neither fight nor accede to Germany's terms. Thereupon he was sent to the Germans once more, after having been chastised for harboring bourgeois-nationalist prejudices, and was ordered to sign on the Germans' terms. The resulting treaty of Brest-Litovsk was even harsher than the one originally proposed by the Germans, but Lenin was by no means dismayed. In submitting to the dismemberment of Russia, he was merely doing what he deemed was necessary for the eventual triumph of the world social revolution.[83]

World War I ended, and Communist revolutions in Europe failed. Here again Lenin was true to his principle of strategic flexibility. The NEP (New Economic Policy) restored practices which were anathema to a doctrinaire Communist of that time: a free commodities market, hard money, even a limited amount of private enterprise in manufacturing. The idea of "socialism" in one country (commonly attributed to Stalin) was the continuation of the same tendency to adjust to historical reality.

The contrast between strategic and tactical flexibility of the Communists on the one hand and their ideological intransigence on the other can be put in this way: The Communist leaders will pursue any course of action if *in their own minds* they can be convinced that this course serves the one Cause.

Observe that the conclusion drawn by our extreme right ("never trust the Communists") is by no means the only one to be drawn from this characterization. With equal justification it can be argued that the Communists can be well trusted to abide by agreements if only they believe that the agreements serve the Cause. Accordingly, an entirely new class of strategic problems can be posed, for example, how to get the Communists to believe that this or that agreement (of "advantage" to us) will actually help the cause of global communism. There is little likelihood that the extreme right will be enthusiastic about looking into these strategic opportunities, mainly because their faith in the reality of the Communists' avowed goal is as unbounded as that of the orthodox Communists themselves. (Anything which the Communist leaders believe will help world communism, the extreme right also believes will help world communism.) It may be, however, that our strategists will be interested in examining the potentialities of a new "game," since it is in line with a whole class of games conceived by them: how to make the Communists believe this or that (mostly threats). The aim of this book, however, is not to propose "better strategies" but to criticize strategic thinking as such; so we will not pursue this line of thought any further.

To return to the essence of the orthodox Communists' ideological intransigence, it is this: The original articles of faith are sacrosanct. These articles relate to the nature of social relations (the class struggle, the role of the state, etc.) to the interpretation of history (the well-known progression of "stages") and to eschatology (the denouement of history). Like any articles of faith, the Communist tenets are reflected most clearly on the verbal level. For instance, Marxism-Leninism is taught, for the most part, like a catechism: To each question (e.g., "What is the role of religion?") there is one correct answer ("Religion is the opium of the people.") As is the case with every dogma, the writings of the founders of the faith are also sacrosanct. It is impossible to get an orthodox Communist to admit that either Marx or Lenin was wrong on any essential point of theory (or on any inessential one, for that matter).

During Stalin's reign it seemed that a dynasty of infallible Defenders of Faith would be established. But this did not come about. At this writing, doctrinal strife is raging throughout the Communist world, and the possibility seems remote that a dynasty of infallible bearers of authority will ever again emerge. It seems that the demands of practical policy have overridden the longing for doctrinaire unity. However, the demands of practical policy have not yet sufficed to make a dent in the original articles of faith, at least not on the verbal level. It is still impossible for an orthodox Communist to admit that whatever insight Marx and Lenin had into the nature of the state, of international relations, of the class struggle, or of religion has a circumscribed region of validity. Even though a primogeniture of authority has not crystallized, matters of doctrine are still discussed with reference to canonized writings and only rarely with reference to evidence. For the basis of orthodoxy is a doctrine incontrovertible by evidence, which makes evidence either for or against the doctrine irrelevant. An incontrovertible doctrine is worthless as a scientific theory, but this epistemological insight escapes the orthodox Communist, as do (ironically) the full implications of dialectics and of the sociology of knowledge, Marx's outstanding contributions to philosophy and to social science.

The deleterius effects of orthodoxy on Soviet science have been discussed elsewhere (91). For the most part, these effects were not crippling. The demands of "life" (as the Russian Communists themselves are fond of saying) have won precedence, and the witch hunts in natural science are now (hopefully) a thing of the past.

However, in the "sensitive" areas, on which the incontrovertible doctrine has a direct bearing, the dead hand of the past still weighs heavily.

Soviet philosophy is still transfixed by the "fundamental problem of philosophy," as Lenin formulated it, according to which only two consistent philosophical positions are possible, namely, the materialistic position (i.e., the correct one) and the idealistic position (i.e., the wrong one). The Soviet philosopher is therefore constrained to reject outright any formulation in which this "problem" is not central or which attempts to reconcile the two positions or to subject them to further epistemological analysis. Thus we find unrelieved hostility in Soviet writings against the entire modern development in Western philosophy, to which they attribute a most unsavory political role as a prop for the *status quo*. The hostility extends to formulations sharply critical of the *status quo*.

For example, semantic analysis, an outgrowth of logical positivism, when turned upon the encrusted myths of free enterprise dogma, has a withering effect. Also the introspective probings brought out by the existentialists expose the pretensions of the self-styled defenders of Christian civilization as delusions or fraud. But both semantic philosophy and existentialism continue to be castigated in Soviet writings, for both are tinged with "idealism," the original sin of philosophy. In this way, Soviet philosophers deny themselves the opportunity of making a common cause with the severest critics of Western "conventional wisdom." It must be conceded, however, that Communist orthodoxy has much to fear from semantic analysis and from existentialism. The dilemma here is the choice between a defense of one's own orthodoxy and joining forces with others who rebel against the established order. Although in practical matters Soviet Communists have shown themselves capable of flexibility and courage, whenever the articles of faith are in danger they exhibit rigidity and timidity.

It is in politics, however, that the Communists are most severely handicapped by orthodoxy. For here the glaring contradictions between the necessities imposed by "life" and the steadfastness of faith demanded by orthodoxy is most pronounced. "Opportunism," as the orthodox Communists see it, means the sacrifice of principles for immediate gains, which is also the meaning of the word in common usage. Opportunism is a heinous sin in the Communists' political ethos. Yet the Communists' indiscriminate choice of partners and collaborators is well known. These have ranged from the Socialists in the ill-fated united fronts of the thirties to the Nazis in the worse-fated accord of 1939. This was not opportunism in the Communists' view, because the First Principles were never compromised. All the arrangements served, or at any rate were meant to serve, the Cause and only the Cause.

This view is, of course, a direct consequence of the incontrovertible doctrine. The consequence of the view, in turn, is the intense distrust of the Communists felt by non-Communists, even those who are quite sympathetic to the social and economic (if not political) aspects of their philosophy. The pervasiveness of this distrust makes it extremely difficult for Soviet leaders to mobilize enlightened public opinion in the West for their peace proposals, which, if taken at face value, appear eminently sensible, humanitarian, and progressive. The Communists' constant compulsion to reassert the incontrovertible doctrine provides the avowed enemies of the Soviet Union, as well as the covert enemies of peace, with ammunition. For what good is peace if it is openly declared to be a continuation of war, and what good is the "coexistence of different social systems" if tolerance of different systems (i.e., an ideological armistice) is disavowed in the next breath? And what good is it to insist that the conflict is to be a "peaceful one," if from the Communists' own mouths we have assurances that in the struggle with the bourgeoisie everything goes, including fraud and betrayal? There may be excellent reasons for believing the sincerity of the present Soviet leaders' bid to the West for peaceful coexistence and competition for the minds of men, but there is no way to convince the unconvinced short of emphatic disavowal of Lenin's heritage. And this cannot be done without abandoning orthodoxy.

In summary, the commitment to orthodoxy is the Russians' greatest handicap not in the sense that the commitment makes them rigid in the pursuit of policy (it does not) but in the sense that it makes it difficult for them to recruit allies among the non-Communists for the positive aspects of their own aims. Of these, the foremost are peace and disarmament. For this goal they could draw enthusiastic support from the vast majority of the world's population. But the support they draw, particularly in the West, is half-hearted and qualified, because the practice of using allies to achieve specific goals and then turning against them is sanctified by the ethos derived from the incontrovertible doctrine.

Second, Russia's rulers could increase the intensity and the sincerity of the support they enjoy of their own population if certain freedoms (in the old-fashioned Western sense of the word) were still further extended, if the de-Stalinization program were bolder and more thoroughgoing.

Third, orthodoxy puts stifling restrictions on the one sector of science which the Russians have unprecedented opportunity to develop, namely, social science. Such development is impossible on the basis of the incontrovertible doctrine, because evidence is irrelevant to such a doctrine, and no science can develop without critical examination of evidence and without constant revision of hypotheses. Even from a purely utilitarian standpoint (aside from the emancipating potentials of science), a mature social science is sorely needed in the Soviet Union.

To see this, consider for a moment the conventional explanations in the West of the many shortcomings of Soviet economy. Some of the shortcomings are in fact emphasized by the Soviet leaders themselves, for example, low agricultural productivity. Now, to advocates of free enterprise the root of this trouble is perfectly obvious: The farmer has been deprived of the source of incentive, namely, pride of individual ownership. The critic of collectivized agriculture, then, would say there is no cure for the ills of Soviet agriculture except decollectivization (as was done in Poland). But this is no solution, as far as the Russian Communists are concerned. Their problem is to create a society where the individual is *emancipated* from dependence on ownership for security and incentives. Here the free enterprise enthusiast will shrug his shoulders and say that it cannot be done. Nor will he understand why it ought to be done—to him pride of ownership is a positive human value. But need it be a positive value everywhere and forever? Cannot a good case be made for regarding the appetite for possessions as a root of social evils? And if a system has already been established dedicated to the eradication of these appetites is it not worthwhile to try to make it work? (Was not our own Civil War, for example, interpreted as a test to see whether a nation founded upon egalitarian principles is viable?) What if this particular Communist hypothesis is true, as has been suspected by many of the profoundest thinkers who never heard of communism, for example, Jesus of Nazareth?

The Communists' problem, then (a formidable one), is to find substitutes for traditional incentives, which have been abolished. But in order to do this sort of thing effectively, knowledge is needed. Such knowledge could be gathered in the course of scientific investigations, that is, experiments guided by theory and theories supported by experiments. There has been no lack of experimentation with incentives in the Soviet Union. But this experimentation invariably had an improvised, sporadic character. Some new line would be announced, and everyone would greet it as gospel and set about to make it work. If the policy failed, there was no way of ascertaining why it failed. Instead of trying to find out, the leadership sought out scapegoats. If the policy succeeded, there was no way of ascertaining the basis of its success; instead the success was credited to an infinitely wise leadership and so the incontrovertible doctrine became even more incontrovertible.

Another example of a missed opportunity to advance social science is the use of the catch-all "personality cult" to explain the social and political repression under Stalin. Classical Marxist analysis is of no help in this matter. But to rely on another mode of analysis (e.g., the psychological) would be an act of heresy even in the post-Stalin climate. Nor is it thinkable to *extend* Marxist analysis, appropriately modified, to a society ruled by a Communist regime, as was done, for example, by Djilas (35). As a result, no analysis at all is undertaken of a social phenomenon which completely dominated Soviet life for a quarter of a century and which has done immeasurable harm to Soviet society and to the Communist cause.

Finally, the Soviet-Chinese schism must be equally embarrassing to Soviet theoreticians for the same reasons as the "personality cult." Embarrassments of this sort would not be serious if policies could be guided by purely pragmatic considerations. But to the Communist, a "theoretical' 'justification of policy is a real necessity. The sanctity of the incontrovertible doctrine makes it necessary to mask revisions of theory by sophistic circumlocutions and so makes it impossible for an enlightened mind to take the theory seriously.

The Communists have learned tremendously from experience. But their fixation on the incontrovertible doctrine makes it all but impossible for them to get a clear picture of what they have learned and to incorporate the new knowledge into a viable theory. Progress in theory always involves refutation or revision of old views and is incompatible with orthodoxy. The Communists' persistent efforts to combine progress with orthodoxy and their chronic dread of "revisionism" must be extremely wearing on the nerves. At times the Soviet leaders resemble a driver who is pushing with all his might on both the accelerator and the brake. I believe many of the glaringly negative features of Soviet life can be traced to this ambivalance, which in turn stems from an inability to distinguish between heresy and blasphemy.

CHAPTER 21

WHAT WE LACK

~~~~~~

Now we must ask what *we* do not have that we ought to have. Whom shall we ask? Shall we ask the Russians, since we have described their lack from our own point of view? Their answer, I am afraid, will not be illuminating. The Russian is most likely to give a stock answer: America lacks what any capitalist country lacks, namely, an advanced social order—socialism. If we press for elucidation, we are not likely to get very far. At most, we shall get the usual recitation of our social ills: racial discrimination, chronic unemployment, monopolies, imperialism, all blamed on a single "cause"—capitalism. Some of the charges against us will be accurate and well known, others false or out of date, still others too vague either to refute or to admit.

Thus the Russian is not in a position to enlighten us about our shortcomings. Turning to Americans, we will find that representatives of the two main political camps (conservative and liberal) will give contradictory replies. The past-oriented conservatives will insist that America lacks what she has lost—her innocence, i.e., the hardy virtues of the heroic age of unlimited money-making. The future-oriented liberals will insist that America lacks what she has not yet acquired— maturity, wisdom, adaptive attitudes to a changed world.

Is there a common denominator uniting the conservative and the liberal views of America's shortcomings? I believe there is. Both see a lack of national purpose. The difference is that the ones bemoan the feeling of purpose that was lost; the others berate our failure to achieve a purpose realizable in the world of today. To put it in another way, the conservatives seem to be complaining that we are succumbing to senility; the liberals see arrested development as the root of our troubles. Aside from the difference of diagnosis, both camps agree on the character of the symptoms.

I think that the malady underlying these symptoms is our inability to find a form of patriotism which would not repel a serious and informed person. Among us patriotism is peddled largely by primitives and takes the form of braggadocio, puerile pugnaciousness, or nostalgia. Few indeed are the men who can combine a genuine faith in our future with a clear vision. For the most part, our clearest thinkers tend to become alienated from anything that is associated with "national goals."

Are national goals as such perhaps features of obsolete tribal loyalties? Suppose a people succeeded in transcending nationalism and became true cosmopolitans. Would such a people lack something in their make-up? I think they would. I think that genuine identification goes in concentric circles. Only if a person accepts *himself* can he identify with those closest to him. It usually takes a good family member to identify positively with a community and a good member of the community to be a good citizen of a nation. Genuine patriots can transcend their nationalism to become citizens of the world but the broader loyalty does not cancel the narrower one.

It is this process of expanding one's circle of identification which is impeded in the United States. I think that the inhibition stems from our cult of competition (or "success" or the "pursuit of happiness") which declares itself constantly, persistently, unblushingly to be the very essence of "our way of life." We expect our sense of patriotism to be nurtured by the realization that our free institutions provide the opportunities for the most intense and uninhibited self-seeking. The freedom which is most frequently and clearly spelled out in the American creed is the freedom to compete.

There was a time, to be sure, when the sum total of competitive efforts contributed to the rapid economic growth of the country. That was when gigantic treasures of our natural resources were first tapped, when technological inventions were in their embryonic stages, when new methods of production and marketing waited to be developed. Having met a challenge successfully (the challenge to develop an empty continent) we now refuse to meet new challenges—to adapt our institutions and our goals to a radically changed environment.

Our first lack, then, is essentially a lack of courage. The epithet "fat and scared" fits us with frightening accuracy. Lack of courage is a dangerous lack, for we are sensitive about it and tend to overreact with reckless pugnacity when confidence and courage are demanded. This recklessness stems also from our second lack, which is even more serious.

Our second lack is a lack of direct contact with war. Our last such contact was one hundred years ago. Since then we have not experienced any war trauma. Some of the more civilized nations of Europe are also in that position, but they have attained it by virtue of giving up the aspiration to achieve great-power status. We, on the other hand, have achieved great-power status. We were the clearest, perhaps the only, real victors in both world wars, in the sense of having derived real "benefits," as they are commonly understood, from those wars, without having had to pay for them in the appropriate currency. In our 188 years of history we have lost 602,000 war dead, a tiny fraction of the price paid by the other great and near-great powers. In World War II we were losing men on the battle field at a rate of approximately three times the rate of slaughter on the highways, that is, within the range of death rates from natural causes. We have had no devastated cities, no starvations or epidemics, no homeless orphans, no streams of refugees. On the contrary, the people at home lived *better* than they had lived in the years immediately before the war. It would be extremely difficult to explain this anomaly to some one who is accustomed to think in common sense terms; who believes, for example, that a country's standard of living ordinarily is related directly to its production capacity for consumers' goods. Thirty years ago we spent next to nothing on war goods and could have put practically all of our capacity into consumers' goods. But that was the time when people scrounged around in garbage cans for scraps of food. On the other hand, at times when enormous production efforts were diverted to the manufacture of weapons, fewer of us were in want than ever before. And this is true today. The fact that we accept a simple "explanation" (the "work-creating" potential of war industry, as if "work" is something we consume), is in itself a conspicuous symptom of our malady.

The lack of realism in these matters stems, I believe, from our lack of direct experience with war. While we have never been a nation with a strong militarist tradition, our ideas about war are more like those of a militarist nation than are the ideas current among people with strong militarist traditions who have had first-hand experience with war. There is more traditional thinking about war among us than among the Japanese, the French, and possibly even the Germans. Let us see how this comes about.

The traditional rationalization of the savagery of war is accomplished by emphasis on the so-called manly virtues, which war supposedly brings out, such as courage, loyalty, self-denial, etc. Now these claims of the warrior to the manly virtues once had a certain justification. There was a time when the soldier had an opportunity to demonstrate bravery and steadfastness in battle. The immediacy of specific identifiable danger did weld people together into small, fiercely cohesive groups. It cannot be denied that under these circumstances war could be pictured to a certain degree as a heroic enterprise.

With the progressive mechanization of war, the heroic features have been disappearing. It takes less determination to fire a rifle than to swing a sabre, to sit in a trench than to charge on a horse. Artillery has hidden the enemy from view altogether. The patriotic component of war has been annulled by universal conscription which makes everyone automatically "patriotic" and so erases the distinction between the brave and the cowardly. Military "gallantry," i.e., a sense of proportion in the use of violence, the distinction between combatants and non-combatants, respect for the patriotism of the enemy, etc., the last quaint vestiges of the age of chivalry, disappeared without a trace in World War II—the war without a fig leaf.

The term "war" is still applied to nuclear war. One need not quarrel with the usage, since the principal denotation of the word, namely, nationally organized violence, is still contained in it. But all the conventional connotations of war have certainly become meaningless. In nuclear war, bravery is meaningless, since the last strands of contact with the enemy have been severed. The warrior has become a component in a "weapons system." He sits at the controls *in comfort,* as a clerk sits at his desk. He watches signals which convey commands totally devoid of drama. He hears no battle cries, no exhortations to bravery and sacrifice. He is not asked to face a withering fire or to charge the enemy. He obeys only the little colored lights that go on and off on his panels. Death may reach him at any moment, of course, but in this respect the situation of the hero is exactly the same as that of the coward. Neither of them looks death in the face; neither can run away. There are no heroes, only victims. The "ideal" of nuclear war is the complete automation of slaughter.

These matters have been called to our attention many times, and we pay lip service to the realization that war has become "unthinkable." But everywhere in the press, in news broadcasts, in speeches, in school, in recruiting posters, war is still represented as the culmination of "defense," in spite of the fact that the instrumental meaning of the verb "defend" (protect) has long disappeared from its referent.

This loss of perspective is observed everywhere, but it is especially crass in the United States. It seems as if the very lack of a military tradition and our national predisposition for automation has helped us accept with callous complacency the prospect of mass murder of populations.

A French colleague of mine called my attention to an ironic twist in the situation.

"Your callousness," he said, "is the strongest evidence of your essential peace-mindedness as a nation."

I expected a sardonic exploration of this theme. But he seemed perfectly serious as he went on.

"A twelve-year-old girl was given an assignment to write about the Polaris submarine. With the characteristic boldness of American children, she wrote a letter directly to the Navy and was given the red carpet treatment. She was invited to headquarters, taken on a grand tour, photographed with the submarine, and awarded the title of Miss Polaris. This would have been unthinkable in France. We are a warlike nation. We have a military caste of officers who still take war and its traditions in dead earnest. The civilian population hates their guts, but they too take war in dead earnest and with opposite effect. If a picture of a child ever appeared in a French newspaper against the background of some military hardware, we would have a national scandal; perhaps a government would fall. The military would see in such a picture an insult to their profession;

the antimilitarists would declare the picture obscene. But you take such things in stride. This shows you are not really serious. You are just playing at war. You are no more dangerous than children who shoot each other with their index fingers."

"Come now," I said. "You would not say that children are not dangerous if they played with loaded revolvers." I still could not decide whether he was pulling my leg. But he seemed to be in earnest. He argued that all our threats are just talk, that the real commitment to war as a way of life has never penetrated into our national psyche, and he went on to describe the deep-seated kindness of Americans, as evidenced by our free and easy hospitality, trust of strangers, willingness to help, etc.

My colleague's observations of our conspicuous positive national traits are, of course, correct and gratifying. His error is in supposing that war-mindedness depends on a war-making tradition with all its trappings. We have fought and won two world wars without the traditions, without the trappings, and, be it noted, *without any thought of conquest*. This makes us guiltless in our own eyes. No one among us is to blame for the wars, no general staff, no officer caste. We have been forced into the wars. We have been slow to respond to provocations, thus giving ample proof of our peace-mindedness. Only when our patience was tried to the breaking point, only when we were actually attacked (the last time, anyway) did we respond, and then unanimously, as a nation. This blamelessness about war (perhaps actually justified in the case of the second world war) is what makes us so terribly dangerous.

Our lack of experience with the realities of modern war is paralleled by our lack of experience with the realities of misery. In spite of the fact that there is real poverty in the United States, it is not conspicuous. Our very poor are actually a moderate minority, instead of the huge majority which the poor have traditionally constituted in every stratified society. In a way, of course, this shift in the distribution of wealth is a remarkable achievement, but it has its dangerous side. Poverty which is not in the public eye vanishes from awareness as a social problem. An American can live out his whole life without seeing a destitute person or an undernourished child; and he may cling to the widespread belief that America has finally eradicated poverty. This sweeping under the rug of our own poverty-stricken sectors makes the "final solution," that is, the genuine eradication of poverty difficult, in spite of the fact that technically the solution is quite within our grasp.

Especially relevant to our analysis is the global effect of our detachment from the acute problems posed by mass poverty. Our lack of contact with the destitute blinds us to the realities of our times. It is not only a matter of a lack of empathy. The nobleman and the merchant of yesterday, who were surrounded by the destitute in full view and in direct contact with them as servants and serfs, had no more empathy for their plight than has the contemporary dweller in sterilized suburbia, who has no such contacts. But the last century at least produced some thinkers who could exert a significant pressure on public opinion. The Victor Hugos, the Harriet Beecher Stowes, the Dickenses, the Turgenievs, those voices of conscience of Western society becoming aware of its own afflictions, spoke to millions about people and conditions that could be clearly seen. Where are the counterparts of those authors, who would tell us about the oceans of human misery in Asia, Africa, and Latin America, to arouse guilt, compassion, or wrath? About all we have in books of large circulation is *The Ugly American,* and even here the message that "gets across" is an appeal to strategy rather than to conscience (69). The lesson, if any, which seems to have been drawn from that book is that our behavior toward the destitute of the world is stupid, that we ought to be more clever (not more compassionate or understanding) in our dealings with those people, whose good will is a stake in the Cold War game.

It is admittedly more difficult to make the well-fed aware of the ill-fed in our day than it was a century ago. The ill-fed are across oceans; their eyes are shaped differently; they speak languages which are not taught in our schools; and they have never performed for us the services which the mammies, the *nyani,*[84] and the faithful retainers performed for the well-fed of earlier days and so could appear to at least a few of them as members of the human race. To see the Chinese, the Koreans, the Cubans, the Vietnamese, the Angolans as human beings requires much greater imagination. To extrapolate the role these people will play in our immediate future requires a feeling for history. The absence of this feeling is our next great lack.

Our lack of a feeling for history stems from a hypertrophy of horse sense pragmatism, the very quality which has made our civilization great and which now threatens it with extinction. It is not fortuitous that America's greatest industrial genius, Henry Ford, said (under oath, for he was testifying in court) that history was bunk. He was echoing what Mark Twain's iconoclastic outburst had expressed so eloquently: History is for moribund Europe; history is musty museums and scoundrel kings; history deserves to be swept away by master craftsmen, shrewd horse traders, and gaunt settlers on virgin lands.

Even our historians characteristically lack the sense of history. The prevailing image of the historian's task among them is to reconstruct events of the past as accurately as possible. There is a tendency to disavow any effort to find a meaning in these events in the sense of tracing chains of connections between them, noting the persistent themes, deducing over-all secular trends. This timid conception of the historian's task is, needless to say, not sympathetic to a theory of history, that is, to a search for patterns and directions, least of all to the tracing of historical analogies. For the strictly descriptive approach to history is committed to the emphasis on the uniqueness of each event. The task of the historian is seen to be uncovering the minute details which make every "faithfully reconstructed" event non-comparable to every other. In short, the strictly descriptive view of history is primarily a reflection of an antitheoretical bias. "History is bunk" is but another way of saying what many of our historians are saying, namely, that we can learn nothing of practical value from history.

I believe we could learn from history, if by "learning" we mean not so much the acquisition of specialized skills as changes of attitude. But perhaps it is the very prospect of having to change our attitudes that seems threatening to us. Perhaps we fear the lessons of history, and this is why we persist in ignoring them.

A case in point is the apparent analogy between the present world role of the United States and the world role played by the Holy Alliance in the decades following 1815. As is known, the alliance of Russia, Prussia, and Austria was the entrenched monarchy's "defensive" response to the ground swell which had started in France as republicanism, had inundated Europe, degenerated into Napoleonic imperialism and receded, leaving every monarch on the Continent in fearful expectation of the next assault.

In drawing a parallel between revolutionary France and revolutionary Russia and between czarist Russia and antirevolutionary United States, I am not proposing to prove anything, least of all that the events of 1815 were "repeated" 130-odd years later when NATO and SEATO were established. In drawing this parallel, I am only directing attention to the correspondences which have suggested it. The key term in the ideological justification of the Holy Alliance was *legitimacy*. The monarchs, in addition to invoking the divine right doctrine now laid claim to their authority on legalistic grounds. In addition to being wicked the revolutions became *illegal*. The putting down of revolutions was therefore not only a moral duty; it was the exercise of police power, justified by the right of a society to protect itself from anarchy. By extending the notion of "defense," the crushing of revolutions could be justified beyond the borders of the allied powers, since a revolution anywhere threatened the established order everywhere. In fact, it was the expectation of military action by the members of the Holy Alliance in Latin America (to help preserve the established order imposed by Spain) that stimulated the promulgation of our own Monroe Doctrine. The doctrine declared that revolutions in Latin America were none of Europe's business.

The United States foreign policy, conceived by Dean Acheson and John Foster Dulles and continued to this day, bears a striking resemblance to that of the Holy Alliance. It too is based on the principle of legitimacy, namely, the legitimacy of property rights. Confiscation of property, then, is prima facie evidence of the sort of revolution which is not to be tolerated and which may be put down by police actions if possible, and by war if necessary.

Now all three monarchies which constituted the Holy Alliance have long since disintegrated. The presently reigning monarchs of northern Europe, on the other hand, sleep well and are most conspicuous at joyous, ceremonial occasions. They have no need of invoking the principle of legitimacy to stay on their thrones. There is also a dwindling number of the other kind of monarchs, reminiscent of the old type. But the legitimacy principle does not help them when they are dragged out of bed and shot or driven out of the country amid curses. No one dreams of rallying all God-fearing nations to their support. A conclusion seems inevitable, namely, that it was not the legitimacy principle that allowed some of the monarchies to survive but rather the wisdom of monarchs who gave up all the power prerogatives of monarchy.

In a way it is gratifying that the Holy Alliance and its police functions are forgotten. But in another way it is unfortunate that its lessons have not been learned by us, who are in the greatest need of such lessons. Our antitheoretical bias stands in the way of our taking seriously the idea that certain patterns may actually recur in history and the possibility that our unqualified support of "democracy" as we understand it (i.e., profit system plus parliamentary formalities) may be a response quite similar to the unqualified support of legitimist monarchies by the despots of yesterday. It does not occur to us that the socialist and communist movements of today may be the counterparts of republican movements of yesterday and that the struggle between legitimacy and revolution may have the same outcome as the earlier struggle between republican national independence and imperialist monarchy.

All analogies can be punched full of holes, and so can this one. It would be silly to identify Harry Truman with Czar Alexander I or Acheson with Metternich. I must therefore reiterate the disclaimer that the analogy between American foreign policy and the aims of the Holy Alliance was not meant to prove anything. It was offered only to stimulate certain questions, in particular, questions concerning the immediate historical role to be played by people without property and practically without rights, people who therefore care nothing about property rights and are concerned only with bettering their lot, putting first things first—more food, better health measures, more education. These people will give their loyalty to those who can get them these things quickly. If in the process of getting them an opportunity presents itself to settle some scores, this can hardly be expected to dampen the enthusiasm of the oppressed. On the contrary, we learn from past events of this sort that an opportunity to settle scores tends to consolidate the loyalty of the oppressed to the revolutionary leaders. Many innocent people fall victims to unjust and excessive reprisals which typically follow upon the heels of a revolution. But we tend to forget (because we usually identify with the well educated and the articulate) that the victims are in the small minority and that they *resemble* the oppressors. This does not by any means vitiate the injustice, but it does make the insurgent masses insensitive to it. It is quite as difficult for the ill-fed to empathize with the well-fed as the other way around.

Now these matters have been repeatedly mentioned among us, sometimes by highly respected public figures. People of essentially conservative persuasion but endowed with long-range historical vision have warned against the stupid, mischievous, and dangerous game of intrigue and subversion which we are playing in order to maintain the legitimacy principle of property rights. They have branded as a national disgrace our propping up of tottering despots and arming them against their own people. So our lack is not a shortage of people with sufficient imagination and a sense of history to see our cruel historical role. Our lack is a lack of a *climate* which would permit our public to take these warnings seriously. Discussions about how the United States and its ideology fit into the historical scene, of our prospects, of our opportunities to re-examine our policies and to chart another course, not so obviously self-defeating, take place almost exclusively on campuses, in weeklies of small circulation, and at forums arranged by very small groups of dedicated people. Millions of us continue to view the role of the United States in the world scene through the eyes of Steve Canyon and Daddy Warbucks.

CHAPTER 22

WHAT THEY HAVE

~~~~~~

The Russians' greatest ideological asset is a positive basis for patriotism, one which allows national feeling to grow out of more limited
loyalties (to self, family, community) on the one hand and permits
patriotism to expand into a broader loyalty—to a culture, to humanity,
to life itself on the other. This statement may come as a surprise to
the reader who assumes that Russia's "totalitarian" regime must
necessarily stifle every loyalty except that to the national state. And
it is true that certain aspects of Soviet *official* propaganda seem to be
directed toward that end. The recurrent blasts against "rootless cos-
mopolitanism" with their antisemitic overtones are well known as
is the denouncement as "bourgeois nationalism" of the manifestations
of pressures for national autonomies.[85] However, in assessing the
positive aspects of Soviet culture, which is the theme of this chapter,
we must distinguish between the official propaganda and what the
Russians are actually taught in their direct contacts with their parents,
teachers, and mentors. The discrepancy between the official picture
of Soviet mentality and the way people actually live and feel is quite
as great as that between our own "official picture" (for which our
mass media serve as a channel) and the reality of ordinary Americans'
lives.

The language of official Soviet propaganda, found in the press, in
decrees, and in speeches is blatant, banal, arrogant, and redundant.
Soviet propaganda sells Soviet society short, quite the way our mass
media sell our society short, making us appear as a nation of sadists,
clowns, and nitwits. In contrast, the indoctrination of the Soviet young
is subtle, imaginative, and pervaded with positive human values. It

belies our stylized picture of Soviet education as a vast brainwashing system designed to make people into obedient robots.

Urie Bronfenbrenner (16) tells of his visit to a first-grade class in a Russian school. The teacher wants the children to sit erect. Instead of saying something like "Now, children, let us see who can best sit up straight," she says, "Now, children, let us see *which row* is best at sitting up straight." This is the first lesson in attitude formation in the Soviet educational system. Before we react defensively against indoctrinating children with "collectivism," let us see what this lesson teaches and whether the individual is indeed "suppressed" to the collective in this context. The teacher's challenge is an invitation to the children to compete. But the unit of competition is not the individual. The unit is a group. Thus the competitive impulse is coupled with a cooperative one. Competition is not stifled. Merely an antidote is provided to what the Russians consider to be a harmful by-product of competition—egocentrism. Whether this by-product is indeed psychologically harmful may be a matter of opinion. But the opinion that it is harmful is a respectable and a defensible one. Stated positively, the assumption is that at all times, even when competing, the individual must relate *positively* to others and to the world.

CHILDREN'S READING DIET

An examination of Russian children's literature is especially instructive in this regard.

An interesting example is a story which tells of two boys who were nicknamed "Here" and "There." (Their real names were forgotten.) Here was so named because he reached out for everything to take possession of it. "Here, here!" was the first cry he learned. There was attracted to everything at a distance and would start crawling *toward* it, pointing and prattling "There, there!" Here grew up to be a sedentary miser, fat, rich, and dull. There was poor all his life. He went away to study and came back to his native village to teach children. When both men died, Here was forgotten, and a monument was erected to There. The inscription said "He was beloved Here because he was always There." To this day, children ask adults what the inscription means. Each adult (who had been taught by There) has a different silent answer. The flier points to the sky; the sailor to the sea; the miner to the bowels of the earth; the scholar to his forehead.

The language and the tone of these stories bear no resemblance to the exhortations, invectives, and pomposities of official propaganda. Simple, poetic, sometimes richly imaginative, often seasoned with gentle humor, the stories give evidence that the "upbringers" of Russian children are devoted and dedicated human beings. (Russian pedagogy distinguishes between "education" (*obrazovanie*) and "up-bringing (*vospitanie*), and the distinction is reflected in different professional specialties.)

Awareness of the non-Soviet world is not absent in children's literature. As a rule, this world is presented in neutral or friendly colors. I have seen Mickey Mouse in Russian comic books. He is introduced to Russian children as an "American," along with the Italian Cipollino and others. I cannot help regretting that no American child is acquainted with the wonderful Russian comic book characters, in particular Doctor Aibolit and the hair-raising adventures he encounters on his missions of mercy.

Translations are an important ingredient in the Russian child's literary diet, beginning with the nursey level. I have seen Russian versions of French, German, and Italian nursery rhymes, also *Mother Goose*. In the illustrations, the French look French, the English look English, etc.

Besides the themes of personal integrity and social responsibility, another theme pervades Russian children's literature, namely, a love of outdoors. Nature lore and elementary natural history are represented by sketches and stories of animal life. For the very young, animals are represented as weaker creatures to be loved and protected. Older children are introduced to hunting lore but always with an emphasis on restraint and responsibility. Exploitation and conservation of wild life are integrated into a wholesome attitude toward nature.

Science is introduced to Russian youngsters as a great human enterprise. Utilitarian aspects are stressed somewhat to the neglect of the ideational, as is the case with us. Also national figures predominate to the neglect of world figures. Michurin, for example, an agricultural inventor like our Luther Burbank, is pictured as a great scientist. However, in Lomonossov, the Russian counterpart of Benjamin Franklin, the Russian youngster is shown an example of the universal thinker, the scientist-philosopher.

Finally and, perhaps, most significantly, Russian children are introduced already in their primers to the native literary classics. First single lines, then selected passages, finally short pieces from Pushkin, Chekhov, and Tolstoy are the vehicles by which the printed page penetrates the mental make-up of the Russian child. I believe that the classics provide an effective antidote to the indoctrination with official dogma, which follows later in life. This antidote can be expected to act in two ways. First, it can act through the broad range of human values and sophisticated social insights which contrast with the narrow tribal loyalties and political primitivism of the official indoctrination program. Secondly (and this aspect is not often noted), the antidote can be expected to act through inculcating a love for language as an instrument of creative thought. For the easily recognized mark of official propaganda is the atrocious language in which it is couched —a grinding, rasping, monotone of pompous idolatry and angry invective. Few styles exceed that of an official Soviet ex cathedra pronouncement in farcical solemnity and sheer boredom. Only American political speeches and editorials occasionally approach this style in the degree of shameless hypocrisy and disregard for reality. (I must say, however, that our consumer advertising frequently surpasses Soviet propaganda in vulgarity.)

Thus the Russian is exposed both to the best and to the worst uses of his native tongue. But his experience with the best use of the language comes first and fills his most formative years. What little contact I have had with Soviet Russians leads me to believe that genuine humanitarian values and a deep feeling for language as an intricate tool rather than a bombastic weapon dominates the Russian's attitudes. In other words, indications are that what his educational system gives him early in life generally enables him to resist the onslaughts he may suffer later when the pressures of the adult world begin to operate.

On the whole, my impressions have been that Soviet reality is much more wholesome than one would suppose it to be if one judged it by the way it is described in the official propaganda. The Soviet child gets an excellent start in life. He is taught and brought up by people who really care about him, and who have invested their fondest hopes in him. Their teaching methods are superb; the social atmosphere in the schools is excellent. Soviet childhood comes closest to the realization of the ideals which the dedicated Communists have contributed to the repertoire of human aspirations.

What this contrast between the climate of childhood and the climate of adult society does to the Russian psyche I have no way of knowing and am not qualified to guess. I suspect that the results are widely different with different individuals. I know from observation that the range of character and outlook among the Russians is very large, quite contrary to stereotyped notions about the grey regimented mass. In the Soviet Union I have met idealists and opportunists, cynics and stoics. The people who stand out (perhaps in my own impressions because of my basic admiration for that land and its people) are the alert, cooperative, and dedicated. They are industrious, but their love of industry has not been tainted by greed, as that love was tainted in the West during the heydays of industrial development. They are disciplined, but their love of discipline is largely a love of self-discipline untarnished by callousness as it has been in militarized societies.

The outstanding positive feature of Soviet society is that it is possible for clear-eyed young people to harmonize wholesome attitudes with national aspirations. And the pervasiveness and genuineness of national aspirations are unmistakable. There *are* modes of living in Russia where humane impulses and creativity do not conflict with cultural reality. One can be a worker or a farmer and feel that one's work has a meaning far broader than as a means of livelihood. One can be a scholar (in a "non-sensitive" field) and feel that scholarship is noble work, almost revered in popular estimation. One can be an artist (again in a field left alone by dogma, for example, the performing arts) and remain close to the broad masses of people thirsting for beauty and feel their genuine gratitude for having bought beauty to them. One can be a teacher or a parent and feel that one

plants in the children bright hopes for the future of humanity. The
fact that the genuine ideals of communism have survived the Stalinist
dark ages attests to their viability.

Every social order, says the Marxist theory of social evolution,
carries within itself the seeds of its own destruction. So it was with
feudalism, when trade nurtured the growth of cities and with them
the growth of the burgher classes, active, reality-oriented, bold, and
industrious, who finally "took over" as the dominant class—the
bourgeoisie. These people established the capitalist system and its
institutions, which, in turn, gave birth to the industrial proletariat.
This class, Marxist theory says next, has become the time bomb
destined to explode the capitalist social order. What will happen after
the Communist social order is established, Marx did not say. But let
us see what his theory implies.

Two conditions are needed for the "seed of destruction" of a
social order to come to fruition, according to Marxist doctrine,
namely, a confrontation of opposites and a social dynamic which
insures the victory of one side. The confrontation of opposites is the
class struggle, and it is always pictured on the basis of incompatible
economic interests. (In modern terms the class struggle would be depicted as a zero-sum game.) The social dynamic is depicted as the increasingly dominant role which the new rising class plays in the
productive process. Orthodox Communists deny that these conditions
can obtain in a Communist state. They would perhaps admit the operation of a social dynamic which brings a "new class" into prominence,
namely, the professional, intellectual, and managerial personnel. But
the Communist theoreticians would deny that a "class struggle" in any
accepted sense is developing between the new class and, say, the traditional blue collar workers, who, let us recall, have been designated as
the newly victorious class following the Communist revolution.

The Communist theoreticians are quite right when they deny that
a "class struggle" is developing between the white collar and the blue
collar workers in the Soviet Union. This is because the new class is
consolidating its power quite naturally without any struggle, simply
by virtue of occupying decision-making roles and receiving the larger
incomes. To resort once more to the terminology of game theory, the
blue collar workers do not envisage the situation as a zero-sum game.

They believe (probably correctly) that class cooperation is in their best interests, that the economic growth of the country as a whole is a far more important source of progress than anything they could wrest in the way of a greater share of the income now, even if this were politically feasible.

So far there is basic agreement between the view expressed here and the official depiction of Soviet society. The views diverge in the matter of the range which a clash of interests can have. Economic bases of conflict are the most obvious ones and have been studied most intensively, especially by the Marxists. Moreover the Marxists are to be credited with tracing other kinds of struggles (e.g., ideological ones) to their underlying economic roots. Anticipating Freud, who viewed many of our stated motives as rationalizations of covert sexual impulses, Marx viewed ideologies as rationalizations of economic interests.

If this explanation of social struggles is viewed as "final," as it tends to be viewed by the orthodox Marxists (quite in the same way as the orthodox Freudians view sexuality as the "ultimate" basis of psychic conflicts), the theory ossifies. For those who have no vested interests in any particular theory, there is no need for the theory to be drained of its creative power. Thus there is no reason why "economic interest" should not be broken down farther and traced to more primitive psychological concepts. Once this is done, bases for conflict other than economic ones can be readily found or, at any rate conceptualized. There is no need, for example, to force the conflicts which arise among members of a family into an economic framework. Also it would be quite embarrassing for Communists to interpret the present ideological conflict between the Soviet and the Chinese factions within the Communist bloc in terms of a clash of economic interests.

I believe that the psychological concept of personal dominance is more basic than the sociological concept of class dominance. The latter can in principle be explained as the social structure originally emerging from a system of interpersonal dominance relations, frozen in a legalized hereditary pattern. If this explanation is correct, then economic power can be seen as simply a *particular instrument* of social dominance, a particularly effective one, because wealth can be passed through generations and serves a function in organizing productive effort. It seems reasonable to assume that the economic basis of power and dominance is important in all social situations where (1) the essential resources are scarce and (2) no emotional compulsions to share the resources operate. But this factor may well be absent where either the resources are abundant or the survival of the group depends upon a distribution of resources independently of economic considerations. Examples are families (children and often the aged are nurtured regardless of their economic usefulness), groups organized to carry out tasks under adverse conditions (exploring expeditions, military units, bands of outlaws), monastic groups (isolated, communally living religious sects, monasteries), etc. Examples of societies based on material abundance are not yet at hand, although they may be on the verge of coming into existence. It is noteworthy that the Communists consider economic abundance to be a prerequisite condition for an industrial Communist society. They also maintain that this condition together with a socialist economic system is *sufficient* to guarantee the absence of social strife; for the only important social conflicts, in the opinion of the Communists, are those derived from (economic) class struggles.

If competition for dominance is taken as the basis of conflicts, and if economic power is viewed as only a particular instrument of dominance, this facile Marxist conclusion is unwarranted. We are not surprised to see power struggles in basically "Communist" social units, such as families, military establishments, and the like, and we need not view the immense power struggles that at times shake the Soviet Union as paradoxical. Finally we can anticipate the intensification of ideological struggles within and between Communist states, a struggle which need not be related to economic interests. As a result, the social order which the last two generations have come to associate with communism, namely, a social order based on the absolute hegemony of a single autocratic Communist party—will be dissolved.

The dissolution of this social order is to be anticipated as a consequence of the social dynamic built into it (quite in the same way as the dissolution of previous social orders has been anticipated by the Marxists.) For the strength of a Communist state depends, in the view of the Communists themselves (even Stalin could not think otherwise), on the strength of the society which supports it. This is where the thinking of even the most authoritarian Communists differs radically from that of their autocratic predecessors. The czarist ruling class demanded only slavish obedience, not active support, from the masses, which is what the Communist leadership demands. The Communist leadership wants the masses to be vigorous, prosperous, and politically aware (i.e., sincerely to share the convictions of the leadership, not merely to bow to their will). Prosperity demands industrialization; industrialization demands the education of the masses; educated masses are bound to acquire habits of questioning the *status quo*.

One might think that the bureaucracy could postpone the revolt against ideological dictatorship by confining the education of the masses to its technological aspects. Indeed the tremendous emphasis placed on technical education in the Soviet Union sometimes gives the impression that this is just what is being done. A closer look, however, reveals that the humanistic aspect of education has remained as important as ever, especially in the formative years. And this brings us to the other factor of the social dynamic operating in Soviet society.

As has just been said, the Soviet Communists bank not on blind obedience but on active support of their program. They discovered (either consciously on intuitively) that the original ideological props of their program, namely, the drama of class struggle on the international arena and the ideal of international proletarian solidarity, were not sufficient to channel the loyalties and energies of the population and to induce them to make the formidable sacrifices which the dizzy pace of industrialization demanded.

Accordingly, when the industrialization program began in earnest, emphasis shifted from themes of international solidarity to those of national loyalty. Still Soviet patriotism remained remarkably free (comparatively speaking) of aggressive jingoist overtones, Aside from certain xenophobic symptoms, there were few regressive tendencies in Soviet national patriotism. It expressed itself mainly in the idea of national defense in the strictest sense, for example, in the historical emphasis upon Russia's purely defensive wars against the

Mongols, the French, and the Germans, coupled with emphatic disavowals of ambitions of conquest. Further Soviet nationalism expressed itself in the idea of national genius. Although this had some unfortunate side effects (the clumsy priority claims in science and invention) on the whole the results were positive. Here we observe the Soviet upbringing process at its best: The inculcation of the love of soil, love of native tongue, love of the great ideas were characteristically Russian. In all of this the nurturing, constructive principle is paramount. A basis is laid for love, not hatred. Thus the resurgence of national loyalty, based on the concept of national genius and encouraged by the Soviet Communists themselves with the view of strengthening the solidarity of the people behind the regime, cannot but undermine the despotic aspects of the regime.

The conflict, then, in Soviet society is *not* between communism and anticommunism. Russia is probably irrevocably committed to communism. But the Russians who take the ideals of communism seriously are finding out that a struggle is developing on other than political levels, namely, on ethical levels. As such the struggle becomes one between humanitarian ideals, to which the great Russian literature has given such eloquent expression and which the Communists claim as their own, on the one hand, and on the other the dehumanized, ossified, ritualized dogma which serves to perpetuate the power of an entrenched bureaucracy.

Given an opportunity for normal development (i.e., peace), it seems to me that Soviet society must gravitate toward the humanitarian end of the spectrum. Increasing economic abundance, rising educational levels, more frequent and more normal contacts with the West are bound to facilitate this trend. Thus the conscience-motivated Russian can be made to feel that he is on the winning side of a struggle, that a victorious outcome will strengthen his society and vindicate the ideals for which the Revolution was fought and for which his people have sacrificed so much. This is a basis for positive patriotism, Russia's greatest asset.

CHAPTER 23

WHAT WE HAVE

Possessions are often a burden, especially if they are coveted by others who have nothing to give in return. On the other hand, some possessions are useful only to the extent that they can be shared with others. It is with these qualifications in mind that we need to examine our most publicized assets, wealth and freedom.

The simple minded among us assume that we are universally admired for our wealth. Yet it is only in special circumstances that the poor admire the rich. Such admiration may be observed in societies where the distinction between the rich and the poor is thought to be in the nature of things. The poor may also admire the rich if the poor can occasionally become rich and can make this transformation an aim in life. Such was the case with us for several generations. Whatever the actual magnitude of our celebrated class mobility had been or has become, we have profoundly internalized its existence as the basis of social justice. We define our society as one with unlimited class mobility; and from this image, I am sure, stems the conviction that it is normal and desirable for the poor to aspire to be rich and, hence, to admire the rich somewhat in the same way that it is normal and desirable for children to aspire to become adults and, hence, to admire the adults.

The basic flaw in extending this idea to apply to the global population stems from confusing the two ways in which the poor aspire to be rich. One way is the American way. A poor *man* aspires to become a rich *man* and so to *join the ranks* of the rich. He hopes, therefore, to be *accepted* by the rich into their circles. He sees his future spouse among them and plans to bring up his children in accordance with their standards and aspirations. When we expect the people in underdeveloped countries to admire us for our wealth, we do so in the supposition that their aspirations to wealth are, as with us, based on the opportunities provided by class mobility; that they are motivated to work hard within the framework of free enterprise competition and eventually to become our equals.

However, there is another way in which the poor aspire to be rich, and this way is the prevalent one throughout the world, The poor *as a class* aspire to overcome their poverty, and this aspiration is perceived by them as being constantly frustrated by the rich, who stand in their way *as a class*. The poor peasant of a feudal or semi-feudal country does not aspire to become a lord. He does not admire the lord and his ways but hates him and makes plans for his removal. (Besides, there is no way for the peasant to become a lord.) By extension, large sections of the masses in underdeveloped countries see the overdeveloped countries of Europe and America as *obstacles* to their aspirations, not as models to emulate. To what extent the stylized picture of the class struggle and imperialist exploitation represents reality is a separate question. The question before us is whether it is justifiable for us to view our wealth as an *asset* in the present ideological struggle. The conventional American view asserts that it is an asset. The tacit assumption in this view is that the aspirations of the world poor can be so guided that they will accept class mobility as the proper channel for these aspirations. The Communists, however, expect the energy of these aspirations to be directed into class struggle channels. The clash between these two views is one of the principal real issues of the Cold War.[86]

Here we discern the bifurcation between the Soviet and the Chinese view. The Soviet view continues to be dominated by the class struggle version with regard to the *internal* dynamics of the underdeveloped countries. Here they expect and encourage social revolutions rather than the establishment of class-mobile societies (which we envisage). On the level of societies, however, only the Chinese expect a revolutionary explosion in which the underprivileged countries, united under the banner of communism, will wage a worldwide struggle against the "imperialists." The Soviets, on the other hand, although they may vehemently deny it for doctrinaire reasons, have come around to accepting the class-mobility view on the world scale.

To restate the Soviet view, internally the aspirations of the poor in capitalist countries should be geared to a class struggle and so directed toward social revolutions (wherever these are feasible); externally, the aspirations of the poor *countries* should be channeled into class mobility, that is, into constructive peaceful efforts of industrialization, education, and competition with the rich capitalist countries. To be sure, the Soviets acknowledge and even emphasize exploitative imperialist patterns on the world scale as obstacles to the development of the underdeveloped countries along socialist paths. However, they seem to believe that national independence, backed by international guarantees, is sufficient to emancipate the underdeveloped countries from imperialist exploitation. The Soviets are confident that in a world of coexistence the new countries will tend to follow the socialist path (perhaps because the Soviets can provide some aid so as to make those countries independent of Western capital investment).[87] The Soviets to dot say (nor is there evidence that they think) that Cuba or Algeria cannot develop peacefully as socialist states until the imperialist colossi are crushed; however, this seems to be the implication of the Chinese view.[88]

I cannot see how the basic realism of the Soviet view can be denied both in comparison with the Chinese eschatology of the world struggle and in comparison with our extension of the class-mobility model to situations where it makes no sense (e.g., in countries ruled by despotic, corrupt cliques of the rich). True, the Soviets do not follow through to all the realistically derived implications of peaceful coexistence, being prevented from doing so by compulsions inherent in their doctrinaire theoretical system. But we, pragmatists that we are, need not be so constrained. If we dare to follow through to those implications, we can really bring to bear our great assets of wealth and freedom upon immediate future history.

In our own historical experience the accumulation of national wealth took place in a climate of relative freedom. Moreover, the ideals of individual freedom were being constantly proclaimed while wealth was being accumulated; and so the two blessings are linked in our national consciousness. We tend to assume that a social system which leaves the maximum initiative to the individual also provides the greatest opportunity for accumulating wealth. Historical evidence indicates the opposite. The nomads usually enjoyed greater individual freedom and social equality than people in urban-agricultural societies, but it is the latter who accumulated wealth. Moreover, this acquisition of wealth was associated with the coercion of large numbers of people rather than with their emancipation. Such was the pattern in the great empires of antiquity. And this is quite understandable, since the *accumulation* of wealth under conditions of poor productivity requires central control; otherwise the people will eat up the surplus. Where work energy is supplied primarily by human muscle, coercion is needed to get extra work out of people. The pyramids, the temples, the irrigation ditches, the palaces, the roads of antiquity could not have been built without slaves. Accumulation was possible because slaves could be coerced to produce *in excess* of what it took to feed them.[89]

Slaves are coerced by whips and threats. But men can also be coerced by circumstances. The serf had no choice but do what was expected of him, because this is the way in which his life was patterned. He was born into a system of social relations in which he had a *station*. Escape was practically impossible, because there was no place to go. And even if there were, he could escape only if he abandoned his station, that is, whatever security he had against starvation and violence.

It is maintained by the Marxists that the capitalist system is also a coercive one, since the worker is presumably coerced to work by his poverty, which, in turn results from the fact that the worker has been separated from his tools, appropriated in the form of machines by the entrepreneur. Each system of coercion, according to Marxist theory, requires its own legal machinery to enforce it. The property rights of the slave owner and the intricate system of feudal rights and obligations were outstanding examples. Curiously, the abrogation of the rights and obligations, as in modern (capitalist) democratic society, is interpreted by the orthodox Marxist as merely introducing another system of coercion. For the freedom which is most zealously stressed and most jealously guarded in "bourgeois" society is the so-called economic freedom, epitomized in the freedom of contract. This means, according to the Marxists, that the worker and the entrepreneur can agree on any wage scale "agreeable" to both. But this is the very essence of coercion in modern conditions, the Marxists point out, because it enables the entrepreneur to force the worker to accept the entrepreneur's terms or starve. The worker can supposedly sell his labor only at the market price of labor, and this market price according to an older theory (the Iron Law of Wages) adopted by Marx, is determined by what it takes to keep the worker's body and soul together and to allow him to rear his replacements. In this way the orthodox Marxist dismisses the "freedoms" found in bourgeois societies as mere trappings whose purpose is to mask the true nature of capitalist exploitation.

Now it is known that Marxist ideas never got a true foothold in America, and the reasons for this seem fairly apparent. First, when the ideas were beginning to spread, the American frontier was still open, and therefore the ultimatum, "Work on my terms or starve" did not apply to the more energetic and enterprising. They could always push on, and so the potential leadership cadres for a radical labor movement were constantly sloughed off. Second, when the frontier was no longer open, immigration to the United States became heavy, and the immigrants became the "raw" industrial labor force (miners, mill hands, etc.), while native Americans moved into middle class positions. The immigrants were largely of peasant stock unpermeated by Marxist ideas. Besides, they were a "self-selected" population. Those who came were strongly motivated to better their *individual* lots. Conditions of class mobility, for which America became justly famous, reinforced the motivation. Upward-mobile people are not receptive to the ideals, nor even to the concept, of class struggle. Third, the extremely favorable conditions (vast resources, energetic labor force, absence of restrictions, security from hostile neighbors) made possible an extremely rapid accumulation of capital. Capital means machinery. While in preindustrial days, in order to produce twice his keep (the excess going to the master or landlord), the worker or peasant had to slave like a beast, in our day to produce several times one's keep has become comparatively painless.

Finally, consider the implication of the Iron Law of Wages itself as it applies to wages in a highly complex industrial society. The law asserts that the worker will be paid what is needed to keep him in the system of production. Leaving aside for a moment the collective bargaining power of the worker, let us assume the Iron Law of Wages to be valid. But in order "to keep the worker in production" nowadays, much more must be given to him than was given to his ancestor in the English mills. The modern worker must be given an education to enable him to acquire certain skills, and so must his children, who will in time replace him. Besides, the role of the "worker" has become greatly differentiated. The wage earners now include a vast population of clerical and managerial personnel. Whatever the "class loyalty" of these people is, *economically* they are of the working class, because their earnings derive from that portion of the "variable capital" (As Marx called it) which is earmarked for wages. Now the salaried manager requires a great deal for this upkeep. He must be schooled and dressed in a way that inspires respect in his subordinates; he must have an expense account; his wife must be socially presentable. Similar demands are placed on even the humblest "wage slaves." To take an example, a young lady receptionist of a respectable firm must present a veritably regal appearance and a cultivated accent. It is quite impossible for salesmen, technicians, clerks, in short, employees who have dealings with people rather than with things, to be dressed in rags and to live in hovels.

The rise of the white collar–professional class has been repeatedly pointed out as a living refutation of Marxist theories. It is noteworthy, however, that the comfortable middle class standard of living is not necessarily a refutation of that part of Marxist theory which pertains to the Iron Law of Wages. For even if the law operated *unimpeded,* middle class standards would still need to be maintained for the middle class, because they could not otherwise function effectively in the productive process.[90]

Where Marxist theory "fails" is in its tacit assumption that the Iron Law of Wages would keep the entire wage-earning class in misery and so prepare them for revolution. But "failure" is an ambiguous term when applied to a theory. Did Newton's theory of gravitation "fail," since it did not explain the precession of Mercury's orbit? Yes, it failed in the strict sense of the word, but only when it was stretched beyond its range of application. Did Darwin's theory of natural selection fail, since the mechanisms of variation assumed by him (in ignorance of mutations) were not operating? Yes, this too was a failure, but Darwin's notions about the mechanism of variation (among which was the Lamarckian idea of inherited acquired characteristics) were not essential to the principal features of his natural selection theory. It is quixotic to imagine that any theory can be a final and total explanation of some class of phenomena. So it is with Marxist theory. It has failed in particulars. But it is not a useless theory because of its failures. On the contrary, if the ardent adherents of the theory were not so intensely concerned with keeping it "pure," the failures of the theory would be its most valuable contributions to our knowledge. For it is precisely the *failures* of a theory which provide a leverage for further development. This happens when the desire to know outweighs the anxiety about "being right."

Let us now resurrect Karl Marx and take him on a tour of America. Let us show him a model factory with its parking lots, landscaped lawns, and tiled washrooms; the workers' suburb; the school where the workers' children go. Let us show him what the $6,000-per-year worker can buy, what his life expectancy is, and the retirement checks he gets from the government and from his union. Let us take Marx to a plumbers' convention in a Statler Hotel and ask him to guess to what social class the participants belong. Then let us tell him. One might guess that Marx will be convinced that sometime around the turn of the century the social revolution occurred in the United States and that the dictatorship of the proletariat has *come and gone.*

Let us allow Marx to persist in that delusion for a while. By properly selecting what we show him, we can confirm his impression. We can select features of our life to make him believe that the state has indeed "withered away," having lost its coercive function. We can point out to him the absence of censorship, of a passport system, and of police surveillance over citizens. We can point out the autonomy of local governing bodies, freedom of assembly and association. For a while, Marx might even nurture a thought that religion, the opium of the people, has vanished. For he might mistake our church congregations for social clubs.

Next, let us bring a dissonant element into our picture. We now show him a strike of dock workers. Before he has a chance to revise his opinion of what American society is like, let us explain to him the issue of the strike. American workers refuse to service a ship which stopped in New York on the way to Cuba.

"Can it be," Marx might ask, "that Cuba is still under tyrannical rule of the capitalists and that the workers of socialist America refuse to have anything to do with that country?"

We whisk him away to Cuba, where he will see evidence of a society in the "dictatorship of the proletariat" stage. The slogans, the meetings, and his own pictures on posters will convince him that the social revolution has just taken place in that country. So far so good. America, obviously more advanced than Cuba, had had its revolution much earlier and had already emerged as a classless society and so lost its revolutionary symptoms. Cuba, economically far behind, is following in America's footsteps. But why should American workers sabotage the efforts of the Cuban workers? And what is all this talk about *Yanqui imperialismo*? Also, what is the significance of the Guantanamo base?

We take old Marx back to the States, and this time we do not tell him where he is. We now show him the seamy side. We take him to the slums of Birmingham, Washington, and Chicago. We let him watch the antisegregation demonstrations. We show him the Pentagon and explain the structure and function of our death industry. We let him read *U.S. News and World Report*. Then we get into our time machine and show him a Soviet concentration camp of ten years ago. We take him back another fifteen years and show him Stalin's liquidation industry. We let him read a draft of the Soviet-German pact of 1939, and then show him Hitler's Germany. We change the scene more and more rapidly, showing him the most glaring contrasts among countries and within countries. When he begins to show evidence of complete confusion, let us take him to his old desk in the British Museum and to the time when he was writing *Das Kapital* and ask him to add a chapter, predicting the history of the next century, based on what he has seen.

There is no way of bringing this magic about, and so we have no way of knowing what he would write. We know that since Marx's days a century of cataclysmic events has destroyed old societies and brought new ones into being. We know there is no way to squeeze these events into a Marxist scheme that will satisfy anyone except those who would persist in their orthodoxy no matter what has to be ignored. Those we cannot reach, and we need not try to reach them. However, there are others who are groping for a historical vision derived from actual historical experience of the last century. Those we can reach, if we do not ourselves fall victims to dogma. Here is where our "antitheoretical bias" can serve us well, if we put it to proper epistemological use. The view that history is bunk is a nihilistic view; but to say that history is a complex process in which several currents can be discerned, some going in opposite directions, and that therefore it is extremely *difficult* to learn from history —this is to make a realistic appraisal based on an open-minded examination of historical facts.

We can point out that the development of American civilization neither confirms nor refutes Marxist theory. It certainly does not confirm it, because so much of what has happened does not fit the oversimplified Marxist scheme. But neither does our recent history refute Marxism, because it took place under conditions so totally different from those which characterized the societies studied by Marx. In fact, even in Europe the conditions which provided the strongest evidence for Marx's theories have largely disappeared.

However, there might be more justification in viewing *global* economic history of the last century in Marxist terms. For here the intensification of exploitation of the propertyless did actually take place, and a progressive impoverishment of the colonial peoples was a result. If there is a genuine proletariat today (people who have "nothing to lose but their chains") it is to be found not where Marx found it, in the industrial cities of Europe, but in the villages of Africa, Asia, and Latin America. But a social revolution on a world scale presents problems undreamed of by either Marx or Lenin (who extended Marx's notions to global dimensions). Lenin could still think of a social revolution being "accomplished" by armed detachments of industrial workers seizing a few telephone exchanges and railway centers and by local committees assuming the authority of the state. To imagine such events on a world scale is to indulge in fantasy. The world's "poor" do not form a single-willed "class" and no elite like the Russian Bolshevik party can command their undivided loyalty so as to be able to chart the course of revolution and of reconstruction. In other words, although national social revolutions are still possible, perhaps even feasible, in underdeveloped countries, a social revolution on a world scale has become too big a job for any organized group to handle. On a world scale, the only promising path to improving the lot of the poor is that of cooperative effort. The nations which have arrived will have to help the nations which have not. Here is the opportunity to vindicate the principle of class collaboration, which is anathema to orthodox Marxists.

In this one respect—on the level of global development—orthodox Marxism will have to be abandoned. Not a power struggle but cooperative effort and good will based on enlightened self-interest and on an awakened conscience (sometimes it is impossible to distinguish between the two) will help bring into being a global society of the sort envisaged by the old-time Communists. Our help will be needed, and therefore our advice will be heeded.

We can give substantial help if we put our wealth to good use. We can give sound advice if we put our freedom to good use. This we can do if we recognize the truly significant meaning of our freedom. Let us see what this is.

Our most precious freedom is the freedom from compulsive conceptualization. The victim of compulsive conceptualization must twist his perceptions in order to force his observations into his preconceived scheme. At times nothing else will do but to shut certain stimuli out from consciousness altogether, that is, to become deliberately blind and deaf. At other times, events must be invented or trivial events blown up to significance. Thus, confronted with a challenge to his system, the compulsive believer lies to himself, and having deceived himself, he will lie to others without compunction, because he does not even know that he is lying. Now we are certainly not free of dogma and of stereotyped evaluations. But our thinkers are not forced into orthodoxy. What orthodoxy we observe in academe, in the organs of public opinion, in the pulpit, etc., has been largely self-imposed by the compliant, the timid, and the dull.

In spite of plentiful instances of intimidation, it is still possible in the United States to resist pressures for conformity. Questioning the established order and established thought patterns and mores, rejecting the legitimacy of self-constituted authority is a tradition that dies hard.

This tradition is still alive in our society, at any rate in the Western World.[91] Our problem is to convince the Communist world that in intellectual freedom we have something that they *need*.

Can the Russians be made to feel a need of intellectual freedom? I think so if their problems are presented to them from their own point of view. They recognize and emphasize the importance of understanding history. The second half of the history of the United States cannot be understood in any of its essentials in terms of Marxist-Leninist concepts. But any one who aspires to the role of prognosticator of history (as the Communists do) must understand these events. He must understand how it happened that, contrary to expectations, the most capitalist of the capitalist nations has achieved also the highest per capita consumption of commodities and a distribution of income whose spread from lowest to highest stratum does not exceed that of the oldest socialist country. Also a materialist has to understand how it comes about that material riches and leisure, undreamed of fifty years ago, have failed to make the life of the American worker joyous and exciting. Evidently it was not only poverty and the monotony of long hours of toil that was responsible for the plight of the industrial worker. Is there something debilitating in the capitalist system *regardless* of the economic inequities it had been supposed to aggravate? Can it be that the capitalist system is even *worse* than it had been depicted by Marx and Lenin? Here is an idea that will actually appeal to a Communist! But once he starts thinking along these lines, he may be led to consider other ideas. Can it be something inherent in the industrial system at a certain stage of development or in the emphasis of the importance of material wealth to the exclusion of other values, or even (let us face it) something inherent in human nature that makes an emotionally satisfying life so difficult to achieve? Whatever it is, the Communists have to know it if they are seriously engaged in the task of building a good society. And whether they are or not, they believe they are.

The Communists, who have committed themselves to planning their economic and social development, would learn a great deal from America if they viewed our development as an object lesson of history: What happens when a capitalist society becomes affluent? In order to do so, the Communists must rid themselves of their prefabricated facile explanations and relearn the dictum, ironically credited to Lenin, namely, "Facts are stubborn things." This can be done only in the climate of intellectual freedom. On this score we can teach them a great deal (as representatives of Western culture, if not specifically as Americans).

If we cherish this climate and nurture our often neglected intellectual freedom back to vigor and make it contagious, we can make it our greatest asset—something that we have and they need, something we would freely share with others and be the richer for it.

CHAPTER 24

THE CASE FOR IDEOLOGICAL DISARMAMENT

Within a few days of each other there appeared a special issue of the *Nation* devoted to a single topic (24) and a news story about a new type of Moscow trial. The juxtaposition of these two is a pertinent illustration of what was said in the last four chapters. Most of the incidents related in the *Nation* had been widely publicized. They were gathered together into a dreary picture of a society to which Polybius's remark may well apply. "In Carthage, nothing which results in profit is regarded as disgraceful." There was the price-fixing conspiracy of the electrical companies, the quiz show scandals, the packaging hoax, the cheating in examinations, all testifying to an atrophy of a sense of honor in our society. Lying, chicanery, and cheating seem to have become normal components of career-building in business and in public life. An attitude of indifference toward dishonesty or its outright acceptance as an instrument of acquisition or advancement seems to have diffused through our population.

The news story, which referred to a new form of judicial procedure in Russia, told of a trial of three youths in a "Court of Public Opinion." The youths had engaged in commercial transactions. Their punishment was exile from Moscow and an assignment to "socially useful work" on outlying farms. It was emphasized at the trial that the young men had not committed any crimes. The court in which they were tried was not a criminal court. A Court of Public Opinion is a new institution in Soviet life, designed to try cases of violation of "moral standards," not violations of law.

One of our social diseases, as Fred J. Cook points out (24), is a climate of public opinion in which anything that is not illegal is condoned. The attitude reflected in the new Soviet "courts" can be viewed as diametrically opposed to ours. Staying within the law does not make you safe. There is also something called public morality. The violator of this morality is called to task.

The contrast between the two sets of mores stems from a fundamental difference in the conceptions of what are proper channels of aspiration for an individual in society. With us the pursuit of private gain is not only tolerated; it is commended. Aggressive, acquisitive ambitions bespeak a person's vigor, his involvement with the culturally accepted values, in short, his worth. To be sure, two constraints on the pursuit of private gain have been traditionally recognized in our society. The acquisitive strategies must be kept within the law, and there must be a recognition of something called "fair play." But fair play is judged by what is *expected* of the individual. Therefore, there is no such thing as a *prevalent* violation of fair play. If a behavior becomes prevalent, it is expected, and everything which falls within expectation is "fair." As for the constraint of legality, it often loses its effectiveness through the constraints put upon law-enforcing agencies themselves. These latter constraints are consequences of our system of justice, which in criminal proceedings puts the entire burden of proof on the state. Another source of constraint upon a system of justice is the tacitly recognized extenuating circumstance. Every legal system recognizes such circumstances.

In any society, extenuating circumstances are those which make the violations of law appear a consequence of yielding to a passion with which the society is in sympathy. For example, in Mediterranean countries, husbands who have murdered unfaithful wives are treated with comparative leniency. In our society the predominant passion is that of private gain. Moreover, in any society, extenuating circumstances are most clearly invoked when the society's most respected members are transgressors. Accordingly, violation of law by respectable business leaders in pursuit of business success are those most likely to be understood and all but forgiven. The infrequency with which such transgressions are brought to trial and the mildness of the punishments imposed contribute eloquent evidence of these attitudes.

In the Soviet Union, on the contrary, the motivation of private gain is an *aggravating* circumstance. A dramatic example was reported in 1962 (4).

An owner of an apple orchard was tried for the murder of a teen-age boy, one of a gang of boys who raided his orchard. The accused depended on his orchard for his livelihood and the frequent devastating raids (which were not mere pranks but large scale operations) drove him to distraction. Once he caught the thieves in the act, whereupon they set upon him and beat him up severely. Complaints to the militia brought no results. In desperation, the man bought a shotgun, and the tragedy occurred when the orchard was again raided. The accused insisted that he gave a warning whistle (this was corroborated by witnesses) and that he fired the shot in the air.

It is almost certain that an American court would have acquitted the defendant in these circumstances if he were brought to trial at all. The Soviet prosecutor demanded the maximum sentence of ten years at hard labor. What shocked the American observers at the very outset of the trial was the brutal interrogation by the presiding judge, which gave one every reason to believe that the verdict had been decided upon in advance. But the greatest shock was to come at the end of the trial. In his concluding statement, the presiding judge stated that the murder fell not into the category of ordinary crime but into the category of *political* crime and that consequently the accused was sentenced to suffer "the highest measure of social defense," namely, death by shooting.

The actual outcome of this affair was an appeal to a higher court *by the prosecuting attorney* and a commutation of the sentence to ten years at hard labor. But the point was clearly made. What is most severely punished in the Soviet Union (next to disloyalty to the regime) is a certain complex of *attitudes*. These are precisely the attitudes which in the United States command the highest social approval: the attitudes which reflect an ambition for economic independence. The orchard owner sought to make his living *outside* the approved channels of participation in the socially organized production process. He became a property owner. No matter that he worked as hard or harder than collective farmers; no matter that his apples were as good or better than those grown on collective farms and that they added to the country's wealth. He developed the *mentality* of a property owner, investing his energies into activities directed at increasing his personal wealth. There was no way to punish him directly for these sins against the established mores, but when the opportunity arose, the accumulated rage against him was released and he was destroyed.

"How many apples would you have lost," the presiding judge kept harping, "if you had spared this young life? Five? Ten?"

Not only do crimes motivated by "greed" evoke the harshest punishments in the Soviet Union. The range of punishable offenses had been extended beyond the bounds prescribed by law. Although the law does not specify a definition of a "parasite," official propaganda does. A "parasite" in the Soviet Union is one who derives his income from private business transactions. Although it is not against the law to purchase an item from a private person, nor to sell one at a price agreed upon, the person who makes *a practice* of buying things to sell at a profit is called a parasite. Although beyond the reach of the law, he has been put within the reach of "outraged public opinion." The recently established courts are empowered to condemn such persons, to expel them from communities, and even to impose sentences such as "to engage in socially useful labor" for prescribed periods of time. Such sentences have the force of law.[92]

Among us "aggravating circumstances" also operate, particularly in certain regions. In the South, punishments meted out to Negroes accused of sexual advances to white women are notoriously harsh. For example, while there is no law forbidding a Negro to look at a white woman in a certain way, Negroes have been lynched for just that.

The dominant society strikes not so much at an individual guilty of an offense against its established mores as at the mentality which threatens the mores. In the case of the American South, the threatening mentality is that of the Negro who makes the bid for equality. But you cannot jail or kill a mentality. You can only jail or kill human beings. Accordingly, any opportunity which presents itself for punishing an individual who *concretizes* the threatening mentality is eagerly seized.

As in Russia, with us too this process extends beyond the bounds set by law. The self-appointed guardians of morality in our society are largely special interest groups, each of which has singled out some aspect of behavior which it finds threatening. All too often their pressures are directed toward the preservation of extremely parochial conceptions of morality. But there are few pressure groups campaigning against liars, chiselers, gougers, or bigots.[93] By and large, everything that is legal is generally also moral, and even some illegal activities carry no stigma of immorality. Our society belies the statement by Justice Earl Warren, "In civilized life, law floats on a sea of ethics." If everything that is legal is also ethical, one has lost the basis of law itself, and ultimately contempt for law must follow.

But how is the concept of what is ethical to be extended beyond the limits of legality? Have the Soviets solved this problem by introducing their Courts of Public Opinion? Most Americans would be repelled by the idea. Unlike the Russians, we would be keenly aware of the inevitable abuses. We would have visions of non-conformists (among whom outstanding individuals are sure to be found) hounded by bigotry and mediocrity. Besides, these courts would be in obvious violation of our Constitution, since they would deprive the condemned individual of "due process." In short we would not *trust* our public opinion to regulate morals. We are proud of the safeguards which still exist among us to protect the non-conformist from the pressure of established convention. The seeming lack of concern of the Russians with the vicious potentialities of the Courts of Public Opinion indicates that they have few misgivings on this score. In fact, the Russians can be expected to exhibit these courts as manifestations of genuine democracy (mass participation in public affairs). Erroneous as this view must appear to us, the fact remains that the courts reflect just the sort of quality of which our society has been deprived. We lack a public opinion concerned with social morality.

THE MORES COMPLEMENT EACH OTHER

One cannot escape the impression that in many fundamental respects the two worlds, ours and the Communists', complement each other. The features of democracy which they lack (restraints on the power of the ruling group, tolerance of ideological diversity) are precisely the features we are proud of. Those necessary features of a complex society which we lack (social responsibility, historical vision) are the foundations of Communist society. This is not to say that either we or they have realized our respective ideals. Brutal and arbitrary power is wielded in many areas of American life. I am sure that greed motivates large sectors of Soviet society. But to the extent that our respective societies have not yet become completely and irrevocably corrupt, the original ideals on which each was founded have remained. That is to say, *whatever* remains of the creative forces that brought our society into being is embodied in the restraint on coercive power of the state and on tolerance of diversity. Of all our much publicized freedoms, the freedom from arbitrary and relentless persecution, the freedom of social criticism, the freedom to seek truth and to speak it without *necessarily* suffering drastic consequences, all these are real.

Of all the trumpeted blessings of the Soviet socialist society, one is genuine: the ideal of the socially responsible individual who participates actively in a collective effort toward a goal ardently desired by all. It is a goal, moreover, which can be reasonably defended as a worthy one for all mankind.

The idea of complementarity of the two worlds has been proposed here to counteract the Devil image which dominates both Russian and American conventional thinking. In the light of the complementarity idea, it is possible to see the source of the Devil image, for it is true that what one world holds sacred the other neglects or even subverts. The Cold War feeds on this incompatibility and rivets the attention of both populations upon it. In the Cold War climate, it becomes next to impossible to accept the idea that each world has preserved a value which the other world *ought* to develop or restore. Our social disease is our social immaturity: We have failed to develop a social conscience appropriate to a complex, crowded society. Their social disease is their political immaturity, a failure to develop political institutions able to cope with the problem of power allocation in a society based on a planned economy. Each world ought to inquire into what can be learned from the other instead of castigating the other for what the other does not have.

A consequence of recognizing the complementarity of the two worlds would be a step toward ideological disarmament. This idea appears in various forms and with various emphasis in the recent peace literature. Osgood's tension-reducing proposals, for example (86), essentially involve steps toward ideological disarmament. However, such a commitment is only rarely encountered. "Voices of reason" on both sides usually urge an end to the arms race in order that the "really important" struggle, namely, the struggle for men's minds, can go on unimpeded by terror. The prevalent theme even among the peace-minded is still "Let us make the world safe for a decisive ideological struggle."

In the light of the complementarity idea, the prospects of an ideological victory of either world over the other seems equally ghastly, if capitalism is represented by the present American society and communism by the present Soviet society. For both societies are diseased even though the nature of their diseases is widely different. Ours is a chronic disease. We are riddled with innumerable festering sores which drain our vitality and to which we have become accustomed. Boredom, apathy, and cynicism are debilitating but not agonizing, because the sensibilities of the victims have been dulled. The symptoms of the Russian social disease are more dramatic and more painful to the victims. The frustrations imposed by tyranny are paralyzing. Terror means bloodshed and crippling fear.

But it seems to me that the Russian disease is easier to cure than ours. The pressures for freedom and dignity of the individual, against the hypertrophy of coercive power, against stifling dogma, exist in the Soviet population and are building up. It seems that by issuing just a few decrees, the leadership of the Soviet Communist party could transform Soviet society. They could release the pent-up creative energies to mix with the heady air of freedom and so stimulate an era of magnificent accomplishment unequaled in history. Our situation is not so simple. American society cannot be revitalized by a few obvious "measures." Our disease has penetrated deep into the psyche of the population. With us it is not a matter of removing restraints but of adding incentives, restoring an aim in life. We do need a "cause" desperately. That is why we have been seduced by the phony self-defeating cause of the anti-Communist crusade.

Perhaps it is true, as seems to be implied in certain psychological theories, that we need enemies. To a certain extent, however, we are free to choose them. Not infrequently our enemies become those whom we have so designated. We could, therefore, try to choose our enemies more wisely. It is not wise to choose communism as our enemy; nor is it wise of the Communists to choose the "bourgeois world" as the enemy. The magnitude of the destructive force which can be marshalled in support of "socialism" and of "Western civilization" is so formidable that only the destruction of both of the "defended" societies can result from a confrontation. So much is obvious. What is not obvious to many is that a victory in the ideological struggle is also an illusion, as it has been in every ideological struggle in history. No ideology has ever vanquished another and remained what it has been. Neither side, therefore, can expect to "win" the ideological struggle in the sense of preserving its own ideology while getting rid of the other one. However, both sides could, if they were willing and persistent, get rid of their own psychopaths. If enemies are needed to fulfill a psychological need, they are readily available. A simple realignment of forces would enable the liberals of both sides to concentrate on their common enemy—the extreme right-Stalinist axis.

How likely is such a program to be adopted by the policy makers of East and West? Not very likely. But this is true of all the sensible programs which have been proposed. The fact that none of them is likely to be adopted or even seriously considered has little to do with their feasibility. It has to do rather with the outlooks and the thinking habits of people who come to occupy decision-making roles. I believe that a program of ideological disarmament is as feasible as the various disarmament and tension-reduction plans which have been proposed. Nor need ideological disarmament interfere with other programs; it can complement them. But ideological disarmament requires even more boldness, imagination, and a propensity for self-appraisal— qualities all but incompatible with those necessary to achieve political success in the United States or in the Soviet Union.

On the other hand, the real risks taken by a Soviet or an American head of state in attempting to implement an ideological disarmament program are not to be dismissed lightly. If a Soviet head of state tried to embark on such a program, he would be staking all, including possibly his life, and the outcome of the risk would be immediately decisive. It is possible that Khrushchev took such a risk when he made his famous speech denouncing Stalin's crimes (64). A proposal to re-examine Marxism-Leninism at its very roots might be an even greater risk. But if he or his successor should win such a gamble, he would win immediately. For there is little doubt that the end of Russia's isolation from the West would be enormously appealing to the Soviet masses, especially if accompanied by sweeping reforms carrying de-Stalinization to its logical conclusion.

An American president embarking on a program of ideological disarmament would be taking a less dramatic risk, because the ensuing struggle would be slower in developing. The President could place technical and constitutional obstacles to the attempts to remove him, meanwhile mobilizing popular support. But his struggle would be harder and more protracted than the Soviet leader's. The Russians would joyously welcome a sudden announcement that America is no longer an enemy and would avidly read the crop of articles in their theoretical journals depicting the "special American form of capitalism as a system particularly suited to the American temperament and an inevitable result of America's historical development." But no analogous announcement can be made to Americans. Americans are simply not told as bluntly as the Russians or the Catholics what their attitudes must be in matters of faith.

A shift in the public conception of communism in the United States requires no less than a thorough re-education. But there are no institutions through which this re-education could be undertaken and no specific channels through which the new ideas could be energetically and persistently disseminated from a central source. An outright creation of such channels (e.g., a Department of Propaganda) is, of course, out of the question. Nor is the outlook promising for using the well-known gambits of news management or techniques of public relations. For this sort of re-education cannot be treated as another selling job. It should aim for results deeper than compliant behavior, and these results cannot be meaningfully assessed as are the results of political and commercial propaganda from surveys, votes, and sales. In the United States, ideological disarmament would be on the level of mass therapy, requiring an approach to conscience and psyche, rather than to reflex responses. Madison Avenue gimmicks simply will not do.

Fortunately, there are now in America many men and women who

would gladly meet this challenge and who could furnish the professional talent and rank-and-file cadres for developing and implementing
methods of undoing the mass-psychological damage inflicted by the
Cold War. This reservoir of talent and dedication is evidenced by
the considerable initial success of a somewhat similar operation, the
Peace Corps. An ideological disarmament campaign could begin
somewhat along the same lines, naturally with the cooperation of the
Soviet Union. A manyfold expansion of the East-West cultural exchange program could be a natural starting point.[94]

Unlike hardware disarmament, some ideological disarmament measures can be undertaken independently of their adoption by the
governments. Although individuals and groups of private citizens cannot dismantle a single bomb, they can contribute to the goal of ideological disarmament by mutual and self-education. Admittedly, there
are more opportunities for such initiatives in the United States than in
the Soviet Union, but the opportunities now existing in the Soviet
Union are not to be discounted. The opportunities can be developed,
provided they are not perceived as direct threats to the power of the
Communist party. It must be kept in mind that the Soviet elite finds
itself in a most difficult dilemma on this score. On the one hand, many
of them fervently desire the end of nuclear terror, because they continue to entertain a vision of a "triumphal victory of communism" in its
humanitarian sense, i.e., the establishment of a Communist society in
the Soviet Union as a shining example to the rest of the world. This
vision is one of abundance and equality, a virtual analogue of the old
American Dream, with "equality" substituted for "opportunity." On
the other hand, the Soviet elite recognize that their power has been
perpetuated by force, by a monopoly of the instruments of molding
public opinion, and frequently by terror. They must be afraid that a
relaxation of tensions may threaten their power, because this power
derives in no small measure from a fear of the hostile bourgeois world
induced in the masses. Thus the Soviet elite need the Devil image too.
But they do not need it as desperately as our military-industrial complex needs it. For it is conceivable that the Soviet elite may continue
in their leadership role even in the absence of the outside threat, e.g.,
as technical, educational, bureaucratic, and managerial elite of a
peaceful society based on a planned economy, while our own military-

industrial complex has no such hopes. Destroy the Devil image, and their role becomes superfluous. On the other hand, while a successful revolt against the military industrial complex is conceivable under the leadership of an enlightened administration in the United States, or at least an active resistance against it is conceivable, the Communist party of the Soviet Union is sacrosanct. It can and will easily crush any overt resistance. A return to terror in the Soviet Union would be a severe blow at any prospect of ideological disarmament.

Thus the ideological disarmament approach involves different problems in the United States and in the Soviet Union. Here the policy (or the movement) can be bolder. The internal enemy (the extreme right) can be easily attacked and the goal of eliminating their influence from public life can be (in fact ought to be) openly espoused. There the approach must be much more cautious. Because of its entrenched position, the Communist party cannot be dislodged as the center of practically absolute power at least in political matters. But because of its ambivalence, the Communist party need not be directly challenged. Rather, the forward-looking faction ought to be helped in the task already half-heartedly undertaken, that of eliminating the backward-looking Stalinists. To reduce the threat to the Soviet Union means to reduce the threat to the hegemony of the Communist party, at least for a long time to come.

CHAPTER 25

CONCLUDING REMARKS

Man has used the knowledge gained from the practice of science to change things to suit himself. He has been immensely successful, largely because "things" are relatively helpless: They do not fight back in a conscious, organized way. To be sure, one can imagine at times that nature "resists" man. Antibiotics and insecticides lose their effectiveness as resistant strains of microorganisms and insects evolve. Occasionally, dependence on technology and hygiene makes civilized man helpless in conditions where the hardier primitive can survive. But the score is still heavily in favor of civilized man. Nature's "weapons" turned against man (if one can talk so), such as depletion of resources and adaptive changes in man's biological enemies, are still no match for man's ingenuity.

Strategic analysis is the application of ingenuity to conflict against a rational opponent. Such an opponent is not helpless. He fights back and generally has the same material and conceptual tools at his disposal. It is therefore unrealistic to expect from the application of "science" the same practically unqualified success in a conflict against equals as has been enjoyed in the conflict against nearly helpless nature. In human conflict, it is not true that the more science we have the stronger we become, because in such conflict only relative strength counts, and this does not necessarily increase with technological potential and strategic cleverness, because the opponent is impelled to make similar gains.

For this reason (among others) many thoughtful and informed persons question the wisdom of continuing the arms race. The stockpiling of nuclear warheads seems to these people especially senseless, since the defensive value of these weapons is admittedly nil, while their alleged deterrent value does not increase with the number of times over that one of the opponents can obliterate the other after both have already been obliterated.

The strategist whom I introduced in the foreword of this book replied to this argument somewhat as follows: "Yes, it is true that there are enough nuclear warheads to kill every man, woman, and child on earth several times over. But this is also true of conventional bombs. There are also enough bullets to shoot every man, woman, and child, and even enough kitchen knives to cut everyone's throat. Admittedly it is more difficult to kill everyone with conventional bombs, still more difficult with bullets, and all but impossible with kitchen knives, unless everyone obligingly stood still. But it can be done, and so there is nothing special about the genocidal potentiality of nuclear weapons."

This observation suggests that there are at least three separate problems involved in the full realization of man's destructive capacity. The first is the availability of weapons. The physical scientists have seen to that. The second is planning for efficient use of the weapons. This is the traditional area for strategy. The third is assuring the willingness to use the weapons.

The degree of willingness required evidently varies inversely with the efficiency of the weapon. It is theoretically possible to kill everyone with a kitchen knife, but the efficiency of this weapon is so low that the project could be accomplished only if the victims cooperated.

It follows that the more destructive the weapons and the more efficient the apparatus of triggering them, the smaller is the degree of willingness required to put them to use. The strategists frequently recognize this when they contemplate the danger of accidental nuclear war. Such a war can occur even though "nobody wants it," and the magnitude of the destruction would be quite unrelated to the intensity of hatred of the opponents for each other.

One of the problems which the strategists have posed is that of making the total war weapon systems both efficient and "safe," a difficult, perhaps impossible task, because the efficiency and safety of weapons systems are inversely related. The neo-traditionalists, perhaps realizing this fact of life, tend to de-emphasize reliance on nuclear weapons and argue for increasing the efficiency of conventional weapons and the willingness to use them.

However, regardless of what kind of arsenal they recommend, the strategists always plead for increasing the willingness and the readiness to resort to violence, because the nexus of their argument is that security is synonymous with strength and strength with toughness.

It seems to me that this is a fallacy. Security against natural dangers can be gained by erecting fortresses against the elements. Security against conquest may at times have been attainable by armaments. But military security becomes a farce if "defense" means the potential and the willingness to wreak total destruction by speaking a few words on the telephone. Quibbling about the meaning of "total" does not help. It is no consolation to be told that "recovery" from a nuclear war is possible. "Recovery" may mean starting the same process over again.

If destructiveness is directly related to the efficiency of weapons and to the willingness to use them, common sense would dictate that security lies in making weapons less efficient and in erecting inhibitions against their use, that is, in physical and ideological disarmament. This argument usually falls upon deaf ears. Nevertheless, the argument must be constantly reiterated.

To begin with, words like "strategist," "decision-maker" and the like refer not to persons but to social roles. These social roles, however, are embodied in human beings. Only rarely do human beings become so completely the embodiments of their social roles that they become completely immune to matters which are of concern to human beings rather than to "actors" in a game of strategy. Some decision-makers may be induced to pay more attention some of the time to the voice of conscience. The resulting changes may be cumulative and autocatalytic.

Second, the orientation of the rulers and of their power derives in great measure from the orientation of the populations whom they rule. This is especially true of politically stable mass states, such as the United States and the Soviet Union. Regardless of the political mechanics, the rulers of both these states achieve their status by a selective process and so reflect the dominant values of their respective cultures. These values change, and to a considerable degree these changes are catalyzed by people capable of analyzing and re-examining the dominant values. These people are diffused throughout the populations of the mass states. They are opinion leaders, writers, educators, and so on. They not only catalyze but also *articulate* the changes of attitude which occur in a culture. One aim of this book has been to point out to these people that the bankruptcy of strategic thinking derives from its own logic. Therefore, when they pit the dictates of conscience against the dictates of strategy, they are not merely pitting sentiments against realism, as the strategists often contend. In stressing the role of conscience in human affairs, the concerned people take a more realistic position than the self-styled "realists," who cannot transcend the limitations of their conceptual scheme. My aim, therefore, has been to strengthen the self-assurance of the conscience-oriented articulate people, hoping thereby to increase their influence on public opinion. Should this result in an autocatalytic process, the climate may change sufficiently to induce, impel, or encourage a revision of current foreign policies.

Third, I have argued that an ideology is essentially a commitment to some particular aspect of the human condition. There are several such aspects, and the validity of one does not negate the validity of others. But in the historical experience of a nation some one aspect is at times singled out and fixated upon. This is especially likely to happen if the aspect in question has played a rallying role in the making of a nation and in the crystallization of its values and beliefs. The beliefs may then freeze into a dogma. Other beliefs appear as threats; and their proponents, as the embodiments of evil. This seems to have happened in the present polarization of ideologies around "capitalism" and "communism."

The maintenance of the balance of terror is rationalized in terms of the polarized ideologies. My aim has been to show that the widely differing ideologies of East and West can be seen as complementary to one another. Both individual freedom and organized collective effort are necessary to man in the present stage of his development. The political systems of East and West are largely the results of attempts to solve one aspect of this problem at the cost of neglecting the other. If this were more widely realized, much of the energy presently expended in a futile ideological strife could be diverted to more constructive purposes.

Finally, I believe it is necessary to make the arguments developed herein regardless of the outlook for success. Conscience, by its very nature, compels people to act on other than pragmatic grounds. To ask what an act compelled by conscience is supposed to "achieve" is pointless. The answer can be only tautological: "Satisfy the demand of conscience." However, even though the immediate pragmatic value of a conscience-driven act may not be demonstrable, in historical perspective it appears that great, irreversible changes in the human condition have been brought about by accumulations of such acts.

NOTES

1. Since this was written, an updated version of the celebrated *Modest Proposal* actually appeared in print (84).

2. The reader interested in the ramifications of this problem and in the mathematical intricacies associated with it is referred to (3) and to (10).

3. The so-called Weber-Fechner Law of psychophysics states that the "just dicriminable difference" between two stimuli is proportional to the magnitude of the stimuli. From this postulate, one deduces that the "subjective" intensity increases as the logarithm of the "objective" intensity; that is, at an ever slower rate with respect to the latter.

4. A scale which assigns ordered positions to a set of objects is called an ordinal scale. A utility scale must be more specific: It should specify the ratios of the intervals between any pair of assigned positions. Such a scale is called an interval scale. On this scale, the choice of unit and of the zero point is arbitrary, but the ratios between the intervals are determined; that is, remain the same regardless of what units or what zero point are chosen. In mathematical language, such a scale is said to be "invariant under linear transformations."

5. Originally, utilities of objects and events were assumed to be inherent in the objects or events themselves, like measurable physical quantities. Later economists for the most part discarded this notion of utility as useless in economic theory. When utility was redefined by von Neumann and Morgenstern, it became entirely dependent on an ordering of risky outcomes.

6. An operational definition is one which defines a thing or an event in terms of operations which must be performed to exhibit what is defined. An operational definition of a "fair die" would be one which specifies a certain observable behavior of such a die. For a thorough discussion of operational definitions see (14).

7. A variable approaches a limit in the mathematical sense if eventually the difference between the value of the variable and a pre-assigned quantity becomes *and remains* smaller than any chosen quantity, however small. This is not true of the fraction of times a four will come up. Although this fraction will ultimately become very nearly ⅙, there is no guarantee against a fluctuation of any size whatsoever after any number of throws.

8. In technical literature, "subjective" or "personal" probability are the usual terms. The reader interested in this topic is referred to the excellent expositions of it in (30, 31, 99).

9. Indeed, the usage of this word has become so broad that its meaning is sometimes seriously perverted. Somewhere I read a statement characterizing a nuclear war as a "zero-sum game," because if it is fought, no one will have anything left. But this is just what makes the "game" non-zero-sum, if the choice is between fighting a nuclear war and not fighting it. In the first case, *both* parties lose; in the second case *both* win or, at any rate, do not lose.

10. Matching pennies is defined here as follows. Players A and B place their pennies as they please. If they match, A wins; if they do not, B wins.

11. A very simple way of calculating both the optimal randomization mixtures and the resulting expected utilities is explained in (129, p. 62). Unfortunately, this method does not work when more than two strategies are available to each player. For a general method of calculating mixed strategies, the interested reader is referred to (123).

12. The mixed strategy so determined is *defined* as the optimal strategy in the formal theory. This is not to say that it can necessarily be justified as optimal in the practical sense. The same problems arise here with respect to optimality as in decisions under risk (cf. Chap. 3).

13. Two prisoners charged with the same crime are held incommunicado. If both confess, both can be convicted. If neither confesses, neither can be convicted. But if one confesses but the other holds out, the first not only goes scot free but get a reward to boot, while the second gets a more severe punishment than he would have got if both confessed. Should a rational prisoner confess or hold out under these circumstances?

The story illustrating the game is attributed to A. W. Tucker. The essentials of the game appeared already in the early experiments of M. M. Flood (44, 45).

14. For an experimental demonstration of what can be expected in response to a trusting act, see (34).

15. We differentiate $x(6-x)$ with respect to x and set the derivative equal to zero:

$$\frac{d}{dx}\, x(6-x)=6-2x=0,$$

which gives $x=3$.

16. We differentiate $x\sqrt{2-x}$ with respect to x and set the derivative equal to zero. We obtain

$$\sqrt{2-x}\ -\ \frac{x}{2\sqrt{2-x}}=0.$$

Rationalizing and clearing fractions, we have

$$2(2-x)-x=0; \quad x=\tfrac{4}{3}$$

Consequently, $y=\sqrt{2-x}=\sqrt{2/3}=0.81$ approximately.

17. On the same basis, Nash distinguished between *cooperative* and *non-cooperative* games. I believe this terminology somewhat misleading, because non-zero-sum games in general have competitive as well as cooperative aspects.

18. A somewhat simpler form of the same game is discussed in (74, p. 90).

19. In non-zero-sum games there is a difference between the *maximin* strategy, which assures for self the payoff which one can get (or better) whatever the other does, and the *minimax* strategy, which holds the other player to his maximin payoff. In zero-sum games, maximin and minimax strategies are identical, but not in non-zero-sum games.

20. It may seem strange that each, in randomizing his (her) strategy, favors the less preferred place. This is so because in searching for the maximin, the two imagine themselves to be playing a zero-sum game, i.e., a game against an opponent who will deliberately frustrate one's attempts to get the largest payoff. This is only a fiction, but it serves as a starting point. Once the maximin strategies are found, the No Sale point is determined, and the bargaining problem comes to the fore.

21. Still another arbitration scheme has been developed by Braithwaite (13). I strongly recommend this charming and perceptive book to the reader interested in the ethical implications of game theory.

22. It might be argued that the DD "solution" of prisoner's dilemma reveals a characteristic feature of a non-negotiable game. I have no

quarrel with this *formal* result; but I still maintain that it is not satisfactory as a normative (prescriptive) solution.

23. I have tried unsuccessfully to trace the source of this story, but its authenticity is not important.

24. Snyder himself is aware of this limitation when he writes, "Finally, assume (a rather drastic assumption!) that the enemy does not increase his own forces to offset our increase" (113, p. 270).

25. In this case, the operational meaning of a probability would be defined in terms of an observed frequency of occurrence of the event in question *within a specified population*. But a single man is not a population.

26. The "intersection" of several classes is composed of individuals who belong to all of them.

27. When the other player's payoffs are considered, the resulting game is the game of chicken (cf. p. 116).

28. It is noteworthy that in one popular exposition of game theory (129), 122 pages are devoted to zero-sum games, while the discussion of non-zero-sum games occupies two pages.

29. Simulations will be discussed in Chapter 13.

30. This whirlpool has a hypnotic fascination for Schelling (101), who returns to the phrase "he thinks that I think that he thinks . . ." with remarkable persistency.

31. The danger of "surprise" attack was de-emphasized by many strategists during the last half of the last decade. This de-emphasis was a by-product of criticism leveled against the doctrine of massive retaliation (cf. p. 185) and of playing up the importance of the capability to wage a"limited war." However, Kahn, in breaking through the nuclear barrier (carrying strategic theory into thermonuclear war and beyond) reintroduced the doctrine of surprise attack with all its ramifications.

32. Cf.. the definition of the "splendid first strike capability" (58, p. 36).

33. This view is disputed by Parsons (88). It seems to me, however, that Parsons is discussing power in a different context from that in which it is understood by strategy-oriented political scientists. K. W. Deutsch (32, pp. 120–122) discusses power as currency. Although he is not explicit on this point, the implication of the analogy is that at least in a given period power is a conservative quantity, i.e., there is just so much of it to go around.

34. The model often used as a paradigm of political behavior is the N-person game, i.e., the game with more than two players. Such a game can always be made zero-sum by the addition of a fictitious player who wins what the others collectively lose, and vice versa. The theory of the N-

person game will not be discussed in this book. For applications to politics (where the stakes of the game are power) the interested reader is referred to (75). Hardly any application has been made of N-person game theory to diplo-military strategy, although the relevance of such a theory would seem to be at least as great, possibly greater than that of the two-person game theory. In simulations, however, (as distinguished from formal theory) more than two nations are typically represented (15, 49, 95). Simulation games are frequently non-zero-sum games with respect to some of the payoffs, but they are usually zero-sum with respect to power distribution.

35. In his book on conflict (101), Schelling devotes a chapter to bargaining, but it revolves almost exclusively around the prominence principle. I have not been able to find other discussions of bargaining theories in the writings of the strategists except in the context of ultimatums and blackmail, e.g. (59, Chap. 6), nor any discussions of arbitration theory.

36. This point is discussed in detail in (92, Chap. 14).

37. In the early years of the Cold War, there was an uproar in the United States about the theft of "atomic secrets" by the Russians. Strictly speaking, there were, of course, no such secrets. Scientific information can be obtained directly from nature by any competently conducted scientific enterprise and so does not need to be stolen. However, the theft of "scientific secrets" is not altogether absurd since it may be cheaper to steal them than to get them by independent investigations.

38. A game of perfect information is one where at all times the results of all previous moves are known to all the players. It has been proved in game theory that every game of perfect information has a saddle point. Chess is such a game. Most card games are not, because the first move is usually made by an extra player called Chance who chooses the initial arrangement of the cards. It is not the participation of Chance, however, but ignorance of her choice that makes card games games without perfect information.

39. Exploitation of the other's strategic mistakes is treated briefly in (74, Chap. 4). On the whole, however, theoretical development in this direction has been meager.

40. This is called "playing the opponent" rather than "playing the board."

41. In this connection see (34).

42. Conventional questionnaires and surveys will be of little help here. In certain important matters, there is little relation between people's verbal responses and their deep commitments.

43. There is little evidence that such applications are made or recommended. In the opinion of some, however, there is some cause for alarm (103).

44. In practice, assessment in complex situations is also a creative act (i.e., a decision, specifically a selection, of what are assumed to be the essentials of the situation). Nevertheless, the distinction between assessment (the processing of information) and decision (choice of action) seems useful.

45. Thus, in the simulations discussed by Guetzkow and others (49), in some variants Nature decided the outcomes of wars more or less arbitrarily; in other variants, in accordance with specified rules.

46. Here I am following Brody's description (15) of Benson's simulation. The interested reader may consult the original source in (6).

47. In a stochastic process, different end states of the system may be reached from the same initial system state. The regularities manifest themselves in the frequency distributions of the end states associated with a given initial state. The so-called Monte Carlo method is essentially a simulation of a stochastic process in which chance events are programmed into the computation procedure.

48. Cf. note 45.

49. A description of the SAGE system, as an example, appears in (43).

50. There has been an extensive use of simulations of this sort in training personnel to man defense systems (such as SAGE).

51. Guetzkow's games seem to be especially valuable in this regard.

52. I hope that my criticism of McClelland's game from the standpoint of pedagogy is not interpreted as casting an aspersion on his views on international relations. I think that his remarks in (78), for example, reveal a profound understanding of the problems involved.

53. Marquis de Sade also stimulated the imagination.

54. The announced payoffs were in points convertible at the rate of ten points for a cent. The subjects were paid a subject's fee of $1.35 per hour with the understanding that any losses incurred in the game would be taken from this fee. Usually subjects won or lost something in the neighborhood of a dollar. On a very few occasions their losses exceeded their pay.

55. Deterministic laws specify exactly what state must follow what state. Probabilistic laws specify only probabilities governing the transitions from state to state.

56. Stochastic processes of this sort are called Markov processes. The essential feature of a Markov process is its complete characterization by

the probabilities of the system's transition from state to state. That is to say, no matter what the initial distribution of the states has been, if certain rather mild conditions are satisfied, eventually the frequencies of the states will be determined entirely by the transition probabilities, not by the initial distribution.

57. Our assumption that all subjects were identical is also clearly untenable. Of these, I believe (on certain technical grounds), the assumption about the constancy of the propensities during the process introduces more serious discrepancies than the other.

58. The stochastic theory of learning developed by Estes (41) and by Bush and Mosteller (17) derives from a probabilistic model of the learning process, based, in turn, on the theory of conditioning. The stochastic learning model gives good results when applied to experiments on animals and human beings in situations where predominantly rote (trial and error) learning occurs.

59. Most of the early work on the prisoner's dilemma was done on this level. Understandably, the frequency of cooperative responses is the most interesting variable.

60. If the assumption of symmetry is abandoned, and individual pairs are considered, the number of parameters or variables on each level is, of course, doubled, a separate parameter being assigned to each subject.

61. In earlier experiments the increase of cooperative choices was not observed, possibly because the sessions lasted no longer than 30–50 plays (80, 105). However, the initial decrease of cooperation, which we also observed in the first 25 plays or so, was observed and reported.

62. This is the Pearson correlation coefficient, an index of the extent to which the responses of the two subjects tend to be alike. Taking a session with an arbitrary number of plays, if CC, CD, DC, and DD denote the numbers of the responses in the four categories, the correlation coefficient for that session is given by

$$\rho = \frac{CC \times DD - CD \times DC}{\sqrt{(CC+CD) \times (CC+DC) \times (DD+CD) \times (DD+DC)}}$$

It is noteworthy that if correlations are computed between the numbers of C choices made by the two members of each pair across the pairs, this correlation turns out to be in the nineties. This result practically refutes any hypothesis which relates the frequency of cooperative choices to some stable inherent tendency in the individual, for if this were the case, the frequencies of randomly paired subjects would not be correlated at all. The conclusion is inescapable that the interaction in the course of repeated plays is the chief determinant of the process.

63. This effect is reminiscent of the instability which Lewis F. Richardson deduced in his mathematical theory of arms races. According to this theory, a polarized international system (such as the opposing alliances in Europe at the beginning of the century and, presumably, the present ones) will tend either toward ever-increasing cooperation or toward a run-away arms race terminating in war. Fortuitously determined initial conditions may push the system into one direction or the other (96).

64. At this writing Adam Yarmolinsky is a special assistant to the Secretary of Defense. Arthur Waskow is a historian affiliated with the Peace Research Institute. The encounter was reported in *Science,* March 15, 1963, pp. 1034–1035.

65. At this writing Jerome B. Wiesner is dean of the school of science at Massachusetts Institute of Technology.

66. A paper treating a similar problem was presented at the International Conference on Arms Control in Ann Arbor, Michigan, in December 1962 and again in January 1964.

67. Compare this principle with the "balance" described in (85), where war has become chronic and the alliances shift every time it looks as if one side is going to lose for good.

68. For typical examples of peace strategies see (42), (125), and (126).

69. The crucial role of self-fulfilling assumptions as a strategic factor is clearly recognized by both Kahn (58) and Schelling (101). However, they treat this factor only as a serious difficulty in designing strategy, never as a ground for questioning the foundations of strategic thinking itself.

71. Recall the gesture of the dollar-a-year men in World War II, which emphasized the sacrifice of donating one's services to the society at large.

72. In this connection, see the vivid portrayal of Naphtha, the Communist-Catholic, an embodiment of the medieval ideals of the anonymous and the communal in (77).

73. Karl Marx has acknowledged these sources.

74. "Conservative" is used here in the sense implied by Senator Barry Goldwater and his admirers.

75. The interested reader is referred to the special issue of the *Nation* on this subject (24).

76. Cf. the excerpt from John T. Flynn's sketch of Franklin D. Roosevelt (*Country Squire in the White House*) cited in (54). After describing

the plight of the country in 1940, Flynn concludes, "If it has all happened that way, it is because Franklin D. Roosevelt is that way."

77. The regular channels of expression for this view are the newspapers and the mass circulation magazines. Occasionally the well-known clichés appear in book form. For a typical specimen see (104).

78. Characteristically, when reference is made to the "working masses" of the Soviet Union, *rabochi* is seldom, if ever, used. The proper word is *trudiashchiyesia* (derived from *trud*). On the other hand, when the working class is referred to (at present this is done only in reference to the workers in capitalist countries), *rabochi klas* is the term.

79. The discovery of the "genetic code" was perhaps the most significant advance in biology in our century. For a popular account, see, for example (27) and (83).

80. The analogy drawn here between social and biological organisms is more than a figure of speech. There are weighty reasons for taking such analogies seriously. The difficulty of drawing a sharp line between biological and social evolution is dramatically demonstrated in (40).

81. The *blazheny* appears in Russian literature in a variety of guises, as, e.g., an idiot personifying a czar's conscience (89), a millionaire prince (37), a young man who takes Christianity literally (36), a selfless middle class woman (20), compassionate peasants (121) and (119).

82. For a keen, perceptive analysis of this dilemma, the interested reader is referred to (70).

83. Lenin's thinking in the Brest-Litovsk affair was bold and creative, and his prognosis, although mistaken with regard to proletarian revolutions, was vindicated with regard to Russia's future, since the treaty was nullified by Germany's defeat. Observe, however, that Trotsky's proposal of non-violent resistance against the Germans was also bold and imaginative, and we have no way of knowing what would have happened if it had been carried out.

84. The role of *nyanya*, the serf nurse, as a source of direct contact between the sensitive members of the gentry and the people, has been much discussed in Russian literary criticism.

85. The break with Yugoslavia in 1948 was on that basis. A similar break with Poland in 1956 was averted after considerable national autonomy was guaranteed to the Poles. Within the Soviet Union, autonomy of nationalities is recognized only in non-political matters, such as language and innocuous expressions of folk idiom—dress, folk art, etc.

86. This is the much publicized "struggle for men's minds," to which many basically peace-oriented people wish to shift the objectives of the Cold War (cf. 126).

87. This is particularly emphasized in (42).

88. Here I must acknowledge that I actually know next to nothing about the Chinese views except from what I read in Western and Soviet sources. I see no compelling reason to give much credence to either. In what follows, however, I assume, for lack of primary sources, that the Chinese views are actually as they have been depicted.

89. This idea underlies the Marxian concept of surplus value, which links power relations in a society to relations emerging from its mode of production and distribution.

90. Actually it was, of course, the motivation to increase the buying power of the masses (to enhance the potentialities of mass production) that was responsible for the entrepreneurs' active interest in raising the workers' wages. At least the American capitalists realized, to an extent, that capital and labor were not always playing a zero-sum game.

91. Nor has the tradition died in those countries of Eastern Europe which participated in the mainstream of Western civilization, notably Poland and Hungary. This became manifest in the dramatic restoration of intellectual freedom in Poland in 1956. Since then there has been some recession in Poland, compensated in part by increasing liberalization in Hungary. There can be little doubt that the ups and downs are reflections of oscillations in Soviet cultural policy.

92. To put it bluntly, a man is tried not for what he did but for who he is. During the Stalinist terror, this conception of "justice" became manifest in the grimmest way. An excerpt from a recent Soviet novel presents a vivid example.

The commander looked at me hard from under his beetle brows as he asked my full name. I told him. Year of birth. I told him. It was in the thirties and I was, let's see just twenty-two then, just a kid. "Well, Tiurin, who are you serving?" "I serve the working people," I replied with a salute. He blew up and banged both fists on the desk, bang. "You're serving the working people, you bastard, but what are you yourself?" I froze inside but kept a grip on myself. "Machine-gunner, first class. Excellent marks in military training and polit. . . ." "First class! What are you talking about, you shit? Your father's a kulak. Look this document has come from Kamen. Your father's a kulak and you've been hiding. They've been looking for you for two years." I turned pale and kept my mouth shut. I hadn't written a line home for a year to keep them from tracing me. I had no idea how they were living at home, and they knew nothing about me. "Where's your conscience?" he shouted at me, all four bars on his collar shaking. "Aren't you ashamed of yourself for deceiving the Soviet Power? . . .

This story is told by one of the inmates in a forced labor camp (115, pp. 86–87).

93. This function is considered to be the province of professional organizations and such institutions as the Better Business Bureau.

94. An outline of such a program is offered in (55). An essentially similar idea was developed twelve years earlier in (94).

REFERENCES

(1) ARENDT, H. *Eichmann in Jerusalem: A Report on the Banality of Evil.* New York: Viking Press, 1963.

(2) ———. *The Origins of Totalitarianism.* New York: Harcourt, Brace, 1951.

(3) ARROW, K. J. *Social Choice and Individual Values.* New York: John Wiley & Sons, 1951.

(4) AZRAEL, J. R. "Murder trial in Moscow," *Atlantic Monthly* (May 1962).

(5) BECKER, G. M., DE GROOT, M. H., and MARSCHAK, J. "Stochastic models of choice behavior," *Behavioral Science,* 8 (1963), pp. 41–55.

(6) BENSON, O. "A simple diplomatic game—or putting one and one together" (mimeo). Norman: University of Oklahoma, 1959.

(7) BERNOULLI, J. "Exposition of a new theory on the measurement of risk" (English translation by LOUISE SOMMER), *Econometrica,* 22 (1954), pp. 23–26.

(8) BETTELHEIM, B. "Eichmann; the system; the victims," *New Republic,* (June 15, 1963).

(9) BIXENSTEIN, V. K., POTASH, H. M., and WILSON, K. V. "Effects of level of cooperative choice by the other player on choices in a prisoner's dilemma game: Part I," *Journal of Abnormal and Social Psychology,* 66 (1963), pp. 308–313.

(10) BLAU, J. H. "The existence of social welfare functions," *Econometrica,* 25 (1957), pp. 302–313.

(11) BLOOMFIELD, L. P. and PADELFORD, N. J. "Three experiments in political gaming," *American Political Science Review,* 43 (1959), pp. 1105–1115.

(12) BOULDING, K. E. *Conflict and Defense: A General Theory.* New York: Harper & Row, 1962.

(13) BRAITHWAITE, R. B. *Theory of Games as a Tool for The Moral Philosopher.* Cambridge: Cambridge University Press, 1955.

(14) BRIDGMAN, P. W. *The Logic of Modern Physics.* New York: Macmillan, 1927.

(15) BRODY, R. A. "Some systemic effects of the spread of nuclear weapons technology: A study through simulation of a multinuclear future." A report on research supported by the Air Force Office of Scientific Research, Office of Aerospace Research, United States Air Force, Contract AF 49 (638)-742 and Research Grant AF-AFOSR 95-63 (February 1963).

(16) BRONFENBRENNER, U. "Soviet methods of character education: Some implications for research," *American Psychologist,* 17 (1962), pp. 550–564.

(17) BUSH, R. R., and MOSTELLER, F. *Stochastic Models for Learning.* New York: John Wiley & Sons, 1955.

(18) CHAPMAN, R. L., *et al.* "The System Research Laboratory's air defense experiments," in (48).

(19) CHEKHOV, A. *The Cherry Orchard.* Baltimore: Penguin Books, 1959.

(20) ———. *The Darling.* Baltimore: Penguin Books, 1959.

(21) CLEMENS, S. *The Connecticut Yankee.* New York: Dodd, Meade, 1960.

(22) ———. *Huckleberry Finn.* New York: Dodd, Meade, 1958.

(23) COHEN, J. *Chance, Skill, and Luck.* Baltimore: Penguin Books, 1960.

(24) COOK, FRED, J. "The corrupt society," *Nation,* June 1–8, 1963.

(25) COOMBS, C. H., and PRUITT, D. G. "Components of risk in decision making: Probability variance preferences," *Journal of Experimental Psychology,* 60 (1960), pp. 265–277.

(26) ———. "Some characteristics of choice behavior in risky situations," *Annals of the New York Academy of Sciences,* 89 (1961) pp. 784–794.

(27) CRICK, F. H. C. "The genetic code," *Scientific American,* October 1962.

(28) DAVIS, R. H., CARPENTER, P. B., and MISSLER, C. W. "A Game for Studying the Problems of Arms Control." SP-799. Santa Monica, Calif.: System Development Corporation, May 11, 1962.

(29) DAVIS, R. H., *et al. Arms Control Simulation.* Technical Memo-

randum TM-(L)-633. Santa Monica, Calif.: System Development Corporation, August 10, 1961.

(30) DE FINETTI, B. "Recent suggestions for the reconciliations of theories of probability," *Proceedings of the Second Berkeley Symposium on Mathematical Statistics and Probability.* Edited by J. NEYMAN. Berkeley: University of California Press, 1951.

(31) ———. "Probability philosophy and interpretation," in *International Encyclopedia of the Social Sciences.* New York: Macmillan (forthcoming).

(32) DEUTSCH, K. W. *The Nerves of Government.* Glencoe, Ill.: Free Press of Glencoe, 1963.

(33) DEUTSCH, M. "Producing change in an adversary," in *International Conflict and Behavioral Science,* "The Craigville Papers." Edited by R. FISHER. New York: Basic Books, 1964.

(34) ———. "Trust and suspicion," *Journal of Conflict Resolution,* 2 (1958), pp. 265–279.

(35) DJILAS, M. *The New Class.* New York: Praeger, 1957.

(36) DOSTOYEVSKY, F. *The Brothers Karamazov.* New York: Grosset & Dunlap, 1959.

(37) ———. *The Idiot.* New York: Macmillan, 1948.

(38) ———. *The Possessed.* New York: Macmillan, 1962.

(39) EDWARDS, W. "Subjective probabilities inferred from decisions," *Psychological Review,* 69 (1962), pp. 109–135.

(40). EMERSON, A. E. "Ecology, evolution, and society," *American Naturalist,* 77 (1943), pp. 97–118.

(41) ESTES, W. K. "Toward a statistical theory of learning," *Psychological Review,* 57 (1950), pp. 94–107.

(42) ETZIONI, A. *The Hard Way to Peace, A New Strategy.* New York: Collier Books, 1962.

(43) EVERETT, R. R., ZRAKET, C. A., and BENINGTON, H. D. "SAGE— A data processing system for air defense," *Proceedings of the Eastern Joint Computer Conference* (December 9–13, 1957). New York: Institute of Radio Engineers, 1958, pp. 148–155.

(44) FLOOD, M. M. "Game-learning theory and some decision making experiments," in (118).

(45) ———. "Some experimental games," *Research Memorandum* RM-789, Santa Monica, Calif.: RAND Corporation, 1952.

(46) FROMM, E. "The case for unilateral disarmament," *Daedalus,* 89 (Fall 1960), pp. 1015–1028.

(47) GARST, J. D. "Conscience on trial," *Nation*, March 24, 1962.

(48) GUETZKOW, H. (ed.). *Simulation in Social Science. Readings.* Englewood Cliffs, N. J.: Prentice-Hall, 1962.

(49) GUETZKOW, H., *et al. Simulation in International Relations.* Englewood Cliffs, N. J.: Prentice-Hall, 1963.

(50) HARSANYI, J. C. "Models for the analysis of balance of power in society," *Logic, Methodology and Philosophy of Science.* Proceedings of the 1960 International Congress. Stanford, Calif.: Stanford University Press, 1962.

(51) ———. "On the rationality postulates underlying the theory of cooperative games," *Journal of Conflict Resolution*, 5 (1961), pp. 179–196.

(52) ———. "Rationality postulates for bargaining solutions in cooperative and in non-cooperative games," *Management Science*, 9 (1962), pp. 141–153.

(53) HART, B. H. LIDDELL. *Deterrent or Defense. A Fresh Look at the West's Military Position.* New York: Praeger, 1960.

(54) HAYAKAWA, S. I. *Language in Thought and Action.* New York: Harcourt, Brace, 1949.

(55) HAYAKAWA, S. I., and RAPOPORT, A. "Communication with the Soviet Union" *ETC., A Review of General Semantics*, 17 (1960), pp. 389–414.

(56) HORVATH, W. J., and FOSTER, C. C. "Stochastic models of war alliances," *Journal of Conflict Resolution*, 7 (1963), pp. 110–116.

(57) ILF, I., and PETROV, E. *Tonia.* Moscow: Gosizdat, 1959.

(58) KAHN, H. *On Thermonuclear War.* Princeton, N. J.: Princeton University Press, 1960.

(59) ———. *Thinking about the Unthinkable.* New York: Horizon Press, 1962.

(60) KAPLAN, M. A. *System and Process in International Politics.* New York: John Wiley & Sons, 1957.

(61) KAUFMANN, W. W. (ed.). *Military Policy and National Security.* Princeton, N. J.: Princeton University Press, 1956.

(62) ———. "The requirements of deterrence," in (61).

(63) ———. "Limited warfare," in (61).

(64) KHRUSHCHEV, N. S. *The Anatomy of Terror.* Washington, D. C.: Public Affairs Press, 1956.

(65) KISSINGER, H. A. *Nuclear Weapons and Foreign Policy* (abridged edition). Garden City, N. Y.: Doubleday, 1958.

(66) KNORR, K. "Passive air defense for the United States," in (61).

(67) KNORR, K., and VERBA, S. (eds.). *The International System. Theoretical Essays.* Princeton, N. J.: Princeton University Press, 1961.

(68) LANG, D. "Profiles: A scientist's advice II," *New Yorker,* January 26, 1963.

(69) LEDERER, W. J., and BURDICK, E. *The Ugly American.* New York: W. W. Norton, 1958.

(70) LEITES, N. C. *A Study of Bolshevism.* Glencoe, Ill.: Free Press, 1953.

(71) LIEBERMAN, B. "Human behavior in a strictly determined 3 × 3 matrix game," *Behavioral Science,* 5 (1960), pp. 317–322.

(72) LUCE, R. D. *Individual Choice Behavior: A Theoretical Analysis.* New York: John Wiley & Sons, 1959.

(73) ———. "A probabilistic theory of utitlity," *Econometrica,* 26 (1958) pp. 193–224.

(74) LUCE, R. D., and RAIFFA, H. *Games and Decisions.* New York: John Wiley & Sons, 1957.

(75) LUCE, R. D., and ROGOW, A. A. "A game-theoretic analysis of congressional power distributions for a stable two-party system," *Behavioral Science,* 1 (1956), pp. 83–95.

(76) LUTZKER, D. R. "Internationalism as a predictor of cooperative behavior," *Journal of Conflict Resolution,* 4 (1960), pp. 426–430.

(77) MANN, THOMAS. *The Magic Mountain.* New York: Alfred A. Knopf, 1927.

(78) MCCLELLAND, C. A. "The acute international crisis," in (67).

(79) ———. "A world politics game" (mimeo). San Francisco State College, 1959, cited in (15).

(80) MINAS, J. S., *et al.* "Some descriptive aspects of two-person non-zero-sum games, II," *Journal of Conflict Resolution,* 4 (1960), pp. 193–197.

(81) NASH, J. "The bargaining problem," *Econometrica,* 18 (1950), pp. 155–162.

(82) ———. "Non-cooperative games," *Annals of Mathematics,* 54 (1951), pp. 286–295.

(83) NIRENBERG, M. W. "The genetic code: II," *Scientific American,* March 1963.

(84) ORANS, M. "On serving your fellow man." *ETC., A Review of General Semantics,* 19 (1963), pp. 389–391.

(85) ORWELL, G. *Nineteen Eighty-Four.* New York: Harcourt, Brace & World, 1955.

(86) Osgood, C. E. *An Alternative to War or Surrender.* Urbana, Ill: University of Illinois Press, 1962.

(87) Osgood, R. E. *Limited War. The Challenge to American Strategy.* Chicago: University of Chicago Press, 1957.

(88) Parsons, T. "On the concept of political power," *Proceedings of the American Philosophical Society,* 107 (1963), pp. 232–262.

(89) Pushkin, A. *Boris Godunov,* in Yarmolisnsky, A. (ed.). *Poems Prose and Plays.* New York: Modern Library.

(90) Raiffa, H. "Arbritration schemes for generalized two-person games," in Kuhn, H. W., and Tucker, A. W. (eds.), *Contributions to the Theory of Games,* II, (Annals of Mathematics Studies, 28.) Princeton, N. J.: Princeton University Press, 1953.

(91) Rapoport, A. "Death of communication with Russia?" *ETC., A Review of General Semantics,* 7 (1950), pp. 83–96.

(92) ——. *Fights, Games, and Debates.* Ann Arbor, Mich.: University of Michigan Press, 1960.

(93) Rapoport, A., and Orwant, C. "Experimental games: A review," *Behavioral Science,* 7 (1962), pp. 1–37.

(94) Rapoport, A., Rapoport, G. G., and Shimbel, A. "Sanity and the Cold War," *Measure,* 2 (1951), pp. 161–174.

(95) Raytheon Company (Missile and Space Division), *Design for a Strategic Model.* BR-1354A. Bedford, Mass.: 1961

(96) Richardson, L. F. *Arms and Insecurity.* Pittsburgh: Boxwood Press, and Chicago: Quadrangle Books, 1960.

(97) ——. *Statistics of Deadly Quarrels.* Pittsburgh: Boxwood Press, and Chicago: Quadrangle Books, 1960.

(98) Riesman, D. (in collaboration with R. Denney and N. Glazer). *The Lonely Crowd.* New Haven: Yale University Press, 1950.

(99) Savage, L. J. *Foundations of Statistics.* New York: John Wiley & Sons, 1954.

(100) Schelling, T. C. "Experimental games and bargaining theory," in (67).

(101) ——. *The Strategy of Conflict.* Cambridge, Mass.: Harvard University Press, 1960.

(102) Schelling, T. C. and Halperin, M. H. *Strategy and Arms Control.* New York: Twentieth Century Fund, 1961.

(103) Schenck, H. Jr., "Computing 'ad absurdum,' " *Nation,* June 15, 1963.

(104) Schwartz, F. *You Can Trust the Communists (To Be Communists).* Englewood Cliffs, N. J.: Prentice-Hall, 1960.

(105) SCODEL, A., *et al.* "Some descriptive aspects of two-person non-zero-sum games," *Journal of Conflict Resolution,* 3 (1959), pp. 114–119.

(106) SHAPLEY, L. S. "A value for n-person games," in KUHN, H. W. and TUCKER, A. W. (eds.). *Contributions to the Theory of Games,* II. (Annals of Mathematics Studies, 28.) Princeton, N. J.: Princeton University Press, 1953.

(107) SHAPOSHNIKOV, B. M. *Mozg Armii.* Moscow-Leningrad: Gosizdat, 1929, cited in (65).

(108) SHAW, G. B. *Androcles and the Lion.* New York: Dodd, Mead, 1935.

(109) SINGER, J. D. *Deterrence, Arms Control and Disarmanent. Toward a Synthesis in National Security Policy.* Columbus, O.: Ohio State University Press, 1962.

(110) SINGER, J. D., and RAPOPORT, A. "The armers and the disarmers," *Nation,* March 2, 1963.

(111) SMOKER, P. "A mathematical study of the present arms race," *General Systems,* 8 (1963), pp. 51–60.

(112) ———. "A pilot study of the present arms race," *ibid,* pp. 61–76.

(113) SNYDER, G. H. *Deterrence and Defense. Toward a Theory of National Security.* Princeton, N. J.: Princeton University Press, 1961.

(114) SOLOMON, L. "The influence of some types of power relationships," *Journal of Abnormal and Social Psychology,* 61 (1960), pp. 223–230.

(115) SOLZHENTSYN, A. *One Day in the Life of Ivan Denisovich.* New York: E. P. Dutton, 1963.

(116) STEINBECK, J. *Grapes of Wrath.* New York: Viking Press, 1939.

(117) SUPPES, P. and ATKINSON, R. C. *Markov Learning Models for Multiperson Interactions.* Stanford, Calif.: Stanford University Press, 1960.

(118) THRALL, R. M., COOMBS, C. H., and DAVIS, R. L. (eds.). *Decision Processes.* New York: John Wiley & Sons, 1954.

(119) TOLSTOY, L. N. *War and Peace.* New York: Grosset & Dunlap, 1956.

(120) TURGENIEV, I. *Fathers and Sons.* New York: Cambridge University Press, 1953.

(121) ———. *Sportsman's Notebook.* Translated by CHARLES and NATASHA HEPBURN. New York: Viking Press, 1957.

(122) U.S. SENATE, *Study of Airpower.* Hearings before the Subcommittee on the Air Force of the Committee on Armed Services,

84th Cong., 2d sess. Washington, D.C.: Government Printing Office, 1956.

(123) VON NEUMANN, J. "A numerical method to determine optimum strategy," *Naval Research Logistics Quarterly,* 1 (1954), pp. 109–115.

(124) VON NEUMANN, J. and MORGENSTERN, O. *Theory of Games and Economic Behavior* (2nd ed.). Princeton, N. J.: Princeton University Press, 1947.

(125) WASKOW, A. *The Limits of Defense.* New York: Doubleday, 1962.

(126) ———. "Non-lethal equivalents of war," in *International Conflict and Behavioral Science,* "The Craigville Papers." Edited by R. FISHER. New York: Basic Books, 1964.

(127) ———. *The Shelter-Centered Society.* Washington, D.C.: Peace Research Institute, 1962.

(128) WEISS, H. K. "Stochastic models for the duration and magnitude of a 'deadly quarrel,'" *Operations Research,* 11 (1963), pp. 101–121.

(129) WILLIAMS, J. D. *The Compleat Strategyst.* New York: McGraw-Hill, 1954.

(130) WILLIAMS, T. *A Streetcar Named Desire.* New York: New Directions, 1947.

(131) WRIGHT, Q. *A Study of War.* Chicago: University of Chicago Press, 1942.

(132) ZIRKLE, C. *Death of a Science in Russia.* Philadelphia: University of Pennsylvania Press, 1949.

GLOSSARY

~~~~~~

N.B. The definitions offered here are neither exact nor complete. They are meant only to serve as reminders of the context in which the words are used in this book.

ABSOLUTE SCALE—A measurement procedure in which the magnitudes are independent of units; e.g., probabilities of events.

ADDITIVITY—A property possessed by measurable quantities whose magnitudes can be meaningfully added when the quantities are combined. For example, the combined weight of Cow A and Cow B equals the sum of the two weights. However, utilities of objects or events are not necessarily additive. The utility of a cup of coffee in which an ounce of salt has been dissolved need not equal the utility of a cup of coffee plus the utility of an ounce of salt.

ARBITRATION—Methods of settling disputes in which disinterested parties participate or principles of equity are invoked.

BARGAINING—Negotiation among partners or opponents in which no disinterested parties participate and no principles of equity are invoked.

BONA FIDE PLAYER—A player in a game who has both alternatives to choose from and a preference rank order among the outcomes.

CALCULATED RISK—A decision based on the calculation of expected gains of the available courses of action.

CONTEST—A situation in which two or more actors strive for incompatible goals, in which the actions of one do not restrict the range of actions of others; e.g., bowling, pole-vaulting.

CONTROLLED VARIABLE—A quantity deliberately held constant in an experiment or in selecting a sample to be observed in order to observe the effects of other variables.

CRITICAL POINT (of a gas)—A combination of pressure and temperature at which the gaseous state is indistinguishable from the liquid state.

DEGREE OF BELIEF—Subjectively estimated likelihood of an event.

DESCRIPTIVE—A theory is descriptive if it states general laws about some class of events. In contrast to normative (*q.v.*) theory, a descriptive decision theory states how people make decisions, not how they ought to make them.

DETERMINISTIC LAW—A law of nature which presumably ensures that a system starting from a given state will with certainty pass through a determined sequence of states.

DIMINISHING RETURNS—A situation in which additional increments of something received bring progressively smaller increments of utility.

DOMINATING STRATEGY (or DECISION)—A course of action which leads to the most preferred outcome regardless of what else may happen or what others may do.

EMPIRICAL QUESTION—A question which can in principle be answered by appropriate observations.

EQUILIBRIUM STRATEGY—A strategy from which a player cannot depart without worsening his position provided the other players remain with their equilibrium strategies.

EXPECTED GAIN—If each of a set of outcomes has a certain probability of occurrence and a certain utility, the expected gain is the sum of the utilities multiplied by the respective probabilities.

FAIR BET—In gambling, a bet in which the expected gain is zero.

GAME—A decision problem involving two or more actors and a set of rules which indicate the sequence in which the actors make their decisions, the range of alternatives open to the actors at each stage, the conditions which terminate the process, and the payoffs to each player, depending on the totality of their decisions.

GAME AGAINST NATURE—A game between two players in which one has no preference rank order among the outcomes.

GAMING—Contrived situations, in which decision-making is exercised under imposed constraints (rules).

"HARD" SCIENCE—A discipline which confines its attention to objectively verifiable events and prescribes rigorous rules of deduction.

INDEX—A numerical value invented for the purpose of quantifying some concept, e.g., "intelligence quotient," "gross national product," etc.

INTERVAL SCALE—A measurement procedure which allows only the determination of the ratios of pairs of intervals between the magnitudes but not the ratios of the magnitudes themselves, e.g., the Centigrade and Fahrenheit temperature scales.

INVERSE PROBLEM—A problem obtained from a given one by interchanging what is known and what is to be determined.

IRREVERSIBLE PROCESS—A process which can normally proceed in only one direction, e.g., the equalization of temperature in an isolated body.

ISOMORPHIC—Two systems (theories, situations) are isomorphic to each other if to each element of one corresponds exactly one element of the other and the relations between the corresponding pairs are preserved.

LOGISTICS—The branch of military science which deals with the movement and utilization of materiel. Applicable also to other activities involving transportation of materiel and scheduling of operations.

MATCHING PENNIES—A and B each put down a penny with either side up. If heads or tails match, A wins; otherwise B. The ancient game of morra is based on exactly the same principle. Each of two players holds up either one or two fingers. If the number of fingers is odd, one player wins; otherwise the other.

MATHEMATICAL FUNCTION—A relationship between variables defined explicitly, so that knowing any value of one allows us to determine the corresponding value or values of the other.

MATRIX—A rectangular array with entries (usually numbers) in each cell, so that specifying a row and a column determines a cell and with it the corresponding entry or entries.

MAXIMIZE—To choose a value of an independent variable to which corresponds a maximal value of a dependent variable.

MICHELSON-MORLEY EXPERIMENT—An experiment designed to determine the velocity of the earth relative to the "ether." Its negative results led to fundamental revisions of the assumptions of mechanics and electrodynamics, leading to the formulation of the theory of relativity.

MINIMAX—A strategy which assures to a player the maximum payoff he can get in a zero-sum game against a rational opponent.

MINIMIZE—To choose a value of an independent variable to which corresponds a minimal value of a dependent variable.

MIXED STRATEGY—A method of picking a strategy by the use of a chance device in which a certain probability is assigned to each of the available strategies.

MODEL—A simplified replica of a system, situation, or event; a set of equations purporting to depict all the essential relations which determine a system or a situation.

NEP—New Economic Policy, introduced by Lenin in 1921 to stimulate Russian economy, permitted limited private enterprise in trade and manufacture.

N-PERSON GAME—A game with more than two players.

NON-ZERO-SUM GAME—More properly, non-constant-sum game (cf. zero-sum game), one in which the sums of the payoffs to the respective players are not equal in all outcomes.

NORMAL FORM—A game is in normal form when all the available strategies of each player have been listed and also all the payoffs associated with each outcome.

NORMATIVE—A theory is normative if it provides rules for finding the best among alternative courses of action. In contrast to descriptive (*q.v.*) theory, a normative decision theory states how people ought to make decisions, not how they make decisions.

OPERATIONS RESEARCH—Investigations, usually mathematical, aimed at finding quantities or courses of action optimal with respect to a set of given goals and under a set of given constraints.

OPTIMIZE—To choose a value of an independent variable to which corresponds a most preferred value of a dependent variable.

ORDINAL SCALE—A measurement procedure which allows only the determination of the rank of a set of objects but not the "distances" between them, e.g., first choice, second choice, etc.

OUTCOME—In a game, the situation resulting at the termination of a play of the game from the totality of decisions made by the players. Each outcome determines a set of payoffs, one to each player.

PARAMETER—A quantity which remains constant in given experimental conditions or in a given sample, but which may vary with the conditions or with the population from which samples are taken.

PAYOFF—The utility of an outcome of a game.

PERFECT GAS—A gas which obeys the law $PV=CT$, where P is pressure, V volume, T temperature, C a constant, at all values of P, V, and T.

PRECESSION—The rotation of the axis of an orbit.

PRE-EMPTION—Making a move (presumably to one's advantage) which would have (presumably) benefited an opponent, had he made it first.

PRESCRIPTIVE—See NORMATIVE.

PRISONER'S DILEMMA—A non-zero-sum game which illustrates the failure of both the minimax principle and of the dominating strategy principle.

PRISONER'S DILEMMA PLAYED TWICE—A game consisting of two successive moves, each made by two players simultaneously, in which each move is a play of Prisoner's Dilemma and the outcome of the first move is announced before the second is made.

PRISTAV—Czarist police chief.

PROBABILISTIC LAW—A law which specifies either the probabilities of a given set of outcomes or the way the probabilities change with time or as a result of preceding outcomes.

PROMINENT STRATEGY—A strategy which can serve as a focal point of tacit agreement to the common advantage of two or more players unable to communicate with each other.

PROPENSITY—An inclination to a given act. A propensity can be quantified by specifying the relative frequency an individual performs the act in question when he finds himself in a given situation (or class of situations.)

PURE GOOD—Something with a utility which always increases with magnitude, hence something one cannot have too much of.

RANDOMIZE—Allow chance to determine one's choices.

RATIO SCALE—A measurement procedure which allows the determination of the ratios between the magnitudes but not the absolute value of the magnitudes unless a unit is specified, e.g., dollars, inches.

RATIONAL—A rational decision is one which can be shown to be a consequence of choosing the most promising of a number of alternatives which have been considered.

REVERSIBLE PROCESS—A process governed by a law such that if the sign of the time variable is changed the law still holds.

RISK—A situation in which the probabilities (not all equal to one) of all possible outcomes of each decision are known.

RULES—The constraints under which decisions must be made. In a game, these may be specified by agreement; or they may be constraints imposed by the nature of the situation itself.

SADDLE POINT—An entry in the strategy matrix of a game which is at the same time the minimum in its row and the maximum in its column (assuming the payoffs are those accruing to the row-chooser).

ST. PETERSBURG PARADOX—A paradox inherent in a game cited by J. Bernoulli as an example of a decision problem in which it is absurd to bet on the theoretically "winning" side.

SCENARIO—A term introduced by strategists to designate imagined situations (usually crises, wars, etc.) contrived for exercising strategic decision-making and to stimulate the invention of alternative outcomes and courses of action.

SECOND LAW OF THERMODYNAMICS—This law states that in a system isolated from its environment entropy can only increase. Entropy can be roughly equated with the amount of "chaos"; hence, isolated systems tend toward chaotic states.

SIMULATION—Replicating certain features of interest in a situation for purposes of study or experimentation.

SOLUTIONS OF EQUATIONS BY RADICALS—An algebraic equation is of the type $a_nX^n + a_{n-1}X^{n-1} + \ldots \div a_0 = 0$, where the a's are constants presumed known, and X is an unknown to be determined. The equation is solved explicitly if it is indicated what operations are to be performed on the a's to obtain X. If these operations involve no more than addition, substraction, multiplication, division, and the extraction of roots, the equation is said to be solvable by radicals.

SQUARING THE CIRCLE—A problem proposed in antiquity, in which it was required to construct, using only straight edge and compass, a square equal in area to the area of a given circle. The problem was shown to be unsolvable in the nineteenth century.

STATE OF NATURE—The "indifferent" player's choice in a game against nature (q.v.).

STOCHASTIC MODEL—A mathematical model of a process in which the variables of interest are sets of probabilities associated with possible outcomes.

STRATEGY—In game theory a composite decision in which a player specifies (usually to himself) what he will do in every possible situation that can arise in the course of a play of the game.

SUBJECTIVE PROBABILITY—A personal estimate of a probability either explicitly stated or inferred from a choice among acts the ascribed utilities of whose outcomes are known.

SURE-THING PRINCIPLE—The principle of choosing a dominating strategy (q.v.) if such exists.

TRANSITIVITY—A relation, symbolized by $\rightarrow$, is transitive if $a \rightarrow b$ and $b \rightarrow c$ implies $a \rightarrow c$. For example, the relations "descendant of," "equal to," and "greater than" are all transitive.

UNCERTAINTY—A situation in which the probabilities of the possible outcomes of decisions are not known.

UTILE—A unit of utility.

UTILITY—A theoretical value assigned to an object or an event. If such a value can be assigned to each of a set of objects or events, it becomes possible to rank them in the order of preference.

UTILITY SCALE—A rule which specifies how the utility of any of a set of objects or events is to be calculated. A scale is assumed to be associated with a particular individual or a class of individuals.

ZERO-SUM GAME—A game in which the sum of the payoffs to the respective players is zero regardless of the outcome. If all the sums are equal, not necessarily zero, the game is called constant sum. The theory of constant-sum games is identical to that of zero-sum games, and the two terms are not distinguished in this book.

INDEX

About the Author

ANATOL RAPOPORT'S primary academic interest is the application of mathematics to biology and to psychology. A professor at the University of Michigan and senior research mathematician at the university's Mental Health Research Institute, he is one of this country's most versatile intellectuals. His most recent book, *Fights, Games, and Debates,* established him as a leading spokesman on applications and implications of game theory. In addition to his work in mathematical biology, Dr. Rapoport is known for his original contributions to semantics, especially his recognition of the importance of language in influencing behavior patterns.

Dr. Rapoport was born in Russia and attended high school in Chicago. He later received degrees in music at the State Academy in Vienna, and for the next several years gave concerts in Europe and the United States. He returned to Chicago in 1937 and four years later received his doctorate in mathematics from the University of Chicago. He then served in the U.S. Air Force before returning to academic life in 1946.